PRINCIPLES OF THE ISLAMIC THEORETICAL MYSTICISM

PRINCIPLES OF THE ISLAMIC THEORETICAL MYSTICISM

Saeed Rahimian

Translated by
Fazel Asadi Amjad
Mahdi Dasht Bozorgi

Ordering Information:
Quantity sales. Special discounts are available on quantity purchases by corporations, associations, and others. For details, contact the distributor at the address below.

Shia Books Australia
www.shiabooks.com.au
info@shiabooks.com.au

ISBN 978-1-911361-16-9

Second Edition 2021

Content

Transliteration

Symbol	Transliteration	Symbol	Transliteration
ء	’	أ	a
ب	b	ت	t
ث	th	ج	j
ح	ḥ	خ	kh
د	d	ذ	dh
ر	r	ز	z
س	s	ش	sh
ص	ṣ	ض	ḍ
ط	ṭ	ظ	ẓ
ع	‘	غ	gh
ف	f	ق	q
ک	k	ل	l
م	m	ن	n
ه	h	و	w
ی	y	ة	ah
Long Vowels		Short Vowels	
آ	a	ـَ	a
ای	ī	ـِ	i
او	ū	ـُ	u
Persian Letters			
Symbol	**Transliteration**	**Symbol**	**Transliteration**
پ	p	چ	ch
ژ	zh	گ	g

At the end of Farsi words, 'eh', '-e', and '-ye' have been used.

Preface

Considering necessity of preparing appropriate Islamic texts in English for the modern world and aiming at satisfying that need, Al-Mustafa International Research Institute (M.I.R.I.) was established in 2009. This centre has accomplished that duty in the best way by producing, translating, and reprinting tens of such appropriate texts. The present book entitled *Principles of the Islamic Theoretical Mysticism*, which is published in Farsi by The Organization for Researching and Composing University Textbooks in the Humanities (SAMT), is among works translated by the Institute.

This book is a textbook for Islamic Mysticism at postgraduate level; nevertheless others who are interested in the subject may gain useful information from the book. We hope that this book should form a link showing the way for those who seek advancement.

We take this opportunity to express our gratitude to "Islam and West Research Centre Ltd" for publishing this book and hope that the latter should form a link showing the way for those who seek advancement.

Al-Mustafa International Research Institute (M.I.R.I.)

Introduction

Mysticism (*'Irfān* in Arabic), which etymologically means a kind of knowledge and perception, can be defined technically as a kind of immediate knowledge and understanding beyond the senses or reason which facilitates the process of overcoming the obstacles and lifting the veils of the heart through a kind of spiritual wayfaring or attraction, and in this way the mystic understands the inner truth, the hidden and the true unity that is hidden behind appearances and diversity. This process follows a spiritual journey and demands the perfection of the soul and is accomplished through self-knowledge and the enlightenment of the interior. However, to explain further the meaning of mysticism or gnosis and its different dimensions and aspects we should look at it in its various connotations:

1. As a kind of "perception", that is an immediate and direct knowledge of the nature of the intuitive knowledge, which leads the mystic to directly experience the very truth and the world of unity or the interior and the hidden part of the world.

2. As a kind of "perspective". In this sense it is a kind of cryptic or intrinsic reading based on the interpretation of the holy texts or literary works and offered as a "mystical reading". Therefore, it stands in parallel to other readings, such as philosophical, jurisprudential and theological readings.

3. As a “method”. This meaning which is usually modified by the epithet “practical” indicates a kind of conduct and a way of living that is marked by going beyond theoretical and practical conventions and manners and acting against routine customs and internal desires to reach an ultimate truth that is hidden behind appearances.

4. As “a set of instructions”, which comes in the form of the mystics’ writings and speeches (in both theoretical and practical dimensions) and is compiled to illustrate the mystical worldview and also the way of wayfaring and its achievements.

5. As “a historical institution”. The external and social manifestation of this institution in Islam is the different Sufi sects and Sufis, which both have had some conflicts and transactions with other social and religion institutions.

Historically speaking what has firstly been called gnosis and expressed in terms such as “the owners of knowledge” and “people of Sufism” is the third meaning and then the second, fourth, fifth and finally the first meanings. But in the present work the theoretical dimension of the fourth meaning (gnosis as a set of instructions and teachings) has been mainly considered. It is known as the intellectual legacy of Islamic culture, and under the title “theoretical mysticism” it has been discussed from different perspectives and explained in prose and verse and in technical terms or symbolic words and concepts.

The Common Principles of Mystical Orders

By looking carefully into the definition and dimensions of gnosis, to call knowledge or a certain kind of knowledge mystical some principles are necessary:

Believing in the degrees of the worlds of existence. The mystical perception claims it goes beyond appearances and the common trend of the universe and penetrates the inner sides.

1. Believing in the degrees of man's understanding. Since the extrinsic sensible knowledge and even rational knowledge (because the intellect is unable to grasp the higher truths of the world) are not considered mystical knowledge but as kinds of superficial knowledge. Therefore, the only way of perceiving the ultimate truths of the world is presential or intuitive knowledge, which, of course, comprises different degrees and stages.

2. Believing in the degrees of man. Mystics usually believe there is a correspondence between man and the world and that man's knowledge of the world is a link between the two. So man as a potential knower has different degrees and by following the mystical way and acquiring mystical knowledge he will attain higher degrees in virtue and character (stations).

3. The degrees, states and knowledge are real. All the mystical orders believe their findings are deep and real accounts of the reality of the world rather than the creation of their fancy or figments of their imagination.

Besides the above principles, which are present in all mystical orders (religious or nonreligious), there is another principle in religious mysticism:

4. The achievements are sacred and divine. The mystical degrees and states find meaning in their attribution to the Exalted Allah (as the object of knowledge, love, fear and hope).

In Islamic mysticism two other principles may be added to the above mentioned principles:

5. It is founded on .... (the science of Names). As it will be seen the beginning and end of Islamic mysticism in its ontology, epistemology and practice (in the sense of adopting the precepts of Allah) is founded on the divine Names.

6. Believing in the degrees of the Qur'an. The Islamic mysticism in a sense is showing [representing] the interior and the inner layers

of the divine verses revealed in the Qur'an. To know these internal aspects one must travel through the existential degrees and human degrees corresponding with the inner sides of the Qur'an.

The correspondence of the degrees of the written book (the Qur'an), the book of creation (the world of being) and also the book of the soul (the existence of man) is one of the distinctions of Islamic mysticism. In Islamic mysticism the way that passes through these degrees and reaches the high stations of gnosis is called the path of *Wilāya* [Sainthood], which by relying on the vessel of affection and love or asceticism and self-control leads the mystic to travel through the divine Names and annihilate himself in the best divine Names and finally subsist in their truths.

Practical and Theoretical Mysticism

Practical mysticism is a set of mystical thoughts whose subject is the essence of the Real and His manifestations, namely His Names, attributes and acts, or His essence in one of its determinations. Qayṣarī's definition of gnosis (both practical and theoretical) as a science includes its subject, questions and uses. He writes:

> It is the knowledge of the Glorified Allah, in regard of His Names and attributes and manifestations, the states of the origin and resurrection, and the realities of the world and how they return to one Reality, which is the unique essence. It is also the knowledge of the spiritual wayfaring and the struggle to deliver the soul of the confinement of the shackles of particularity and its union with its Origin and for it to accept the attributes of absoluteness and universality.

Accordingly, the questions of gnosis could be described as follows:

1. Explaining the emergence of diversity (relating the world to the Real and describing the process of the world's descending).

2. Explaining the manifestations of the Names and attributes.

3. Explaining the way diversity returns to unity (the process of the world's ascension).

4. Explaining the way of returning (mystical wayfaring), which is related to practical mysticism.

So, the questions of gnosis are the manifestations and the qualities of the essence of the Real, which are His Names, attributes and acts. In other words, the two essential questions of gnosis are: 1. "What is monotheism?" (the question of the oneness of existence and its related issues) and 2. "Who is a monotheist?" (the question of the Perfect Man and its related issues). The first part deals with two important arguments:

1. Proving the existence of unity, and

2. Explaining diversity, whose end is the knowledge of the Real and its "method" relies on the findings of the mystics, the texts of the divine revelation, the speeches of the infallible and also the intellectual arguments that confirm the intuitive and experiential findings and systematize and explain the mystical worldview and answer the objections made to it.

The subjects and questions of theoretical gnosis or mystical worldview could be divided into five essential parts:

1. Mystical epistemology (preliminary issues),

2. Mystical ontology,

3. Mystical theology,

4. Mystical cosmology, and

5. Mystical anthropology.

Practical mysticism means going through the stages of human perfection according to a special method and plan in order to approach Allah and attain the divine knowledge and the highest ranks of *wilāyat* or sainthood (the rank of the real certainty and union of union).

Islamic mysticism first appeared as practical mysticism and the ways of mystical life in the first two centuries at the beginning of Islam (in the two forms of asceticism and love), and then by compiling the mystical achievements of the mentioned mystics in written compendiums, the thoughts and writings of the people of this way became well-known.

Whereas the capital of the practical mystics is nothing other than a pure heart and pure intention in their deeds and the experience of all the spiritual stages begins and ends with this capital, theoretical mysticism in respect of learning and teaching depends on many sciences, such as logic, philosophy and theology and knowing the speeches, findings and achievements of the mystics. Theoretical mysticism in this regard is similar to theoretical wisdom or metaphysics, though it has some essential differences with it, too. Muṭahharī writes:

> Mysticism in this part like divine philosophy attempts to interpret and explain existence. Of course, philosophy in its demonstrations depends only on intellectual principles, but mysticism employs, technically speaking, intuitive principles and in its argument and only then explains them in the language of the intellect. Rational philosophical arguments are like questions which are written and studied in the same language, whereas mystical arguments are like issues translated from another language. That is, the mystic, at least as he claims, explains whatever he sees by the eyes of his heart and all his being in the language of the intellect.

The difference between theoretical mysticism and other Islamic sciences could be explained in the following way:

In regard of subject, the subject of philosophy is the reality of existence, for theology it is the religious dogmas, and for mysticism it is the essence of the Real and one of its determinations.

In regard of methodology, the method of philosophy is rational; for theology it is intellectual, traditional and sometimes experimental, etc.; and for mysticism it is both rational and intuitive and sometimes traditional.

In respect of objective, the objective of philosophy is the knowledge of the qualities, necessaries and divisions of existence; for theology it is proving the religious dogmas; and for mysticism it is the knowledge of the Names and attributes of the Real and the inside and the secret of the world.

Mullā Hādī al-Sabzawārī following Mullā 'Abdul Razzāq al-Lāhījī divides the owners of the knowledge of the realities of the things into four groups. The first group is the theologians who adjust their views to the exterior of the religious law, the second and the third groups are the those who don't care about the agreement or disagreement with the religious law, and they either mainly try to fight against the self and purify their internal being—who are the Sufis—or confine themselves with thinking and intellectual explanation and demonstration—these are the peripatetic, and the fourth group has gathered both ways and they are the illuminationist. Al-Sabzawārī believes the last group is entitled to the favor of the Real and apparently he thinks the transcendent philosophy of Mullā Ṣadrā and his own philosophy belong to this group (the Illuminationsit).

There are some reasons why theoretical mysticism began to be recorded and written down by the third century A.H., which reached its climax in the seventh century by Muḥyī al-Dīn Ibn 'Arabī:

1. The epistemological reason. The human's need to affect a harmony among the different dimensions of his existence and

perception, namely his heart and intellect and experience, made him to try to offer an inclusive, rational and consistent explanation of his experiential knowledge and intuitive truths as much as he can.

2. The illusion of contradiction. The difference in the expressions of the mystics which sometimes occur due to the difference of their stations and experiences and also their existential capacities apparently leads to their disagreement and makes them appear to some as contradicting themselves and speaking irrationally.

3. The accusation of disbelief. Some misapplied expressions or extravagant speeches, which rise from either defective experiences or incorrect translation of intuitive knowledge into speculative knowledge, and sometimes are incompatible with the exterior form of the religious law cause misunderstanding among the people of the religious law.

4. The suspicion of meaninglessness or being unfounded. The peculiarity of the mystical experiences and in consequence the difficulty of finding mental concepts corresponding with their experiential achievements and finally the inability of verbal expressions and phrases to explain intuitive truths induced the suspicion that the intuitive findings are meaningless and the achievements of the mystics rationally are unfounded. This suspicion was mainly advanced by some philosophers, theologians and scholars of *ḥadīth.*

Qayṣarī on the necessity of gnosis and the reason why he composed his treatise on this subject writes:

> Although this science is essentially experiential and only the people of rapture and intuition know it, yet since I found the people of exoteric sciences think it has no solid foundation and is useless and believe it is made only of

> poetic imaginings and idle talks with no evidence or it is a claim to spiritual revelation that cannot be understood, I have explained the subject, questions and principles of this science in this treatise.[1]

He adds, "If in this treatise we offer a proof or evidence, it is only to convince them (the people of exoteric sciences) by referring them to their own science, for they do not accept the revelation of the people of intuition and, more, misinterpret those verses and traditions which have mystical implications."

5. An instructional necessity. The necessity of guiding the disciples and making them aware of what they may find on the way and experience during revelation, manifestations and observations, and also the necessity of explaining and learning the religious dogmas to prevent any misunderstanding or misinterpretation were other reasons for composing the science of theoretical mysticism. Ṣā'in al-Dīn Ibn Turkeh on the uses of theoretical sciences in gnosis and that learning sciences and increasing one's perceptive abilities are not incompatible with relieving the heart writes that there is no problem in this view, but there will be a problem if they think theoretical sciences will bring one to the intended purpose or they are necessary in the mystical wayfaring and that wayfaring is dependent on them. But if they say it is not an obstacle in the mystical way or maximum they hold it as a preparation and help in this way they are not incorrect. The author of *Tamhīd al-Qawā'id* states:

> Preparing the holy place by enthusiastic intellectual acts is not a hinder; rather it is useful in bringing to surface what is hidden in it of knowledge and wisdom

1. *Rasāel Qayṣarī*, The treatise "Resālat Al-Tawḥīd wa Al- Nubuwwat wa Al-wilāyat", 7.

> when the sanctified power prevails over the physical powers and continues to dominate the two faculties of fancy and imagination....[1]

Some of the commentators on *Tamhīd al-Qawā'id* hold acquiring such sciences is necessary and add: "Because the mystical way is difficult, to prevent wandering in the delusions and errors of the imagination the wayfarer before setting out must be informed of the rational laws which separate the truth and falsehood and distinguish between the station and the road. So the way of purification is not independent from the way of demonstration.

The above mentioned factors and the necessity of conversing and communicating in the language of the people or the wise people have led to the formation and composition of theoretical mysticism.

Theoretical mysticism before Ibn 'Arabī was not systematic and it was confined to the speeches and aphorisms of the Masters and their extravagant speeches, which they presented in verse or prose, or their interpretations of the Qur'anic verses and Prophetic sayings, especially in the speeches of mystics such as Ḥallāj, Khwāja 'Abdullāh Anṣārī, Junayd, Sahl al-Tustarī, Abū Ṭālib al-Makkī, al-Tirmidhī, Aḥmad al-Ghazzālī, 'Ayn al-Quḍāt, 'Aṭṭār and Najm al-Dīn Kubrā. However, with Muḥyī al-Dīn Ibn 'Arabī (d. A.H. 638) these disorganized intellectual principles found considerable order and coherence and turned into a complete worldview and coherent thought system as a substitute or a supplement for philosophical and theological movements in grasping the truths of the world and understanding the sciences of Islam. After Muḥyyi al-Dīn theoretical mysticism left its impact on most mystics, orders, Sufi methods, and also philosophers and

1. Ṣā'in al-Dīn Ibn Turkeh, *Tamhīd al-Qawā'id*, 262.

even theologians and commentators. Moreover, the technical terms and principles offered in Ibn 'Arabī's worldview, his method of interpretation of the sacred texts and his mystical experiences have influenced the mentioned disciplines, so that four centuries after him Ṣadr al-Muta'allihīn al-Shīrāzī (d. A.H. 1050), being influenced greatly by Ibn 'Arabī's views, introduced his transcendent Philosophy as one of the most perfect philosophical systems in Islam, which in a sense is the fruit of the fusion of ratiocination, mysticism and the Qur'an, and with much endeavour explained rationally those issues which even Ibn 'Arabī thought can have no rational explanation. Still theoretical mysticism is pervasive, especially in the books of Ibn 'Arabī and his followers, such as al-Qūnawī, 'Abd al-Razzāq al-Kāshānī, Qayṣarī, Ibn Fanarī, Ibn Turkeh, Jāmī, Shabistarī, Lāhījī, and Sayyid Ḥaydar Āmulī as the original sources of understanding the mystical worldview in the classical and educational system of theoretical mysticism and research on it.

What follows is an account of this worldview as understood by the writer. The arguments, on the basis of what has been said so far, are presented in five parts which deal with the principles of 1. Epistemology, 2. Ontology, 3. Theology, 4. Cosmology, and 5. Anthropology in theoretical mysticism.

The Root and Origin of Theoretical Mysticism in Islam

Although some Orientalists speak of the influence of Eastern religions and sects and the Indian mysterious cults in India or the impact of Neo-platonic mysticism as some of the important sources of Sufism, the question remains whether with all the existing sources (such as the Qur'an, tradition, and Islamic supplications) is it necessary to look for an outer source. As the Christian George Geordaq states, it is much astonishing to see a man standing beside the river or sea and then to think from which pond or pool the man has filled his vessel ignoring the river or the sea. In our discussion it is also more logical first to consider the claims of the people of knowledge [= the mystics] who claim they have taken their sciences from the holy Qur'an and the outer and inner sides of its verses, the narrations of the sources of infallibility and also their invaluable spiritual experiences, though naturally and logically enough there are some general similarities among them mainly because mysticism depends on divine inspiration and all religions including Christianity, Brahmanism, Judaism and Islam, share the common source of divine emanation. In short, Muslim mystics, besides their mystical experience, mention the Qur'an and tradition as the buttresses of their mystical insight and support and evidence for their worldview and their life and conduct.

1. The holy Qur'an. As examples we may refer to the following cases:

- The verses which describe Allah as the first and the last and the exterior and the interior and indicate the divine absolute unity.[1]
- The verses which describe Allah as light[2] and speak of His manifestation.[3]
- The verses which emphasize the closeness and companionship of the Real.[4]
- Verses which indicate the actual perishing of all things[5] and

1. (57: 3). '*He is the First and the Last, the Manifest and the Hidden, and He has knowledge of all things.*'
2. (24: 35). '*Allah is the Light of the heavens and the earth.*'
3. (7: 143). '*When his Lord disclosed Himself to the mountain, He leveled it, and Moses fell down swooning.*'
4. (57:4). '*He is with you wherever you may be, and Allah sees best what you do.*'
5. (55: 26). 'Everyone on it [on the earth] is ephemeral.'

the essential self-sufficiency of Allah and the continuous dependence of beings on Allah.[1]

• Verses which indicate that Allah encompasses everywhere and everybody.[2]

• Verses that indicate somehow the combination of divine transcendence and eminence.[3]

• Verses that speak of the heart's vision[4] and meeting Allah[5] and seeing the heavenly dominions.[6]

• Verses that mention the superiority of Adman (man) over angels for receiving the divine Names.[7]

• Verses which clearly speak of the unity of the divine acts.[8]

• Verses that indicate that the other world in relation to this world is the interior one[9] and emphasize the importance of the knowledge of certitude.[10]

• Verses that indicate intuitive knowledge.[11]

---

1. (35: 15). *'O mankind! You are the ones who stand in need of Allah, and Allah – He is the All-sufficient, the All-laudable.'*
2. (2: 115). *'To Allah belong the east and the west: so whichever way you turn, there is the face of Allah!'*
3. (42: 11). *'Nothing is like Him, and He is the All-hearing, the All-seeing.'*
4. (53: 11). *'The heart did not deny what it saw.'*
5. (18: 110). *'Whoever expects to encounter his Lord – let him act righteously.'*
6. (6: 75). *'Thus did We show Abraham the dominions of the heavens and the earth.'*
7. (2: 31). *'He taught Adam the Names, all of them.'*
8. (8: 17). *'You did not throw when you threw; rather it was Allah who threw.'*
9. (30: 7). *'They know just an outward aspect of the life of the world, but they are oblivious of the Hereafter.'*
10. (102: 5-6). *'Were you to know with certain knowledge, you would surely see hell.'*
11. (18: 65). *'They found one of Our servants whom We had granted a mercy from Ourselves, and taught him a knowledge from Our own.'*

- Verses that explain the role of God-fearing in acquiring knowledge and awareness.[1]
- Verses that discuss the different external and internal degrees of the believers.[2]

2. Tradition. It includes certain *ḥadīths* that indicate the following points:

- Existence is particular to Allah.
- The Real is seen by the heart.
- The difference in the degrees of the companions of the Prophet(S), the saints and the believers.
- The closeness due to supererogatory acts.
- The purgatorial and heavenly vision of some believers.
- Describing knowledge as the divine light that is reflected in the heart.
- Lifting the veils for the infallible or their companions.
- Describing the infallible as the Perfect Men and the medium of the divine emanation (they are the hand of Allah, the face of Allah).
- The exterior and interior(s) of the Qur'an and counting the interiors of the divine Book.
- The firm connection between self-knowledge and the knowledge of God.
- The impact of sincere devotion on gaining knowledge and the flow of wisdom on man's tongue.
- The *ḥadīth* of *iḥsān* [Arabic for "righteousness"] as a rank higher than Islam and faith and defining it on the basis of the vision of God.
- Some holy *ḥadīths*, such as "the hidden treasure" and "the creation of Adam on the face of the Real" and many other cases

---

1. (2: 282). '*Be wary of Allah and Allah shall teach you.*'
2. (3: 163). '*They have ranks with Allah, and Allah sees best what they do.*'

which are given as evidence in the books of the people of knowledge [= mystics].

- Some transmitted prayers, especially those dealing with the divine Names, as the effective pillar in all the worlds.
- Some *ḥadīths* that stress the necessity of secrecy and that some sciences must be kept hidden.

Although there may be some disagreement on the interpretation of some verses and their explanation or on the documents and explanation of the narrations, what is important here is the mystics' dependence on the Book and tradition rather than judging the truth or falsehood of this dependence. As researchers have also shown, the spirit that exists in Islamic mysticism and Sufism has essentially an Islamic tinge and color and differs with the so-called mysticism in the East and West in language, notions, form and in some cases content and essence, which must be discussed in its right place.

The relationship between Religion and Mysticism

Irrespective of the root and origin of Islamic mysticism and Sufism, one may ask what kind of relationship is there between a religion and its mysticism. Is there difference and separation, opposition and disagreement, absolute correspondence, supplementation, and etc. between them? In this book besides discussing this subject in general and explaining its different and various aspects, we mainly give emphasis to the relationship between Islam and Islamic mysticism.

So that for the asked questions to be precise the subject of question should be clear. For if we separate the three meanings of religion into those of certainty, verification and historical realization, or to put it in other words religion in the first degree (the holy texts of religion), second degree (the scholars' different interpretation of religion), and third degree (the historical realization of religion in the society, history and its institutions), and on the other hand if we take into consideration the five aspects of mysticism which we have mentioned already, we will reach to different answers (the result of the assessment of the relationship among those three positions and these five aspects). To put it briefly we will discuss the question in the form of five arguments:

1. The relationship between revelation and intuition (the cognitive aspect of mysticism). Some mystics concerning this point have maintained that revelation and intuition are one in nature, that is, of the nature of intuitive knowledge[1], though they somewhat differ in degree, kind of object and some corollaries. Some others claim that the reality of revelation is unknowable and inaccessible and the relation between the two is one of difference or at least it is unknown.

On the relationship between the written revelation, namely the text of the divine book, on the one hand and the achievements of the mystics, the mystics believe the intuitions and the visionary experiences—like other empirical or rational apprehensions of the interpreter—are like clues for better understanding the divine Book and knowing it in detail and depth.

2. The reality of religion and mysticism (from a pedagogical perspective). The relationship between the religious instructions and mystical instructions is complete inclusion, for religion-

1. In this regard, Mawlānā says:

"The inspiration of God is not like astrology or geomancy or dreams - and God best knows what is right.

The Sufis in explaining [their doctrine] call it [the Divine inspiration] the inspiration of the heart, in order to disguise [its real nature] from the vulgar." *Mathnawī*, Book IV, Verses No. 1852- 1853.

besides esoteric knowledge and mystical truths- has other dimensions, such as jurisprudence and exoteric rules, social laws, ethics and the major dogmas.

3. Religion and mystical readings. Since the sources of religion (the Qur'an and tradition) are comprehensible and could be read in different ways, certainly the second dimension of mysticism (mystical perception) could be considered as one of these readings, and in this respect it is understood as an approach to religion in general, as the theo-philosophical approaches and even the exoteric understanding of the Salafies, Hanbalites, the exoterics and the traditionists have the same relation with religion.

4. The pious and mystical life. The mystics hold that the third aspect of mysticism (as a method, or practical mysticism) is one of the ways to piety, though they add it is not the only way. For them ascetic exercises, fear, hope, love and knowledge are some of the ways to piety and they believe the distinctive feature of mysticism is the fusion of the religious law, mystical order, and reality or, to put it in other words, reaching the truths through commitment to the essence and orders of religion and at the same time preserving and practicing the exterior forms of the religious law. Of course, the ways of mysticism are various, such as mysticism that is based on love, ascetic practices or fear; mysticism that is disposed to supplication, intoxication, self-reproach, or religious dogmas; mysticism that is witty, indifferent or unworldly; and mysticism that is founded on spiritual attraction, wayfaring, and etc.

5. The institution of religion and the historical institutions of mysticism. Perhaps the highest opposition that existed between the fifth aspect of mysticism, namely the orders and sects of mysticism, *khānqāhs* [Sufis' places of worship], and the manners and customs of the Sufis, and the institutions of religion, mosques, theologians, the judges and enforcers of the religious law throughout history, and the stories told of excommunications, accusations of heresy and punishments were related to this aspect. No doubt that the causes of such conflicts were sometimes the misconceptions and bigotry of the advocates of the religious law and sometimes the offensive extravagant words of some Sufi sects or their swerving from the religious law.

Accordingly, we may conclude that in order to explain the relationship between religion and mysticism and to reach a clear answer we should separate their different aspects. Nevertheless, it seems, at least according to some of the above-mentioned aspects, we can modify mysticism with a particular religion, such as "Islamic mysticism".

Questions

1. Explain the five common meanings and aspects of mysticism.
2. Explain the historical order of the different meanings of mysticism.
3. What are the common principles of the mystical orders, religious mystical orders and Islamic mystical order?
4. How does Qayṣarī define mysticism?
5. Why has theoretical mysticism been introduced as a discipline since the third century?
6. What are the similarities and differences between theoretical mysticism and philosophy?
7. What are the main sources of theoretical mysticism in the Muslim world?
8. What is the relationship between religion and mysticism? Explain its different states.

Chapter One: Epistemology of Theoretical Mysticism

Epistemological Principles of Mysticism

The epistemological tool in gnosis is the heart and its method is "purifying the inner" and cleansing the inside as the preliminary steps to "the mystical experience", and the source of this perception is the whole universe, from the soul of the mystic to the outer horizons of the world. Since the mystical experience is known as a kind of "inner experience", it seems necessary, besides knowing the characteristics of the inner experience, to know the features, kinds, precepts and the position and the degree of the credibility of the mystical experience. It is also important to have an estimation of the causes of the deficiency of the intellect in knowing the truth, the relationship between the intellect and the heart, the conditions of attaining the mystical experience and its impediments, and finally certain issues, such as the language of mysticism and interpretation with the mystics.

It seems, at least to the writer, the first general but relatively systematic plan for the epistemology of the mystics was introduced by Ibn Sina in the ninth and tenth sections of *al-Ishārāt* and the second was offered by Ibn 'Arabī in the introduction of *al-Futūḥāt al-Makkiyya*. The followers of Ibn 'Arabī have discussed and added, though not very systematically, this subject to their works.

The Intellect, the Heart and Revelation

It is necessary to consider one epistemological point discussed, though not coherently, in the works of the mystics to prevent some errors and misunderstandings, namely the relationship among the intellect, the heart (intuition) and revelation (transmission). Explaining this connection will help to explain the connection of the religious law, the mystical Order or the path, and Truth more clearly in the doctrine of the mystics.

For the intellect various meanings have been mentioned in the Islamic sources, some of which come within the domain of practical reason in philosophical sense, some others within the domain of theoretical reason, and some others essentially belong to that of intuition and the heart. One of the first explanations of the intellect's meaning in Islamic traditions is found in the words of Imām 'Alī (A.S.) in *Nahj al-Balāgha* where he divides the intellect into the natural and the acquired and gives primacy to the natural intellect (which is innate and inborn). Mawlānā on the basis of this *ḥadīth* writes:

> "Intelligence consists of two intelligences; the former is the acquired one which you learn, like a boy at school."[1]
>
> "The other intelligence is like a pearl and coral: its fountain is in the midst of the soul."[2]

In the Islamic sources the intellect is praised as a divine blessing and is known as the tool of acquiring knowledge, the criterion of distinguishing between right and wrong, the evidence of God, and the tool of gaining paradise and worshipping God. On the other hand, what is counted blameworthy is cunning, deception,

1. *Mathnawī*, Book IV, Verse No. 1960.
2. Ibid, Book IV, Verse No. 1964.

inducing doubts and misgivings, temptation, and playing tricks, which are wrong and inappropriate uses of the intellect that lead their practitioners to perdition.

Moreover, if in the words of the mystics we see that sometimes reason, knowledge and demonstration are praised and sometimes reason, thinking, philosophy and argument are looked at with disdain, sometimes reason is thought to be opposite to intuition and the heart's vision and sometimes supporting it, sometimes it is imagined as meddling with the religious law and sometimes it is considered one of the sources of the divine law, we should know these verdicts are issued in relation to the different aspects of the intellect or the different classes or ranks of people.

To illustrate, the intellect in theoretical mysticism stands opposite to the heart but in practical mysticism it is opposite to love; besides, the intellect in the first meaning, meaning acquired intellect, which is the means to reach acquired sciences, is divided into two kinds:

Practical reason (one of the sources of knowledge) by which we distinguish between good and evil.

Theoretical reason, which is the means to understanding and the agent of perceiving the universals (in an epistemological sense), is both one of the tools and one of the sources of knowledge, whose role in the process of knowledge is to analyze the achievements of the sources of knowledge, such as sense, intuition, revelation and practical reason and also to investigate its other attainments in the later stages.

Therefore, so far that the intellect analyses the products of the mentioned sources it cannot be opposite to those sources of knowledge, as it is not in the nature of a tool to question the subject of its work. Moreover, as a source of knowledge, if the intellect limits its activity to its own domain and the products of its knowledge and does not deny what lies beyond its reach, it will not be opposite to the other sources. Of course, since the intellect is a measuring tool it can highlight the errors of the other sources, but in fact this error finding is in a sense a correction of its own error as a dominant faculty rather than the error of the sense or that of experience and intuition.

As some philosophers and mystics have mentioned, error occurs at the stage of the intellect's judgment rather than in the report of the sense or intuition. Reason, nevertheless, can know its limits and admit its ignorance and brings man to the verge of nonintellectual and argues for certain issues which he cannot have a deep or true understanding of them. This is the intellect that understands its limits, and as it was said it stands in no opposition with the sensible or intuitive findings or the teachings of the revelation, for there is no disagreement between intellectual and beyond-intellectual (but not anti-intellectual) issues; rather such intellect can elucidate sensible experiences, explain mystical experiences, and interpret the revelation-based attainments of the Prophets. Indeed theoretical mysticism was put down on record as the result of the intellect investigating the mystical experience, as philosophy, mathematics, and empirical sciences have been the result of the intellect's investigation into the attainments of other sources and tools of knowledge.

On the other hand, if reason, as a source of knowledge, acknowledges its limits and boundaries and is not too conceited to speak of what lies beyond its perceptional power, it will not be incompatible with intuition or revelation.

In short, as it was mentioned, at least on three occasions the mystics have looked down and even condemned the intellect: first when it claims an exclusive right to knowledge and asserts it is the only way to truth. The foot of the rationalists here is said to be wooden and there is an unbridgeable gap between reason and love and the range of their perception. Mawlānā writes in *Mathnawī*:

"The leg of the syllogisers is of wood:
A wooden leg is very infirm."[1]

He also writes in one of his odes:

"The intellect says the six directions are the confinements and there is no way out,
Love says there is a way which I have travelled many times."[2]

Ḥāfiẓ states:

"In a workshop where there is no entry for wisdom and knowledge,
Why should a weak mind offer a bold judgment?
For us who suffer death from the pain of love and the thirst for wine,
The only remedy is either a friend's union or clear wine."[3]

The intellect in such a state may deny what it has not attained (or it is inaccessible or above-intellectual), which is a false conversion (meaning not existing because it is not found or not seen).

"The speech of water, the speech of earth, and the speech of mud are apprehended by the senses of them who have hearts [the mystics].
The philosopher who disbelieves in the moaning pillar [*ḥannāna*] is a stranger to the senses of the saints."[4]

***

"The sagacious are the point of the compass of

1. *Mathnawī*, Book I, Verse No. 2128.
2. *Dīvān Shams*, Ode 132.
3. *The Poems of Ḥāfiẓ Shīrāzī*, trans. 'Alāiddīn Pazārgādī, Ode No 186.
4. *Mathnawī*, Book I, Verse No. 3279- 80.

> existence, but love knows that they are wanderers in this circle."[1]
>
> Moreover, the intellect in this state instead of coming closer to its aim of perfection and knowledge gets farther from it. Mawlānā in the story of the dreaming archer compares him to Philosophers. He describes the archer's state:
>
> "O you who have provided yourself with bow and arrows, the prey is near and you have shot far.
>
> The philosopher killed [exhausted] himself with thinking: let him run on [in vain], for his back is turned towards the treasure.
>
> Let him run on: the more he runs, the more remote does he become from the object of his heart's desire.
>
> That (Divine) King said, "(those who) have striven in (for) Us": He did not say, "(those who) have striven away from Us," O restless one."[2]

The second occasion is when "the imagination" prevails over reason; the mystics believe this is one the most important obstacles in the way of mystical wayfaring:

> "Understandings [strong] as mountains have been submerged in the seas of imagination and the whirlpools of fantasy."[3]

Some mystics hold that mysticism is "setting the imagination right", whether imagination is defined as the faculty that perceives the particulars (pure formal percepts or both formal and cognitive precepts, which in the latter sense also includes illusions) or in a more general sense (the faculty that imagines and

---

1. *The Poems of Ḥāfiẓ Shīrāzī*, trans. 'Alāiddīn Pazārgādī, Ode No. 193.
2. *Mathnawī*, Book VI, Verse No. 2354, 2356 – 2358.
3 *Mathnawī*, Book V, Verse No. 2654.

manipulates the particulars or creates illusory forms and meanings) in the two dimensions of conception and assent, which dominates the life of most people. Accordingly, even those who understand the rational explanation of a proposition are sometimes influenced in their action or life by the imagination.

People both in their reflection and action take the particular findings and sometimes few personal experiences as their standards and in consequence in speculation they cannot perceive the universals and in action they are affected by the imagination and fancy. We will see that the faculty of imagination not only leaves its effect on the intellect, but also dresses the intuitions in clothes which are sometimes appropriate and in other times they are inappropriate and end in the distraction of the wayfarer.

The third occasion is when a person is in the state of seeing (witnessing and vision) or he can be in that exalted state, but he replaces "vision" of the heart with the "intelligence" of the intellect. In that case, which is counted a decline (from witnessing certainty to knowing about certainty), turning to the intellect is held blameworthy by the mystics, too. Rūmī writes:

> "Thou hast never perceived a Maker except by means of a thing made: thou art content with a syllogism.
> The philosopher multiplies links [consisting] of [logical] proofs; on the other hand, the elect [the mystic] is contrary to him [in this respect].
> The latter flees from the proof and from the veil [between himself and God]: he has sunk his head in his bosom for the sake of [contemplating] the Object of the proof.
> If to him [the philosopher], the smoke is a proof of the fire, to us [mystics] 'it is sweet [to be] in the fire without the smoke."[1]

---

1. *Mathnawī*, Book V, Verses No. 568 – 671

It is in such a state that the opposition between love and reason is discussed:

"Let thinkers be far from the lovers,
Let the smell of furnace be far from the breeze.
If a rationalist comes he will say there is no space,
But if a lover comes he will say one hundred welcome.
It is the circle of love and let the strict intellect,
Be spent in loving.
Until reason reflects and thinks,
Love reaches to the seventh heaven."[1]

Ḥāfiẓ also says:

"The sacred court of love is much loftier than that of reason,
And only someone can kiss that threshold who has his life in his sleeve."[2]

In short, the attraction and charm of the intellect can maximum take man to the threshold, but it finds no way into that court.

At the end it should be mentioned if a sensible finding like seeing a stick in water broken, or an intuition like finding hell pleasurable, or a transmitted tradition advocating, for example, determinism is in disagreement with the "certain" principles of the intellect, the intellect then is free to correct those instances. In that case the intellect either adopts a correct interpretation that is in harmony with other certain findings or rejects the contrary case or suspends any judgment on the question.

On the relationship between transmission, namely revelation and *ḥadīths*, and intuition Ibn 'Arabī states: although the certain and necessary text and transmission of the religious law are a standard for evaluating the mystics' spiritual experiences and

1. *Dīvān Shams*, Ode No. 172.
2. *The Poems of Ḥāfiẓ Shīrāzī*, trans. 'Alāiddīn Pazārgādī, Ode No. 121.

expressions, yet as we will see in the discussion on the criterion of the validity of the mystical experience these intuitions and spiritual experiences can be a clue for the interpretation of the uncertain text (whether uncertain in its origin or meaning) or determining its meaning or shifting from its surface meaning.

The Explanation of Ibn 'Arabī

To further illustrate the relationship between the intellect, the heart and the religious law and their agreement, it is important to explain the doctrine of Ibn 'Arabī and to quote some of his words. Ibn 'Arabī emphasizes on the two functions of the intellect which in consequence have two different implications. He states the intellect in "action" is finite but in "acceptance" is infinite. By this he intends there is difference between reason as a tool of knowledge and reason as a source of knowledge, which he calls "the mind" [thinking], and contends the intellect in the position of action (or the mind) has a certain limited field of action beyond which it can't understand any more, and it admits to this limitation under certain conditions. In this case reason or the mind beside the sense, intuition and revelation is one of the sources of human knowledge, but in the position of acceptance (accepting from another source, such as the sense, heart or revelation) there is no limit or boundary for it as it can take, accept and sometimes analyze knowledge from every other reliable source, such as the sense, revelation or the heart. The intellect in this respect is an imitator and a consumer.

Having explained this point, he criticizes some thinkers and philosophers and adds, "It is strange that they are ready to accept that the intellect is an imitator or a consumer of the five senses, taking its knowledge from them, but they are not ready to say the intellect could be an imitator or a consumer of revelation and the religious law or the heart's perceptions, whereas the possibility of error in the last two cases is less than the first one.

He believes that another limitation of the intellect is that it cannot comprehend the logic of "He is and He is not" and the simultaneous contradiction, which will be explained.

The example of the last group is some philosophers or shallow scholars who only on the ground that the content of revelation or the implications of intuition is unusual deny them or think they are less possible. Ibn 'Arabī, therefore, divides the people of the intellect into two groups:

The owners of the common and conventional intellects who depend on their intellectual findings and, therefore, cannot understand nonintellectual issues.

The owners of the enlightened intellects who acknowledge the intellect's insufficiency and limitation and, therefore, they are somehow guided to the nonintellectual mode. Moreover, their intellectual findings agree with the divine law and are compatible with the heart's perceptions. He believes the latter group through their enlightened intellect (which is connected to the universal intellect) can go beyond the intellectual mode and grasp the heart's perceptions and the world of intuition. For Ibn 'Arabī the interests and precepts of the religious law are also of the beyond-intellectual sciences.

Ibn 'Arabī calls the findings of the intellectual reflection "the science of reason" (like proving the existence of paradise and hell), the achievement of taste and experience of knowledge "the science of states" (such as drinking from the fountain of paradise in the imaginal revelation) and the attainment of divine gifts through the holy Spirit, which is particular to saints and prophets, "the science of the secrets" (like believing in the oneness of existence). The content of the science of the secrets is also of two kinds: either it is perceived by the intellect (like believing in the hereafter) or the intellect cannot grasp it and it is attained by spiritual revelation (such as understanding the states after death). In the latter case, it turns to either the science of states, but in a more certain and higher form, or the sciences of traditions (or transmission), which are based on the information given by the infallible on the hidden worlds (like what a person cannot understand by either intellect or intuition, but he believes in it through revelation).

Moreover, Ibn 'Arabī calls the sciences that are particular to the mystics and located in their heart "the science of specialization" and states the particular science of the people of the Real deals mainly with seven questions, which when understood appreciating the truths will be easier. The questions are:

Knowing the divine Names,

Knowing the manifestations of the Real,

Knowing the discourse of the Exalted Allah, which comes in the language of the divine laws (on the ambiguous and the anthropomorphic attributes of the Real),

Knowing the perfection of existence and its deficiency (knowing the best of orders and that even the seeming defects indicate perfection),

Knowing man's reality (and knowing his weakness, dependence and insufficiency in the process of self-knowledge),

Knowing the causes of imaginal revelation and knowing the conjunctive and disjunctive imagination (the way meanings appear in corporeal forms and vice versa), and

Knowing the diseases and their remedies (spiritual diseases, whether in speech, acts or states) which is necessary in practical wayfaring.

Ibn 'Arabī in different places of his works refers to those special sciences which are the outcome of nonintellectual perceptions and that he has experienced, such as the science of letter, the science of the scales, the science of the stations of the righteous, the science of the secret of destiny, the science of the incarnation of the spirits, and the science of unity.

The Knowledge of the Mystical Experience

Although "mystical experience" is a new term which first was suggested in modern theology in the 19th century and some studies have been done on its characteristics, kinds and precepts, yet its referent, namely mystical revelation and intuition, has been discussed for centuries by the mystics in different religions. Here, the writer attempts to present a combination of two of the mentioned methods.

Experience is a kind of immediate confrontation, which according to the kind of induction and function has different kinds and implications, such as:

Worldly experience (or sensory experience), which is of different kinds, such as:

Daily experience: different experiences which an individual has every day of the events and incidents in his surroundings.

Professional experience: It results from the repetition of a scientific or practical work, and it makes the work for the experienced person easy.

Scientific experience: such experiences are no longer sporadic or irregular but take the form of a science and a scientific discipline with certain definitions and principles.

Aesthetic experience (approbation): It is a live experience which stirs the feelings (but not necessarily knowledge and awareness) and is accompanied with excitement and quaint marvel but not any feeling of sanctity, devotion, glorification or commitment (as seen in the religious experience).

Moral experience: It is a feeling of exaltation and high spiritual position along with a calm conscience which results from doing a moral deed or acquiring a good attribute or moral precept. This feeling may be permanent or impermanent and its acquisition may be easy or difficult. This feeling is neither necessarily edifying nor accompanied with the elements of sanctity, devotion or submission.

Although the last two experiences have some similarities with the religious and mystical experiences, considering their import and characteristics and the definition and features of the inner experience and also the religious and mystical experiences that will be discussed later, they have also some noticeable differences with them. This is not to say that in the process of one event and incident different experiences may be present, as some theories have been offered since a long time on religion, mysticism, ethics and art and the unity of their origin and essence, which could be discussed in its right place.

Inner experience: Any kind of inner feeling and state or immediate and direct personal perception accompanied with a live confrontation and presence of the experienced that unintentionally and passively (though with deliberate preparations) leads to acquiring knowledge or evoking a special feeling, and the time of its beginning and end is set by the granting cause, is called inner experience.

Besides religious and mystical experiences, this definition includes the true vision or that which is seen in usual dreams, though formed by the imagination, and also the inner experiences of the individual in artificial sleep (hypnotism), under the effect of telepathy or some other psychological or Para-psychological phenomena that result from introspection or concentration, and even the temptations of the self or Satan.

Note 1: The epithets "immediate" and "direct" that modify perception mean it should not have any inferential relationship with the individual's previous knowledge, whether intuitively, such as spiritual revelations or inspirations, or acquired, like conjectures and guesses.

Note 2: Influencing the external world through inner meditation and demonstrating extraordinary issues outside the world of the soul, when accompanied by the features mentioned in the definition, can be included in the inner experience (or at least accompany it).

Religious experience: Whenever a personal cognitive perception that is immediate and direct comes with a (conscious) inner feeling and is accompanied with a confrontation and a feeling of connection with an exalted Being (God) or His supernatural manifestations (angels, Prophets, intimate servants [saints], etc.) and completes submission to the subject of the experience and requires or embraces religious traditions and sciences, in function it is a religious experience. It has the following features:

A feeling of objectivity and reality, which leads to the person's religious perfection and firmness in faith (adding to one's knowledge) besides fascination or wonder in regard of the known objects.

A sense of commitment and responsibility along with a feeling of sanctity, awe, reverence and peace which ends in glorifying the subject of the experience or praising and worshipping Him.

The religious experience which is often non-spatial and atemporal, in the mind of the person undertaking the experience and at the stage of turning into concepts and expressions, is expressed in religious terms. It is important to mention a few points here:

Besides the Prophets' revelation and mystical experiences this definition also embraces other states and habits, such as the desire to pray and supplicate, the feeling of hope and trusting Allah, the habit of God-fearing and justice, the true vision, inspiration and heavenly feeling (as put in the words of Rudolf Auto, with the three features of dependence on the absolute, yearning and awe), or a spiritual change or a physical change accompanied with spiritual conversion connected with religious manifestations, such as healing, repentance and guidance.

There is difference between the religious experience and religious insight. Religious insight is a kind of consciousness and understanding that is gained because of certain usual or unusual incidents and confirms and enforces the individual's religious faith. It is similar with the religious experience in creating a sense of commitment and inducing peace, but since there is no direct or live confrontation with God or the ultimate truth or His manifestations, and it is merely a mental conjecture or an inspiration like poetic inspiration or a moral inference of one incident, it is not counted as a religious experience. Religious insight may have a natural aspect with a religious interpretation or a supernatural aspect.

Religious experience as a term was introduced for the first time by Schleiermacher (d.1832), the German theologian, as the essence and the foundation of religion. Some hold that it was the result of a sort of apology and polemics against the rationalists' objections to Christianity. He believed that the essence of religion is an inner feeling and an attention to the infinite, and religion in substance is a feeling and yearning for the infinite being and the religious conduct, dogmas and acts are of secondary importance. For him, religious teachings are accounts of the religious sensibility and religious experience manifested verbally and expressed in words and sentences. After Schleiermacher a lot of researches have been done and many works have been written on the features of the religious experience and its validity, attributes and relationship with the mystical experiences.

The religious experience sometimes provides for the realization of another religious experience or a mystical experience, as repentance and its state may lead to a higher rank of faith and the experience of its joy.

Mystical experience: The mystical experience may be discussed from the two perspectives of comparative mysticism and Islamic mysticism. The features of mystical experience from the viewpoint of comparative mysticism are: a unifying vision; a feeling of certainty or reality (in the sense of independence from the mind and subject); a feeling of success, cheerfulness and satisfaction; a feeling that what is perceived is holy, sanctified and divine; and paradoxical, ineffable and affecting the individual's life.

According to William James, the two fundamental features of mystical experiences are indescribability and epistemological value, and their two dominant features are passiveness and transience. To put it in Stace's words, besides the above features inward or spiritual mysticism (in contrast to outward or horizontal mysticism) it has some other characteristics, such as the annihilation of individuality and the ultimate unity.

From the viewpoint of Rudolf Otto of the three kinds of relationships, namely I/ it (relationship of absence), I/ you (relationship of presence but without unity), and I/ I (relationship of presence along with oneness and unity), the last two experiences are similar to [the nature of] the experiences of presence. Otto calls the second experience (I/ you) the heavenly experience with three prominent features: a feeling of dependence on the absolute, a feeling of fear and awe, and a feeling of yearning for the object of the experience. He further maintains that the I/ I relationship exists in mystical experiences. For him these experiences are two kinds of religious experiences.

For the most Muslim mystics, the mystical experience is a kind of religious experiences, that is, they believe the way of mystical order and reaching the truth is found within and inside the divine law and it is like the core and the essence of religion. Accordingly they hold the true mystical states, in contrast to the manifestations of the self and the emergence of the hidden inner forces or spiritual and satanic temptations that contribute nothing to the perfection of the soul, are dependent on going along the road of the religious law.

Many of the mystical experiences and the stations of the mystics result from improving features and virtues discussed in religion, such as the station of satisfaction, trust, patience, which are of the mystical stations and of the fundamental pillars of the religious moral precepts.

Therefore, the mystical experience (for the Muslim mystics) is those inner and religious experiences in the form of a state, a station or immediate knowledge and at the same time mysterious with all the features of the religious experience (such as confronting a transcendent being or its manifestations, a feeling of sanctity, and commitment) and also a feeling of objectivity in the cognitive experiences that require the purgation and exaltation of the man of experience (the wayfarer) and induces a kind of change (enduring or short lived) in his life and adorns him with the divine moral attributes; finally it ends in the experiences of annihilation and subsistence. This experience has the following features:

It is achieved through *wilāyat* (friendship), love, purification and self-knowledge along with applying methods like introspection, inner concentration, remembrance, reflection, avoiding distractions and passing thoughts, purgation and spiritual adornment which are accomplished in the process of wayfaring or through spiritual attraction at the very beginning of the spiritual journey.

Its subject is the Real's manifestations in essence, Names and acts in the shape of lights or divine forms that are seen or spiritual or formal revelations.

Its ultimate end is the experience of annihilation and subsistence (intimacy due to supererogatory acts and intimacy resulting from obligatory acts) and the individual's manifestation of the divine Names and attributes.

Its dominant characteristics are the following:

It is delightful, soothing, invigorating and reviving.

It is ineffable and indescribable unless in symbolic terms.

It belongs to the indistinguishable unity and entails the individual's annihilation (it is the knowledge of the indefinite and indescribable Absolute).

It is paradoxical and in consequence perplexing (the simultaneous negation and affirmation of the existence of the world).

These experiences have different kinds and descriptions, including:

It is sometimes accompanied with unconsciousness, attraction, intoxication and bewilderment and sometimes with consciousness.

It is sometimes transient and sometimes enduring.

It is sometimes the experience of union with the beloved and sometimes separation and its consciousness.

It is accompanied sometimes with intimacy and sometimes with awe and fear.

It is accompanied sometimes with delight, intoxication and joy and sometimes with dejection and sadness.

It ends sometimes in a firmly-rooted attribute (a station) and sometimes in a transient state.

According to this definition, every inner experience (such as the experience of the non-religious ascetics) is not necessarily a religious experience, and a religious experience (such as having the desire to pray) may not be a mystical experience. Nevertheless, some inner experiences are both religious and mystical, such as reaching the station of trusting God or showing sincerity in worship. Of course, if mystical experiences could be realized in a non-religious environment, the relationship between the inner experience and mystical experience would be only a relationship of complete inclusion. The relationship among the three kinds of inner, religious and mystical experiences in a mode of complete inclusion is shown in the following diagram:

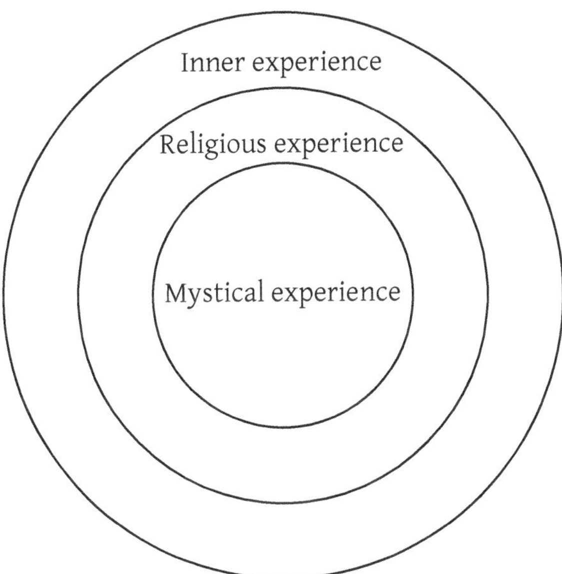

From the mystics' viewpoint the most important philosophy of prescribing the divine worship in the religious laws (the stage of the religious law) is preparation for the fulfillment of the religious experience (the stage of mystical Path), which in turn when it is firmly established and under certain conditions it can finally end in the mystical experience of unity (the stage of truth).

Revelation and the Mystical Experience

On the relationship between revelation and other mystical experiences, such as inspiration and spiritual revelation, it should be noted that although both are communicated by God and are of the nature of intuitive knowledge[1], the mystics contend they also have some differences in:

1. The content of the message. Revelation comprises laws and is compulsory, whereas other mystical experiences do not have such content.
2. Evidence: The content of inspiration and acting according to it is evidential only to its receiver, whereas revelation is a complete evidence for others too, and therefore unlike inspiration it must be announced and made public. This point in turn leads to another characteristic of revelation, namely "commitment".
3. Restriction: Revelation, which is one of the characteristics of Prophethood, is restricted to the prophets, but inspiration, which is one of the features of the intimate friends of Allah, is open to all.
4. Intermediacy (a dominant feature): Revelation is often received through an angel, but inspiration often has no intermediary and occurs in a special way.
5. Infallibility: In the experiences of revelation and the Prophets' revelation not only is knowledge and its reception by the Prophets free from error, but also its expression in the language of the intellect and putting it in the mould of words and phrases is not

---

1. Mawlānā says: The Sufis in explaining (their doctrine) call it (the Divine inspiration) the inspiration of the heart, in order to disguise (its real nature) from the vulgar."
Take it to be the inspiration of the heart, for it [the heart] is the place where He is seen: how should there be error when the heart is aware of Him?" *Mathnawī*, Book IV, Verses No. 1853- 1854.

open to any mistake. Accordingly, the content of revelation is not necessarily affected by the culture of the time.

6. Intuitiveness: Another important difference between revelation and inspiration from the viewpoint of Ibn 'Arabī is that revelation, Prophethood and in consequence divine laws are thought to be of the intuitive sciences, whereas sciences resulting from God-fearing (such as inspiration) are among the acquired sciences.

Another difference is the necessity of undertaking the last journey of the four mystical journeys (the journey with the Real among the people or the journey with the people to the Real) in Prophethood, while it is unnecessary in other mystical experiences, and moderation in speech and refraining from extravagant speeches in explaining the experiences of revelation, which are counted as two dominant characteristics of the Prophets' experiences. Other suggested differences, however, such as the clear and detailed nature of revelation, and the assurance it gives and the information it offers of the history of the people in the past and future, cannot clearly distinguish between revelation and other mystical experiences.

On the differences between inspiration and intuition and revelation Āshtiyānī in his commentary on the Qayṣarī's introduction to *Fuṣūṣ al-Ḥikam* writes:

The difference between inspiration and revelation is that in the revelation to the Prophet(S) the angel which is the source of sciences and truths—with the help of Allah—and by conferring cognitive forms expands the heart and relieves the soul of the Prophet(S), is seen and known by the Prophet(S), that is, the Prophet(S) is aware of the medium ... but this does not occur in inspiration. The inspired only perceives the subtle form of the angel, which is a superadded form. Apparently the difference between these two stations is related to the intensity, weakness or perfection of the light and its absence. The difference between revelation and inspiration according to the views of the verifying mystics and Qayṣarī's account is due to four factors:

First, inspiration is sometimes provided by the knowing King without the intermediation of any being, that is, it results from the particular existence of the Real with the objects. However, revelation is transmitted by the angels and their testimony to the Prophet's soul and, accordingly, the holy *ḥadīths* are not counted revelation.

Second, revelation as a kind of intuition includes spiritual intuition... whereas inspiration is pure spiritual intuition.

Third, revelation is one of the characteristics of Prophecy, but inspiration is of the characteristics of the saints.

Fourth, as it was explained (at the beginning of the discussion) the Prophet(S) does not receive revelation unless he knows the cause and the reason of the knowledge gained through revelation. (Moreover,) one of the conditions of revelation, unlike inspiration, is its communication."

The Cognitive Aspect of the Mystical Experience

Since the cognitive value of theoretical mysticism is rooted in mystical experiences and the mystics' intuitions, in this chapter it is of vital importance to consider the possibility of knowledge in mystical experiences and its different modes and the degree of its validity. The question here is the cognitive aspect of those mystical experiences which refer to a mystical meaning. Accordingly, first we will consider the nature of the mystical experience and the qualities of intuitive knowledge and also the validity and authority of the mystical experiences and their criteria. We will also discuss the kinds, the principles and the obstacles in the way of such experiences, and finally we will look into the language of mysticism.

The Nature of the Mystical Experience

There are some principal views on the nature of the mystical experience and its relationship with certain dimensions of human existence.

1. The Emotional View. According to this view, the mystical experience has no cognitive content value and, therefore, it can be neither confirmed nor contested. As Schleiermacher says, the religious and mystical experience is in a way to feel dependent on the absolute or a power that is distinct from the world, and it is ineffable because emotions have no cognitive or conceptual value. Rudolph Otto also associates celestial feeling with the feelings of dependence on a superior being, fear and humility, and desire and love for an exalted being.

Objection: Although this view explains some of the characteristics of the mystical experience like ineffability, as Iqbal Lahuri emphasizes in his *The Reconstruction of Religious Thinking in Islam*, it cannot explain the true or false claims of the mystics on the basis of pure emotions, for emotions in the stage of experience and practice are devoid of concepts (though in the stage of demonstration and reporting they are expressed in the form of concepts). Therefore, this theory is incompatible with the cognitive side of the mystical revelations and religious experiences.

2. Quasi-sensible **Perception View.** The religious experience has the same structure of the sensory experience, albeit at a personal and spiritual level; that is, it has the three sides of perceiver, perceived and perception. For in sensory perception the external reality (the objective reality) shows itself to man in a way that he can perceive. According to Alston in both kinds of experience in the process of description neither the observer (perceiver) nor the acts of perception (perception) is considered, and the reality of the thing or the phenomenon (the perceived) is presented through certain concepts. Of course, the differences of the two kinds of experience, such as the universality of the sensory experience on one hand and the personality of the mystical experience on the other, the detailed and worldly nature of the sensory experience and its taking the form of certain qualities in contrast to the general (mysterious) nature of the mystical experience and its refrain from taking any definite form are not hidden from the proponents of this theory. To these some other differences may also be added:

- The truth and accuracy of a certain mystical experience, unlike sensory experiences, cannot be easily estimated.
- Although both mystical and sensory experiences at the stage of demonstration abound with theories, the mystical experiences compared to sensory experiences are much more open to interpretation.

We will see that this view in its emphasis on the relationship and similarity between the two kinds of experiences has been able to answer some of the objections made to the validity and authority of the mystical experiences.

Objection: Although the mystical and the sensory experiences are similar to each other in some respects, and duly on they may say this view is closer to reality than other views, this view also cannot explain the nature of the mystical experiences, for evidently if we consider the mystical experience (from an cognitive dimension) a kind of intuitive knowledge, in this experience we cannot propose the three elements of perceiver, perceived object and perception independently. Moreover, unlike the sensory knowledge, which is considered to be acquired knowledge and is open to error in the stage of experience, intuitive knowledge in the stage of experience is infallible, for in such knowledge the known by essence and the known by accident are untied whereas in acquired knowledge they are different. Nevertheless, these two kinds of experience are similar in their fallibility in the stage of expression. That is, in the process of moving from intuitive knowledge to the world of concepts and then putting the concepts into words and expression there is the possibility of error and mistake in correspondence and expression, and so it is in the expressed sensory experiences.

The other similarity between the two kinds of experience is that they are both selective and cannot probe the depth of the subject of their knowledge. One other objection to this view is that if the validity, authority or the certainty of the sensory perception (external senses) is not accepted, according to this view there will be no way to explain the authority or the validity of the mystical experience (unlike some other views).

3. The Interrelatedness of Experience and Interpretation View. This view contends that mystical states and experiences are influenced by previous essential concepts and ideas and argues man's concentrations are the efficient cause (origin) or formal cause (mould) of such experiences. According to Pradfoot, the mystics do not come to any special knowledge or intuitions, but rather it is the mystic's beliefs that create his revelations, like dreams which are rooted in the past experiences and expectations of the individuals. As evidence this view refers to the differences that exist among the mystical or religious experiences of different beliefs, religions and sects.

Objection: Although it may be true to claim that some intuitions are rooted in the beliefs of the mystic, like some visions or intuitions, it should be noted that this is not true about some others, that is, it is in the process of the mystical or religious experience that the individual's convictions are developed, as in dreams some are true and looks into the future, which is totally unknown to the person and duly will make him believe in such a future. Even the religious mystics for whom at the beginning the texts of Ibrahimic religions may not confirm the unity of the Real and the world, but rather indicate their separation, following their experience of the "unity" they begin to see a different meaning in the verses and to have a different interpretation.

On the difference of the mystics' experiences in different religions it should be noted that this is only difference in application or expression and does not injure the common origin of their experiences. Rūmī writes:

> "The disagreement of mankind is caused by names: peace ensues when they advance to reality [denoted by the name]."[1]

Moreover, the difference in expression is sometimes due to the level of the mystic's perception and capacity and the intensity of his existence and knowledge rather than any essential difference in the nature of the experience. To explain further, it should be said that the influence of the concepts and accumulated knowledge is manifested at the stage of expression and not at the time of intuitive experience, as in sensory perception also the different expressions and interpretations emerge only after the sensation. Accordingly, separating the three stages of "perception" (understanding in the domain of intuitive knowledge), "conception and assent" (explanation in the domain of the mind and concepts speculatively) and "expression and interpretation" (in the domain of language and words) will help to eliminate any confusion in the discussion, because the effect of the earlier knowledge is manifested in the last two stages rather than the first one.

4. The Illusion View. It imports that mystical experiences are mere effusions of the mind and the manifestations of the human

1. *Mathnawī*, Book II, Verse No. 3680

unconscious in his consciousness and necessarily do not indicate anything real. Moreover, in nature they are not different from the mental illusions produced by drugs or opium.

Another form of this view is that the supernatural explanation of these experiences is due to the expectations or presuppositions of the individuals, and since the experience accompanies interpretation, it is the interpretation of such experiences in the context of the person's particular ideological system that makes the experience mystical or religious, whereas the same experience may appear no more than an illusion in the context of another person's ideology.

Objection: Despite some superficial similarities between the states of the mystics and those of the deluded, the mystical experiences in respect of function, knowledge and structure, which will be discussed in the section on the principles and criteria of the mystical experience, are essentially different from the other states (see appendix 1). Moreover, this view cannot explain the characteristics of some mystical experiences, such as intuitive experiences that foresee the future or true dreams (besides the ineffability of some other experiences).

5. Intuitive Knowledge View. In this view the cognitive side of mystical experiences is explained on the basis of intuitive knowledge, for this knowledge with its special features can explain the main characteristics of mystical experiences, such as being personal, the feeling of objectivity throughout the experience, indescribability of the subject of the experience, and the experience of unity. The characteristic features of intuitive knowledge are:

- Immediacy (compared to concept, sensation or thought): In a logical division based on negation and affirmation, knowledge is either gained indirectly through concepts or directly, that is, either the known object is present for the knower or only its form and concept. The former, as an example, is a person's knowledge of himself and his states, such as sadness, happiness, fear, love and his perceptive and sensory faculties, and the latter, again to give an example, is the person's awareness of his or others' shape, colour and other qualities.

- Infallibility: Since error occurs in the stage of correspondence between the reporter and the reported object, and in intuitive knowledge there is no concept or form to describe an external object, no doubt infallibility, certainty, assurance and truth will be some of the features of intuitive knowledge. So one cannot doubt his psychological or inner states, such as pain, sadness or joy.
- Doubt: According to the subject of the intuitive perception or the features and existential degree of the perceiver or the other factors contributing to intuitive knowledge, this knowledge will be strong or weak and clear or obscure. Sometimes intuitive perception even goes unnoticed, for example when pain is forgotten because of looking at an absorbing scene.
- Being personal: Unlike speculative knowledge and sensory experience which from a conceptual perspective they are universal and experimental, intuitive knowledge is restricted to the perceiver, which is a part of his being, and is intertwined with his existence.
- Conceptualization and interpretation: Although there is no place for conception and assent in intuitive knowledge and in the stage of experience and realization it is not mixed with concepts, yet when it is communicated to the mind it takes the shape of concepts and mental forms and becomes the subject of reflection, such as definition, reasoning and interpretation. These mental activities which aim at producing speculative knowledge on the findings of intuitive knowledge in the

domain of conception are called "conceptualization" and in the domain of assent are named "interpretability". To explain further, every intuitive finding, such as my existence, pain, grief, joy and other states and faculties, first its meaning is probed in the mind, namely it is defined and classified conceptually, and second concerning its application and interpretation its terms are explained and analyzed. For example, "Pain is of the nature of qualities," "Knowledge is of the category of quality," "Knowledge is of the category of relation", "My existence is a substantial existence," or "My existence is immaterial". Evidently in this stage error in application may happen or the terms are confused, as some have claimed the self (soul) is material or knowledge is of the category of relation. It is in this stage that some errors in the mystical revelations happen.

The last stage is related to the relationship between concepts and expressions, that is, in expressing what is understood intuitively and then transferred to the world of concepts, certain words and expressions are borrowed from the world of language or they are coined, which act to inform the addressee of the subject of knowledge. Evidently, in this stage, error in choosing the right words, sentences or terms may lead to transferring incorrect concepts, aims and findings. So, the following stages follow each other respectively:

Intuitive knowledge → conceptualization → explanation → verbal expression

To sum up, the view which can give a positive clear description of the cognitive aspect of the mystical experience and the characteristics of such experience, like immediacy, infallibility, being personal, communicability, and hierarchy, is the view of intuitive knowledge.

A Few Points

1. Intuitive knowledge, by essence, cannot accept dichotomies such as conception and assent, and also by essence it cannot be said either true or false, and error cannot be attributed to it. Therefore, it is also classified neither as self-evident nor speculative (though it is the origin of self-evident knowledge), and all these divisions are accidentally attributed to it following its shift to speculative knowledge and the world of concepts and expressions.

2. Intuitive knowledge is of two kinds: universal and particular. The first kind like the knowledge of the self and its states and faculties is related to all, but the second, such as spiritual revelations and inspirations, are particular to certain people and achieved under special conditions. Mystical experience belongs to this kind of knowledge.

3. Acquired knowledge as self-evident or speculative falls into different degrees and so is speculative knowledge sometimes definite and sometimes conjectural. Intuitive knowledge likewise has different levels according to its intensity or weakness and clarity or obscurity. Some kinds of intuitive knowledge are clear and direct spiritual revelation and intuition, while some others are vague and need explanation. Of course, the obscurity of the latter may be due to their shift to acquired knowledge.

4. Some scholars argue unconsciousness is one of the features of intuitive knowledge and believe that concentrating on intuitive knowledge and consciousness would eliminate it immediately and turns it into acquired knowledge. However, the fact is unconsciousness is not one of the inherent features of intuitive knowledge, and as much as consciousness of one's self and existence while reading a book is counted intuitive knowledge, this very consciousness and awareness of it and self-inspection

(knowledge of knowledge) and reflection on and understanding mystical revelations are also instances of intuitive knowledge. Of course, as was said before, mystical experiences come by themselves and cannot be induced deliberately, but this aspect is related to the involuntary agency of the origin of these experiences rather than the formal and cognitive aspect of these experiences.

5. The difference between this view (intuitive knowledge) and the second one (similar with sensory perceptions) is clear for those who are skeptical of sensory sciences, for their skepticism necessarily does not extend to include intuitive knowledge, as Descartes extended his doubts to all sensible things but stopped doubting in the domain of intuitive knowledge (his existence, perceptions and even his doubt). Moreover, according to some of the views mentioned above the mystical experiences relate to personal, psychological and uncertain issues in the real world.

Two Objections to Mystical Experiences

1. The falseness of some kinds of intuitive knowledge. Some have argued that error may occur in issues which are known intuitively; therefore, by this probability such experiences are either not intuitive or visionary experiences and intuitive knowledge are open to mistake. For example, time may seem different for two people (for one expecting an event or a person longer but for the other shorter). These two perceptions are gained intuitively, but one or both of them may not correspond with reality (the real time spent).

Answer: This objection does not deny the cognitive value of the mystical experience, for that which is perceived intuitively is not time itself since time is outside the person and his self, but the expectation of the person or his awareness or ignorance of the passing of the seconds or (what is technically called psychological time). Accordingly, error happens in the interpretation of mystical experiences rather than the perception of intuitive and visionary issues, as in sensory perception philosophers locate error in the stage of judgment, interpretation and application rather than perception. For example, the error of a person who sees a mirage is due to his misjudgment of seeing "the fractured light in the steam that exists in the air" and "seeing or the existence of water" rather than in seeing something.

2. The unknowability of the ineffable. One of the objections made to the intuitive and visionary issues is that they are ineffable and unknown. To explain, we always gain new knowledge because of our previous knowledge, and a thing which is not founded on past knowledge or there is no word or concept for it, will not be knowable.

Answer: It is not necessary to always base knew knowledge on previous knowledge; otherwise there would be endless regress. Self-evident sciences and intuitive knowledge itself are counted as cognitive principles (fundamental dogmas). Moreover, if the mystical experiences are ineffable and unknown, it is because they are different from conventional knowledge and the incompatibility of the mystics' knowledge with the current expressions and concepts used by people, rather than being absolutely unknown and essentially ineffable. In the section on the language of mysticism this will be discussed in detail.

The Kinds of Mystical Experience

In comparative mysticism, based on their different aspects, mystical experiences may be divided:

1. On the basis of the medium of the experience. Suin Burn inductively divides the experience of God or the ultimate truth in the following way:

a. Through the medium of a sensible thing considered as general and common, such as the experience of God by looking at a Saint's statue or by looking at the sunset.
b. Through the medium of a sensible and general but unconventional thing, like a burning bush that does not burn.
c. Through the medium of a personal and describable thing, such as the experience of God in vision or spiritual revelation.
d. Through the medium of a personal but indescribable thing, such as understanding the presence of God in things.
e. Through no sensible medium, such as understanding the undifferentiated unity.

2. On the basis of the object of the experience. Stace divides mysticism into the horizontal (external) and the spiritual (internal) and writes:

The essential difference between the two is that the horizontal looks and contemplates the outside through the senses, whereas the spiritual journey looks inside and at the soul. Both journeys end in knowing the ultimate unity or as Plotinus says, "the true unity" ... The horizontal mystic who employs his physical senses sees the diversity and plentitude of the external objects—the sea, the sky, etc.—in a different light through his mystical perception and finds and sees the One or unity manifested in them. The inward-looking mystic, however, tries by extinguishing the physical senses and eliminating the sensory forms, conceptions and thoughts from the tablet of his mind to reach the depth of his essence. He claims that in the hidden corners of his soul and in the rest and silence he finds "the real One", with Whom he is united in origin, but not in the form of unity in diversity (as happens in the horizontal states), but rather in the form of One where there is no diversity or plurality.

In Islamic mysticism also there are different classifications of the mystical experience; some are based on the subject of the experience; some on its origin and circumstances; some on its intensity, weakness or kind; and some on its accompanied effects and states. Of course, these classifications may overlap and partially resemble each other. In the following we refer to some mystical experiences on the basis of the mentioned criteria.

1. The object of the experience

a. Formal and Spiritual Revelation: What man experiences by the inner five senses in the imaginal world and is accompanied with forms similar to the sensory forms is a formal revelation and according to these senses is divided into the following kinds:

- Visual revelation, like seeing the forms of the incarnated spirits and also spiritual lights.
- Aural revelation, such as hearing the voice of the angel by the Prophet.
- Olfactory revelation, such as smelling the breath of the Merciful from the direction of Yemen by the Prophet(S).
- Tactile revelation, such as feeling the power of God when it touches the body.
- Taste revelation, such as drinking milk in a true vision and interpreting it as knowledge.

These revelations sometimes happen together and sometimes come single. They often are accompanied with awareness and knowledge and, therefore, they are associated with spiritual revelations. However, those truths which have no form and are revealed to man in the form of pure meanings fall in the category of "spiritual revelation", which are of different ranks and kinds:

- Conjecture: the emergence of meanings in the rational faculty with no use of premises or deduction.
- The holy light: the appearance of meanings in the rational faculty through reasoning (the lowest rank of spiritual revelation).

- Inspiration: the manifestation of one of the meanings to the heart of the person.
- Seeing by heart: the manifestation of one of the truths or one of the spirits to the human heart.
- Spiritual seeing: the manifestation of one of the truths to man's spirit.

Note. The formal revelation is also divided in two kinds:

1. The revelation of sensible quantities in the form of the world of quantity.
2. The revelation of imaginal quantities: The imaginal world is the first thing which is revealed to the wayfarers, and the different sensible and non-sensible revelations happen in this world.

b. Worldly and Otherworldly Revelations. These two kinds of revelation are also formal revelations (and are often accompanied with spiritual revelation). According to the experience in question, if it concerns worldly events and the incidents of this world, it is called monasticism. The mystics because of the importance they must give to the other world and even only to God, they are recommended to pay no attention to this kind of experience, which is sometimes called enticement.

c. Annihilation and subsistence. Jāmī defines the experience of annihilation as follows:

"Annihilation means because of the overwhelming manifestation of the Real to the interior there no longer remains any awareness of anything other than Him, and it is not hidden that the annihilation of annihilation is implied in annihilation.... This annihilation is the result of unity (unifying the interior), namely extricating the mind from any attachment to anything other than the Real, both in seeking and desire and in knowledge and understanding. In other words, no longer other desired and loved things are desired or sought after, and all known and comprehended objects are removed from the vision and no awareness remains other than that of the Exalted Real to the extent that at the end even the awareness of one's annihilation should vanish from one's consciousness, for even awareness of annihilation is awareness of something other than the absolute Reality. Such an absolute annihilation is not merely a mental state of man, but it is the fulfillment and the prevalence of the Absolute over the limited, as with the rising of the sun all the stars disappear. Therefore, as some verifiers explain, annihilation is not merely a human experience, that is, man is not the agent of the experience, but the agent of the experience is the absolute Reality (the face of Allah). In other words, man's experience of annihilation is the realization of Reality in him and the predominance of his interior over his exterior. The metaphysical and cognitive importance of annihilation is that it shows all determinations return in reality to the source of purity and indeterminacy. Therefore, from an epistemological viewpoint annihilation is to see the reality of things, because being in origin and in its pure form is absolute and unlimited, and as soon as it takes the form of a thing it is no longer itself.

In the stage of annihilation man observes how worldly things lose their apparent solidity and finally vanish in that infinite, unique and absolute being, but in the stage of subsistence the same things from the same absolute undifferentiated reality emerge with all the details, but this time as absolute manifestations and objectifications.

Annihilation is the beginning of "the mode" of sainthood, and according to the rank of the wayfarer it is divided into three levels: annihilation in essence, namely observing that existence is the unique existence to the Exalted Real; annihilation in attributes or understanding that the attributes of perfection are confined to the attributes of the Real; and annihilation in acts, or seeing that all acts are limited to the action of the Real. These levels follow each other, as it will be explained in the section on the different kinds of manifestations.

Subsistence, which is defined as witnessing God's sustenance of all beings, refers to a spiritual rank where the entire world, which has vanished so far in nonexistence and lost in the absolute unity of "being", once again emerges from the depth of nonexistence, and the diverse phenomenal world with its endless variety once again is made visible. In this stage, the same things which in the state of annihilation had lost their apparent solidity come to view again, but they have already lost their essential and substantial self, that is, they no longer appear as self-dependent entities but rather as absolute inner determinations perceived by the hearing and seeing of the Real (the proximity of the supererogatory acts).

d. Knowledge of certainty, objectified certainty, and real certainty. If of the three well-known terms, knowledge of certainty is related to the highest degree of acquired knowledge, the other two terms are related to intuitive knowledge and mystical experiences in the specific sense of the terms. In other words, a person in the stage of objectified certainty sees the truth by the eye of the heart in the form of intuition and spiritual vision, but in real certainty he becomes one with the truth. Each of these ranks are attained respectively one after the other, as influenced by verse seven of *Takāthur* Rūmī writes:

"Knowledge leads to vision, O knowing one:
If it (knowledge) became intuitive certainty, they would see Hell."[1]

Real certainty is also defined as witnessing the truth in its

1. *Mathnawī*, Book III, Verse 4123.

highest form, in a way that it cannot be exceeded (in Kāshānī's words it is to see the unseen as one sees the sensible).

e. Intuition, vision and seeing. In this classification, according to Kāshānī's definition, the first of the divine attributes and truths or truths of creation that dawns upon the wayfarer through a subtle curtain and in the form of a transparent veil of one of the divine Names, which is qualified by a term or an attribute, is called "intuition". If the same truths appear to him with no manifestation or attribute but along a special feature, they are called "vision". However, if there is neither a feature nor distinction but only the appearance of the objectified essence, it is called "seeing".

2. According to awareness and its intensity and weakness

a. On the basis of the level of the mystical experience: The kinds of mystical experiences according to the level of the experience are divided into:

- **Vision and intuition.** The manifestation of objectified forms and meanings in the state of sleep is called "vision" (dream), in wakefulness "revelation", in trance (in a state between sleep and wakefulness) "event", and sobriety (which is particular to the perfect) "seeing". As was said already all the mentioned states come to man and they cannot be induced willingly and the person of experience is overpowered by the mentioned states.
- Mixed and pure. Each of the kinds of the mystical experience (such as vision and revelation and event) may happen in one of the three possible forms:
  - Immaterial. That which is seen by the eye of the heart happens exactly in the seen world, and the imagination does not temper with it, as in the true vision and pure revelation there is no place for falsehood.

- ○ Imagined. That which the spirit sees in the event or vision, the soul or the imagination dresses it with an appropriate form and sees it in that habit. Such a revelation or vision is an imagined revelation or interpreted or deciphered vision and to understand it there is need for an interpreter.

- **Pure imagination.** Whether a dream or an event, it is mere mental suggestions and personal imaginings which prevail over the heart and prevents the soul from contemplating the unseen world. This state in sleep is called confused dreams and in others it is called false event.

b. According to the rank of the person undertaking the experience. The mystics divide the human ranks to seven levels parallel to seven subtle points, and have mentioned for each level of the soul's perfection some corresponding intuitions, such as material (natural) revelations, revelations of the heart, spiritual revelation, inner revelation, and essential revelation, which respectively result in awareness of the hidden issues of the worlds of nature, imagination (heavenly kingdom), spirit and intellect (omnipotence), Names and attributes (divinity) and the station of absolute unity. Moreover, the mystical intuitions according to the spiritual growth of the wayfarer and the orientation of his perception (tending to see diversity, unity or inclusiveness, namely unity in diversity and diversity in unity) are divided into the intuitions of the people of division, people of gathering, and people of the gathering of gathering (second division). This classification is explained in the following.

In the station of gathering attention is given to the Real without considering the creatures; in the station of division the creatures are seen in the Real. In other words, the station of gathering is awareness of the existence of the world and man as manifestations of the essence of the Real, where the manifest and the agent of manifestation are united. The station of division is to know that the existence of the Real is God, which entails the differentiation between the manifest and the manifesting. The station of gathering of gathering, however, is to know the self and the world in the mirror of the Real (by essence) and to know the Real in the mirror of the self and the world (by accident). In this station neither the creatures are the veil of the Real nor is the Real the veil of the creatures.

To explain further, division at first stems from the tendency of mankind to distinguish between the absolute (the Real) and the world of manifestations. Thus reality is divided into two completely distinct parts, the absolute and permanent and the relative and changing, and this view which is based on dualism is called "division". However, for the person who has attained annihilation the world is totally different and there are no essential distinctive marks that separate things from each other and, in fact, there is no awareness. When the perceiver disappears, all determinations and apparent qualifications of things in the external world also vanish, and there only remains the absolute Reality, which is called "the station of gathering".

The highest station is that of subsistence; the mind which in the previous station had stopped working resumes its act of understanding, and things which had been gathered in the station of unity once again are separated into determined diversified beings. Thus this station is called "division after gathering" or "the second division". The essential difference between the first and the second division, however, is that in the first division things are separated from each other distinctly and everything is seen as independent, but in the second division there is no pure diversity, for in this station all the special distinctive marks of things are no other than determinations of the absolute unity, and the unity and purity itself eliminates all existential differences. In this station diversity is unity albeit unity with certain essential aspects. This station is called "the gathering of gathering".

On the other hand, the difference between this station and that of annihilation (gathering) is that unity in the station of annihilation is simple with no aspects, whereas in the station of gathering of gathering it has essential aspects and determinations.

According to Ibn 'Arabī, the views of those who have attended the station of gathering of gathering are the most valid, for the people of this station have "two eyes" and have probed the different interiors and the exteriors of both worlds.

3. According to the effects and states attending the experience

The mystical state or revelation, whether it is permanent or impermanent in time, conscious or unconscious, a dream or a waking vision, bewildering or reassuring, accompanied by silence or speech and wordiness, invigorating or weakening, coupled with intimacy and hope and joy or awe and fear and dejection, is of different kinds. For the people of knowledge each of these has a name and certain attributes, though they cannot be explained in detail here.

The divine manifestations are projected on the heart of the wayfarer in the form of various lights, which are recorded and interpreted in the different treatises of the mystics. As an example we refer to the fifteen lights mentioned in *Ḥikmat al-Ishrāq* and Suhrawardī, the Master of the Illumination Philosophy, believes the Illumination epistemology induces them in the wayfarer. Suhrawardī contends the lights reflected from the higher world and function as the elixir of knowledge, power and control of nature and are divided into the following:

1. A light that reflects on the novices; it is pleasant but impermanent.
2. A light which is higher than the first; it is more like lightening but fearful.
3. A light that is enjoyable and soothing; it reflects on the heart of the people of knowledge and arouses a delightful feeling in them, like when warm water is poured over their heads.
4. A light which is strong and overwhelming; it remains fixed and stable for a long time and numbs the mind.
5. A light that is extremely enjoyable but it is not like lightening; it is evoked by the power of love.
6. A burning light which is evoked by the power of might, and sometimes it terrifies the novices.
7. A bright and absorbing light which is seen brighter than the sun and it causes immense joy.
8. A bright and pleasant light which lasts for a long time and is imagined to be connected to the hair.
9. An occurring light which is both painful and delightful.
10. A light which seems to be settled inside the brain.
11. A light that the soul sheds on all the dimensions of the human spirit and seems as if it makes the body its shield.
12. A light that is accompanied with might and force and looks as if something has been demolished over man's head.
13. A light that snatches the soul and suspends it; it reflects the purity of the soul in different ways.
14. A light that is felt invested with a weight beyond human's endurance.
15. A light that moves and shakes the body and the soul so much as if man is in danger of being cut into pieces.

4. According to the origin of the experience

In this classification the origin and the source of the mystical experiences and the cause of the passing thoughts and inspirations or intuitions and manifestations are considered.

a. The kinds of suggestions and inspirations. Suggestions are discourses that reflect in the heart and derive from different sources. According to their source, they have different names.

- Divine suggestion: It is when the origin of the address is the divine presence.
- Angelic suggestion or inspiration: It is when the origin of the address is one of the angels.
- Personal suggestion or hunches: It is when the origin of the address is the self.
- Satanic suggestion or temptation: It is when the origin of the address is Satan.

Although the mystics stress the total denial of suggestions in order to prepare the heart for divine vision, they discuss the kinds and standards of suggestions with elaboration since the last two kinds are counted obstacles.

b. The kinds of Manifestations. Manifestation is defined as "What appears to the hearts of the hidden lights". The use of this manifestation in practical mysticism is in epistemology and in theoretical mysticism is in ontology. This manifestation stands in contrast to veiling. Its main element is "light", but in revelation it is unveiling. These lights on the ground of their origin are divided into three kinds.

- The manifestation of essence: Its origin is the essence and it causes the annihilation of the essence of the wayfarer and makes him see the existence of all beings in the unique existence of the Real. The vision of these manifestations is called "intuition".
- The manifestation of attributes: Its place is the best Divine Names and the perfections of the essence. It leads to the

Wayfarer's annihilation in the attributes and makes him see all the attributes of perfection in the Exalted Real. Such a vision is called "revelation".

• The manifestation of acts: Its source is the act of the Real and His holy emanation which leads to the annihilation of the acts, unity in action and reducing all acts to the one act of the Real. Such a vision of the mystic is called "presence".

Validity and Authority of the Mystical Experience

In this section we discuss whether mystical experience is supported by belief and dogma, first for the mystic himself and second for others, and then by reviewing the standards of truth and falseness in mystical experience and also the possibility of difference in view or error in the inner experience we will answer some objections in this regard.

The Ground of the Validity and Authority of the Mystical Experience

Is the belief based on the mystical experience reliable or not? In other words, is such experience in terms of "truth" and "acceptability" reliable? Since among the different views on truth, here the one based on correspondence with reality is accepted, the validity and reliability of the mystical experience is both possible and is supported epistemologically. On the other hand, according to the theories on the nature of mystical experience we can accept the significance of the mystical experiences in explaining theoretical mysticism—that is, coming to logical truth (correspondence with reality), which is different from moral truth (correspondence with belief)—when we either relate them to intuitive knowledge and assume they are infallible, or at least assume they are in the same level with the sensory perceptions and have the same degree of credibility or conventional certainty (like Alston's theory). Therefore, this discussion can be followed in two ways:

a. The authority of the mystical experience for its undertaker: Since the undertaker of such experiences is certain of his object, belief in such mystical statements is reliable, and even it is the very proof and reliability.

b. The reliability of the mystical experiences for others: In this concern also those mystical experiences which are common, like perceptional and sensory experiences, and therefore experienced frequently that there is no probable agreement of falseness on them, they are reliable for others too, especially when they are reported by a mystic, whose life, as the Master of Illumination states, is the evidence of his truthfulness. Such observations in certainty and objectivity are no less than that of the observations of an astronomer and his reports to the scientific society and other people. William James argues that in effect the mystical states are like the direct experience of truth and are as valid as the sensory perceptions for us. Moreover, the gap existing between the first person singular (I) and the second person singular (you), one possessed with intuitive and the other with acquired knowledge, is not so big to make their destination different in this respect. Indeed in acquired knowledge a man may make an error in his judgment and then correct it, but in direct experience where the very object of knowledge is found, error does not occur. Even in sensory experience error happens only in subsequent judgment at the stage of application and interpretation.

Now considering the differences that sometimes exist in intuitive knowledge, namely intuitions or expressions following spiritual visions and also the opposite sayings of two mystics, what is the criterion of the truth of these mystical experiences? Before giving an answer to this question, it should be noted that the difference in mystical experiences and their explanation sometimes relates to their intensity or weakness and their clarity or obscurity and sometimes to the difference in the station and rank of the mystic or his attitude and convictions. As Shabistarī writes:

"Since meanings are according to the spiritual station,
There is a problem in the people's understanding."

Of course, the possibility of error necessarily does reduce the validity of perception, as errors that occur in sensory experiences neither decrease from their credibility nor obliterate their reliability, so far that there is a standard for distinguishing the true and false.

On the reliability of the mystical experiences Ibn 'Arabī maintains that reports on the knowledge of the secrets may come through two ways:

1. The infallible (such as the Prophet), and in this case their truth is certain and necessary.
2. Other than the infallible (such as the mystic), in this case their truth is probable, provided that they should be neither impossible nor contrary to any of the principles of the religious law. Then we would be free to accept them or not.

To put it in other words, there is no harm in accepting the speech of a just person, and if we assume the person is unjust but his speech is right, we can accept him in one way or another. More, even if we are not assured of the truth of his speech, we may stop and keep silent, but we cannot reject him.

Ibn 'Arabī is also aware that since there are only few recurrent traditions and many of them are conjectural in their implication he discusses some cases where the intuitions and revelations of the mystics are used as a context for interpreting and commenting on or changing the exterior meaning of a tradition.

The Criterion of Truth in Mystical Experience

a. From the viewpoint of the person undertaking the experience. In this regard, Muslim mystics have offered some criteria to distinguish the true and false experience and separate the divine and angelic experience from the egotistic and satanic one.

- **Teacher**: The interpretation of the mystical experiences, including those intermixed with the imagination, is the responsibility of an experienced and knowing person who is fully aware of the stages and stations, the world of the imagination and the demonstration of the supernatural meanings in concepts and forms and knows the complexities of the wayfarer's soul and can find out the truth or error in the wayfarer's representation of reality.
- **General standards**: Such as constant remembrance, withdrawal from the sensible objects and purifying the inner from considering anything other than God. On the difference between angelic and Satanic suggestions it is also said that the Satanic suggestion calls to disobedience of God's order, whereas the angelic suggestion encourages devotion and reproaches man on committing prohibited and illegal acts. On the difference between the suggestions of the self and Satan it is stated although both of them are false, the former calls to desires and it is not satisfied unless it reaches its desires and needs. The latter, however, does not suffice with a certain suggestion or direction (such as desires), but rather it aims at diverting the disciples' heart from God and His remembrance and therefore there is variety and change in it.

On the difference between divine inspirational suggestions and other suggestions, it is said that divine inspirational suggestions in strength supersede other suggestions and by their special power they invariably control and defeat all the other suggestions.

b. From the viewpoint of others. For others the credibility of mystical experiences depends on issues such as consensus and agreement, compatibility with certain reason, and agreement with established tradition.

- **Consensus and agreement:** As sensory experiences are tested by universality and consensus, the religious and mystical experiences are also measured in this way. As it was said those experiences which are repeatedly reported and there is no suspicion of the connivance of falseness in them are counted valid (whether they are sensory or inner experiences).

One of the objections made to this criterion is that mere consensus is not enough for the validity of an experience, as in a sensory experience it is also possible that all the people who suffer the same disease may see things in a certain colour, say yellow, or all those who press hard their eyelids may see things double, but these perceptions are not necessarily true. The answer to this objection is that in such cases there is no consensus and, therefore, other cases must be considered, and as in sensory experience the way to prove the objectivity of the experiences is changing the states and conditions and eliminating those factors which may interfere and produce a special sensation.

- Compatibility with the certain reason: This is a suitable criterion for ascertaining the validity of the mystical experiences. To explain, for it to be true a mystical experience doesn't necessarily need to be rational; rather it is enough that it is not contrary to reason. Indeed most of the mystical experiences fall within this domain, namely they are trans-rational. Apparently this is the reason why some mystics encourage the wayfarers to learn and teach rational sciences, such as philosophy and theoretical mysticism. In such cases the claimed issues are either rejected or interpreted.

- **To Agree with the accepted and plain tradition:** This is also one of the criteria of distinguishing falseness, that is, compatibility with the religious in theory (knowledge and the principles of religion) and practice (religious commands and laws) is counted necessary in true mystical experiences. Therefore, for a Muslim mystic any element contrary to established religious law would indicate the sensual origin of the inner experience. Of course, incompatibility with conjectural tradition necessarily does not invalidate the revelation, because when context is certain, it is the suspected appearance that must be interpreted.

Note: The last two cases can be a general standard for both the undertaker of the inner experience and others (the third criterion, however, it is only for the believers in religious dispensations).

Objections to the Argument

There are some general and particular objections made to the validity of the mystical experience, its religious support and its criteria, such as:

1. Repeatability: Since the mystical experiences are unique, they cannot be studied or tested by others. Therefore, in respect of validity and religious support they are not like sensory experiences.

Answer: Bergson in answer to this objection writes that, first, even scientific observations are particular cases and they are organized by a discoverer or an observer, such as an astronomer, for example. Second, it can be said the inner experience is also in a way repeatable and can be studied, that is, it can be said that even if the study and investigation of scientific and empirical events is not possible now, it would be possible potentially and in the world of reality, in answer we would say although other people actually and practically do not share the mystic's journey, in reality they can take such a journey and there are some people who would follow the way of mysticism to the end or at least a part of it.

2. Delusion: One of the objections made to the authority of the consensus (and indirectly repeatability) in mystical experiences is that considering the effect of opium, such as, for example, seeing unreal shapes and things by those who take Santonine, consensus is not enough in this kind of experience, and even if this issue is not a proof of falseness, falseness is probable, as it is probable in sensory experience.

Answer: First, as was mentioned before, to prove the objectivity of such experiences we must change the conditions and eliminate those factors which may interfere or affect the experience, as it is done in sensory experiences. In that case consensus in the mentioned examples, such as taking Santonine, would be meaningless. Second, there are some essential differences between mystical experiences and the hallucinations stimulated by narcotic drugs.[1] For example, the mystical way mainly aims at removing suggestions and fancies rather than escalating or encouraging them and, in fact, the mystics regard suggestions as obstacles on the way and believe imagination is one of the bandits of the mystical way.[2] In other words, the mystical way is purgative

---

1. In this regard, Mawlānā says:
   "In order that for a while they may be released from sobriety [consciousness], they lay upon themselves the opprobrium of wine and minstrelsy. They are fleeing from selfhood into selflessness either by means of intoxication or by means of [some engrossing] occupation, O well-conducted man." *Mathnawī*, Book VI, Verse No. 225 and 227.

2 "Understandings [strong] as mountains have been submerged in the seas of imagination and the whirlpools of phantasy." *Mathnawī*, Book V, Verse No. 2654.

rather than decorative or corrupting, and it attempts to remove the obstacles rather than turning to actions such as drug consumption. Second, the life style of the mystics and their liberating way indicates the difference between their experiences and those of others. Third, practically mystical experiences are the causes of peace, excellence and assurance, and the mystics always seek to repeat such experiences, whereas the consumption of drugs is only the cause of loss and regret. Moreover, in many of the mystical experiences, correspondence with reality can be explored and tested, such as true vision, which on repetition in the external world, there would be no doubt in the truth. Finally, the mystics have paid much attention to the mind's health and even they have given some medical prescriptions to this subject.

The Causes and Impediment of the Mystical Experience

From the viewpoint of the mystics the heart is the means to knowing the truths, the unseen world and unity, and it is acquired through objectified certainty. It is like a mirror and it is the duty of the wayfarer to remove the dust from it and to polish it more.

> "Every one, according to the measure of his spiritual
> enlightenment, sees the things unseen in proportion to
> how much the heart's mirror is polished.
> The more he polishes, the more he sees and the more

←

"A hundred thousand awful and terrible ships have been shattered to pieces in the sea of imagination." Ibid, Book V, Verse No. 2659.

"The *qibla* of the gnostic is the light of the union [with God]; the *qibla* of the philosopher's intellect is phantasy." Ibid, Book VI, Verse No. 1897.

"The world of imagination and the phantom of hope and fear is a great obstacle to the traveller [on the mystic's way]." Ibid, Book V, Verse No. 2648.

"Imagination and opinion are the bane of the particular [discursive] reason, because its dwelling-place is in the darkness." Ibid, Book III, Verse No. 1558.

> visible does the form [of the things unseen] become to him."[1]

The obstacles in the way of intuitive perception also stop the reception of manifestations and the hidden lights and the reflection of the truth in this mirror. On the other hand, what promotes this perception also prepares the heart to receive the truth and its light. From the mystics' perspective the most important obstacles in the way of intuitive perceptions and mystical experiences are: being occupied with diversity and fancy and suggestions, negligence, committing sins (whether in action or intention) and prohibited things, spoiling the rights (of Allah, people, and the self) which darkens the heart, seeking the world and indulging sensuous desires and companionship of people unfitting for the mystical way, and finally egotism, dependence on the limited and deficient reason, scienticism and too much reliance on acquired science.

In contrast the most important causes, factors and preparations of the mystical experience are: eagerness, denial of suggestions, avoiding sins, quitting fancy, concentration and self-inspection, remembrance, contemplation, solitude, reticence, abstinence, vigil, asceticism, devotion and supererogatory acts of worship, having a mentor, and finally affection, which, the mystics say, like alchemy transforms the traits of the wayfarer and provides him with the above mentioned requirements in their highest degree and promotes him to the station of annihilation and subsistence.

> "Love is that flame which, when it blazes up, it consumes everything else but the beloved."[2]

---

1. *Mathnawī*, Book IV, Verse No. 2909 – 2910.
2. *Mathnawī*, Book V, Verse No. 588.

The Language of Mysticism

Evidently the mystics insist on keeping the secrets of the Real and the necessity of not displaying and hiding the mystical experiences and emphasize the infallibility of the experience. On the other hand, they have elaborated much on their achievements and have written thousands of books and treatises expressing their ideas and notions in different styles and genres (symbols, extravagant speeches, poems and prose), in each pursuing a special aim and function. The question is how these contrary views and measures could be justified. In this section, four points are discussed respectively: the reasons the mystics keep secrets, why they cannot do it, why they speak, and finally the nature and functions of the verbal modes of the mystics.

The Reasons the Mystics Keep Secrets

There are some reasons why the mystics are ordered to keep secrets and they do not want to tell the divine secret:

- **Secrecy**: The very secrecy of an issue makes it a pledge between the holders of the secret and known initiated, and displaying it is counted disrespectful. So, as the hand of the Real stops the pretenders from finding their way into the circle of secrets (or private spectacle), He also reproaches the person who once when he gets familiar with the secret does not hide it from the strangers;

  "The pretender wished to come and gaze at this private spectacle,
  But the invisible hand came and checked the excluded stranger."[1]

Therefore, keeping the secrets is one of the duties of the wayfarer.

1. *The Poems of Ḥāfiẓ Shīrāzī*, trans. 'Alāiddīn Pazārgādī, Ode No. 152.

"Tell not the rival the secret of love and intoxication;
So let the ignorant die in pain and selfishness."[1]

Mawlānā says,

"To learn the secret of the Unseen is fitting for him (alone) who can seal his lips (and refrain) from speech."[2]

"Gnostics, who have drunk of the cup of God, have known the mysteries and kept them hidden."[3]

- **Fervor:** Whenever a secret is ascribed to God it comes accompanied with the term "fervor". The relationship of God with every person is personal and exclusive. This relationship is a love relationship and at the same time unique and God is in fervor of His love, of the states He bestows on the mystics and His secret. This fervor makes keeping the secret of God necessary and that the mystic should seek the Real for Himself and nothing else.

"The ardour (or fervor) of love cuts the tongue of the select short,
How come the grief of his secret fell on the tongues of the commons?"[4]

This fervor has another manifestation in the mystic, that is, the lover is also in fervor of the beloved and His Name and His relationship with others, and even in some stages he cannot endure the love of others for his heavenly beloved.

"I felt jealous when you were admired by the whole world,

---

1. Ibid,Ode No. 437.
2. *Mathnawī*, Book III, Verse No. 3380.
3. Ibid, Book V, Verse No. 2239.
4. *The Poems of Ḥāfiẓ Shīrāzī*, trans. 'Alāiddīn Pazārgādī, Ode No. 111.

But one can't brawl day and night with all creatures of God."[1]

Sincerity: Not only is secrecy considered one of the factors and grounds of mystical experiences and states, but since speaking of the mystical states may affect the wayfarer with conceit or hypocrisy or arrogance, it would be also closer to the state of purity and sincerity not to display to others the mystical experiences (unless to the Master and the guide).

- **The demands of the state and position:** There are apparently two contradictory sayings which are well-known among the mystics:
  - He who knows Allah his tongue is tied.

Mawlānā says,

"Whosoever has been taught the mysteries of the Truth [or the mysteries of the Divine action], his lips are sealed and closed."[2]

- He who knows Allah cannot hold his tongue.

Ḥāfiẓ says,

"All this honey and sugar that is poured with my words,
Are the reward of the fortitude granted with the beloved's love."[3]

These two sayings could be interpreted as referring to the mystic's two positions and states, or two ways of looking at the Names of beauty (which causes wordiness and intimacy) and the Names of sublimity (which ties the tongue and ends the speech). In the former the demand of the time and state or position is

1. Ibid,Ode No. 136.
2. *Mathnawī*, Book V, Verse No. 2240.
3. *The Poems of Ḥāfiẓ Shīrāzī*, trans. 'Alāiddīn Pazārgādī, Ode No. 183.

silence (of course involuntarily and as a result of the manipulation of the Real or because of selflessness and perfection rather than willingly) and the latter calls for speaking and unveiling.

> "By reason of (inward) sweetness I sit with a sour face: from fullness of speech I am silent."[1]
>
> "Love wills that this Word should be shown forth: if the mirror does not reflect, how is that?"[2]

The other interpretation is that no matter what the mystic says in his explanation of his findings or by writing books, treatises, poems and songs it is as if he has said nothing or has said only one of a thousand. In other words, if his description appears to others lofty, deep and detailed, for him everything which is of the category of language and words is small and inferior and is no more than a pot's portion of the water of the sea. Rūmī measures his speech by the demand of his inner state:

> "From within me a hundred sweet-breathing silent ones put their hands on their lips, signifying, "It is enough."[3]
>
> "I will throw word and sound and speech into confusion, that without these three I may converse with thee."[4]

And he remains waiting for a permission and order from the Unseen:

> "Afterwards, maybe, permission will come [from God]: the secrets that ought to be told will be told.
>
> "With an eloquence that is nearer [to the understanding] than these subtle recondite allusions."[5]

---

1. *Mathnawī*, Book I, Verse No. 1760.
2. Ibid,Verse No. 33.
3. *Mathnawī*, Book IV, Verse No. 2061.
4. *Mathnawī*, Book I, Verse No. 1730.
5. *Mathnawī*, Book VI, Verse No. 6 -7.

Maintaining order in the society: Another advantage of the mystics' secrecy is preserving the order of life and people's routine life, which according to Rūmī is based somehow on ignorance, which is the bed of the gradual and willing development of people:

> "Now that we have become acquainted with the conditions and degrees [of the spiritual world], a seal has been laid upon our lips.
> Lest the mysteries of the Unseen should be divulged and [thereby] the life and livelihood [of the mortals] be destroyed,
> And lest the veil of forgetfulness should be entirely rent and [the meat in] the pot of tribulation be left half-raw."[1]
> "Forgetfulness [of God], O beloved, is the pillar [prop] of this world: [spiritual] intelligence is a bane to this world."[2]

Preventing others from error: Another reason the mystics refrain from explaining their achievements is the possibility of misunderstanding or deviation of those who do not understand their aims.

> "I would have explained this [matter] with [eager] contention, but lest I fear some [weak] mind may stumble.
> The points [involved in it] are sharp as a sword of steel; if you do not have the shield [of capacity to understand], turn back and flee!
> Do not come without the shield against this adamant

---

1. Ibid,Verse No. 3524 - 3526.
2. *Mathnawī*, Book I, Verse No. 2066.

> [keen blade], for the sword is not ashamed of cutting.
> For this cause I have put the sword in sheath, that none who misreads may read contrariwise [in a sense contrary to the true meaning of my words]."[1]
> "I have told it summarily, I have not explained it (at length), otherwise both (thy) perceptions and (my) tongue would be consumed."[2]

Perhaps the ambiguity and many-sidedness of the mystics' poems and speeches is due to their compassion for the people, so that everyone should grasp the meaning of their speech according to his knowledge and understanding.

Cautiousness: To preserve his life, which is the mystic's endowment to achieve perfection in this world, he commits himself to secrecy and concealment, especially when the social conditions and the narrow-mindedness of the intolerant may accuse him of blasphemy and atheism and inflict him with punishment, as Ḥallāj and 'Ayn al-Quḍḍāt were accused and punished by the exoteric people.

> "Do you know what the harp and lyre utter?
> They say: 'Drink wine secretly, for punishment is given for it'."[3]

The Ineffability of the Mystical Experience

It seems an analysis of the relationship between the worlds of

---

1. *Mathnawī*, Book I, Verses No. 690 - 693. Mawlānā in this regard says,
   "O you who are drunk with the wine [of love], you are on the edge of the roof: sit down or [else] descend, and peace be with you!" *Mathnawī*, Book IV, Verse No. 2146.
   "Dam the torrent [of ecstasy] when it runs in flood; else it will work shame and ruin." *Mathnawī*, Book I, Verse No.1743.
2. *Mathnawī*, Book I, Verse No. 1758.
3. *The Poems of Ḥāfiẓ Shīrāzī*, trans. 'Alāiddīn Pazārgādī, Ode No. 200.

reality, concepts and words (external world, mind and language) is a prerequisite for a meticulous study of the causes of the ineffability of the mystical experience. Therefore, we begin the discussion with the explanation of a linguistic theory.

Linguists discuss a theory titled ethnic linguistics, in the sense that there is a mutual relationship between intellectual and cultural models and linguistic models, and the names of things do not consider only the one-to-one correspondence between things and names. To explain it further, it suggests the mind in the work of classification and naming things is not totally passive but it is active, that is, every word and name stems from the particular classification of things and also the division of the categories in the mind, and this categorization of the mind is also dependent on man's perspective on reality (for example, whether his perspective is essential or existential) and makes him divide the categories, for example, into ten or four categories. Therefore, the difference in the classification of things among nations, stems from their different experiences of the world which makes them classify and divide the world in different ways.

The problem of the untranslatable words in languages and cultures and the impossibility or difficulty of translation of some texts is due to the activity of the mind or a special perspective that stands between one thing and its class and name. Accordingly, the concepts are the materialization of our perspective on the world, and the words are the manifestation and reification of those concepts. These concepts and terms are sometimes the common legacy of a nation and sometimes the result of the attitude of a certain group or even a particular individual.

According to some researchers, our immediate experience of reality is essentially a unified and undiversified one. According to ancient Greeks it is primordial matter, meaning agitation, or according to recent philosophers it is existence, a shapeless matter in which everything loses its colour and determination, that is, it is a bare and wax-like mass. It is the human mind which out of this undifferentiated whole creates separate and independent forms, and in the light of the attitudes, perspectives, desires, mental inclinations of a nation and society the system of words is shaped and enriched. The mind by drawing countless lines and intersections on the shapeless mass of existence produces the concepts as an intermediary between the mind and reality. In short, language and the word system is the result of the divisions and classifications already made by the concepts of the world and reality.

According to what is said above, evidently the mystic's inner change, which leads to a new perspective, presents him with a new world of experience. He has experienced existence in a new way, and in consequence to express himself he must follow a new classification and categorization in his mind. This new worldview is the result of his inner development; according to Iqbal Lahuri when the soul changes the world changes, too. In the process of this change in perspective, for example, an attitude that is founded on diversity, essences and the effects and looks from below at existence changes into an attitude that sees nothing but unity, existence, the cause and looks at being from above. Therefore, following the change of concepts, the words change. Indeed borrowing from current and common words or coining a new term is a subtle and at the same time dangerous work, which has some consequences for the mystics and Sufis.

In sum, the experience of annihilation or the vision of the undifferentiated unity and the fading of determinations and the illusory and finding the world nothing but a mirage or a dream—as was discussed in the question of annihilation and subsistence—speak of the awesome and grand experiences that transform the conceptual and verbal system of the mystic altogether. Therefore, the ineffability has always been counted as one of the characteristics of the mystical experiences. In a diagram the discussion could be summarized as follows:

Inner change (the development of insight) → change of the conceptual order (worldview) → change of language (word system)

Following this introduction, we discuss other causes and reasons why mystics cannot describe their mystical experiences. Of course, this inability does not mean there is an intellectual impossibility or it is useless; rather it means description is ineffective and difficult, either because of language or the speaker or the addressee, or a combination of all of them.

1. The limitation of language and concepts (the problem of language): Language is a tool for communicating intentions and expressing inner meanings. It is arbitrary and depends on agreement among people or between the speaker and the addressee. Therefore, understanding the established meaning of the words is secondary to understanding the concepts by the two sides. So, the problem of language in communicating the mystic's experience returns to the problem of finding concepts for his achievements.

The mystics find the words too little for meanings and look at the concepts used for expressing the mystical achievements as a wire net or a thumbnail to measure the water of the sea. In such a state, according to Rūmī, an explanation of such knowledge, instead of shedding light, would darken the reality of existence and defeat the cause.

> "O breath of [phenomenal] existence, whatsoever words thou mayest utter, know that thereby thou hast bound another veil upon it [the mystery]."[1]

---

1. *Mathnawī*, Book III, Verse No. 4726.

Therefore, he asks God to grant him a wordless discourse and wishes that existence should open its mouth and reveal its secrets to all people.

> "Wishing that Being had a tongue, that it might remove the veils from existent beings!"[1]
>
> "O God, do thou reveal to the soul that place where speech is growing without letters."[2]

He now and then leaves his speech unfinished so that the audience by quitting the present state and getting into a new existential state prepares himself to receive inspirational and divine [holy] knowledge.

> "Mystery cannot be compressed into letters,
> The Red Sea is not contained in a jug."[3]
>
> "Another thing remains (to be said), but the Holy Spirit will tell thee the tale of it, without me."[4]

2. The narrowness of understandings (the problem of the addressee): Should the mystic deliver himself in one way or another from the first problem and find some forms, expressions and concepts appropriate to his experience, he will face another problem which is called by some as "the spiritual blindness of others". He would be like a person who tries to describe the colours and show their differences to a born blind. Rūmī writes in this concern:

> "If the people were not veiled [from the Truth] and gross, and if their throats [capacities] were not narrow and feeble,
> In [my] praise of thee I should have done justice to the

1. Ibid,Verse No. 4725.
2. *Mathnawī*, Book I, Verse No. 3092.
3. *The Mystic Rose Garden*, Verse No. 54.
4. *Mathnawī*, Book III, Verse No. 1298.

> reality and expressed myself in another language than this [I should have talked in another way other than this ordinary language]."[1]

Ḥāfiẓ also says:

> "O Lord, where can I find a confident of secrets so that one day,
> The heart may narrate what was said and what was heard?"[2]
>
> In any case, the mystics deem "not being a confidant" the biggest obstacle in the way of communication and intimacy and mutual understanding, and in conversely they find "sympathy" more important in mutual understanding (understanding of each other's concepts and words) than speaking the same language.
>
> "Oh, many are Indians and Turks that speak the same language; oh, there are many pair of Turks that are strangers [to each other].
>
> Therefor the language of mutual understanding is different indeed: to be one in heart is better than to be one in language."[3]

3. Emotions (the problem of the speaker): Some of the mystics' states are of the nature of emotions and likings, states such as love and desires, joy of union and pain of separation, whose intensity and kind is most likely hidden form others, and like many other emotions, such as anger and happiness, they cannot be defined or expressed other than by general expression, and in a sense they must be experienced rather than heard. The following verses describe such an impossibility:

---

1. *Mathnawī*, Book V, Verse No. 3-4.
2. *The Poems of Ḥāfiẓ Shīrāzī*, trans. 'Alāiddīn Pazārgādī, Ode No. 243.
3. *Mathnawī*, Book I, Verse No. 1206 – 7.

"I have suffered such a pain of love that can't be explained;
I have tasted such a poison of separation that can't be explained. "[1]
"The pen does not possess such a tongue to divulge love's secret;
The narration of one's desire is beyond the limit of explanation."[2]

Rūmī also states:

"In that quarter where love was increasing (my) pain,
Bu Hanifa and Shafii gave no instruction." [3]
How much (more) of these phrases and conceptions and metaphors? I want burning, burning: becoming friendly with that burning!"[4]

It should be understood nevertheless that the mystical states which are accompanied with emotions like contraction and expansion, or separation and union, both result from a kind of knowledge and are associated with a special understanding of the self and the beloved. Therefore, this factor by itself cannot explain the ineffability of all mystical experiences, especially cognitive experiences.

4. Wonder and secrecy of the experiences: The most important reason of the ineffability of the mystical experiences, as was mentioned, is their subject and known object, which strike the mystics with wonder and awe. It is that great truth—different from common concepts, knowledge and conventional expressions familiar to most people's minds and even the mystic himself—

---

1. *The Poems of Ḥāfiẓ Shīrāzī*, trans. 'Alāiddīn Pazārgādī, Ode No. 270.
2. *The Poems of Ḥāfiẓ Shīrāzī*, trans. 'Alāiddīn Pazārgādī, Ode No. 442.
3. *Mathnawī*, Book III, Verse No. 3832.
4. *Mathnawī*, Book II, Verse No. 1762.

which all of a sudden like a dazzling flash astounds him with an undifferentiated unity or a vacuum-like state and eliminating all determinations amazes him by the unfamiliar states and objects, an amazement beyond knowledge rather than beneath it which is associated with ignorance. Rūmī says:

> "How should I - not a vein of mine is sensible -
> describe that Friend who hath no peer?"[1]

Thus, at the moments of experience, speaking of such a state and knowledge would be impossible. According to Plotinus, observation stops the way of language, and Awḥadī Marāgha'ī states:

> The day I do not see His face I can speak of my state,
> but this moment that I see Him do not ask me.

Mawlānā compares the state of the mystic in such a situation to a curtain which tries to put aside another curtain, but as blood cannot be washed by blood, how can one of man's (who is one of the determinations of existence) own modifications, namely of language, which is the interpreter of his intellect, unveil the infinite existence? Indeed our interpretations of the mystical experience is no other than pulling the veil of concepts and conjectures over reality and imposing diversity upon pure unity. In such a state not only language and words do not bring one any closer to truth, but for an intuitive perception of the reality it is a calamity and an impediment.

> "O breath of (phenomenal) existence, whatsoever words thou mayest utter, know that thereby thou hast bound another veil upon it [the mystery].
> That utterance and [that] state [of existence] are the bane of [spiritual] perception: to wash away blood with blood is absurd, absurd."[2]

---

1. *Mathnawī*, Book I, Verse No. 130.
2. *Mathnawī*, Book III, Verse No. 4726-7.

> "Before this Sun, which is exceedingly radiant, every guide is in reality a highway rubber."[1]

This is why for the mystic silence is more illuminating than any speech.

> "Although the commentary of the tongue makes [all] clear, yet tongueless love is clearer."[2]
>
> "In [keeping] silence our [inward] speaking [of Him] is [only] made more evident, since the desire [for manifestation] is increased by suppression."[3]
>
> "To utter words (concerning Him) is to shut the window (through which He reveals Himself): the very act of expression is the concealment (of Him)."[4]

Of course, the highest fortune of the correct, unambiguous and illuminating expression that does not hide the true meaning belongs to the few mystics, who have attained the station of gathering and have gathered in themselves both meaning and form. They even in the highest degree of intoxication and in the zenith of their dazzling states and experiences do not open their mouth to speak extravagantly, but rather dress the meanings in proper words.

> "In such (mystical) intoxication (as his) the observance of respect will not be there at all; or if it is, 'it is strange."[5]
>
> "To combine the (outward) form with such a deep (inner) meaning is not possible, except on the part of a mighty (spiritual) king."[6]

---

1. *Mathnawī*, Book VI, Verse No. 702.
2. *Mathnawī*, Book I, Verse No. 113.
3. *Mathnawī*, Book VI, Verse No. 697.
4. Ibid,Verse No. 699.
5. *Mathnawī*, Book III, Verse No. 1394.
6. Ibid,Verse No. 1393.

Indeed, sometimes the mystics in their state of bewilderment speak of the trans-rational nature of their knowledge, and Ibn 'Arabī in explanation says it is so because reason is founded on the law of non-contradiction and the law of the excluded middle, whereas the mystics' knowledge is founded on trans-rational experiences, which cannot be grasped by the intellect. As evidence he mentions some cases. One is the essential relationship of the Real and the world mentioned in the holy Qur'an: 'You did not throw when you threw, rather it was Allah who threw' (8:17), which is expressed in a form gathering negation and affirmation. The other is the question of causality; he explains the intellect decrees that the cause cannot be the effect of that which is its effect, whereas this is admitted in the science of manifestation, which says the cause as a cause cannot be understood without understanding the effect as an effect, and the former is dependent on the latter, and in a sense they are interrelated. Another case is the truth of self-knowledge mentioned in the Prophetic tradition "He who knows himself knows his God". In short, it is in this station of wonder that the conventional principles are disrupted and speech comes to an end. Mawlānā says:

> "How should poesy and rhyme come to me after the foundations of sanity are destroyed?
> "Tis not (merely) one madness which I have amidst the sorrows of love; nay, but madness on madness on madness."[1]
> "If a single mote of reason and consciousness is [remaining] with me, what is this melancholy madness and distracted speech?"[2]

1. *Mathnawī*, Book V, Verse No. 1893-4.
2. *Mathnawī*, Book V, Verse No. 1908.

The Reasons the Mystics Speak

Despite all the obstacles there are and their claims that they do not want to or cannot express mystical experiences, as it is seen often, they have spoken much and have written poems, books, treatises and many compendiums on their observations. In the following some of the motivations and reasons they have for doing that are discussed:

The demand of the state or stations: In some states and stations the mystic is like a mirror and he cannot but reflect the light which he receives. In other words he is like a reed which has no sound of its own other than what the player blows in it. He believes all the words and debates belong to his Beloved. In this station the mystic is the example of "He who knows Allah cannot hold his tongue." The same love which was attended with so much fervor exhibits itself now and seeks to attract all others. Rūmī says:

> "Love wills that this Word should be shown forth: if the mirror does not reflect, how is that?"[1]
>
> "We are as the flute, and the music in us is from thee; we are as the mountain, and the echo in us is from thee."[2]
>
> "We are as the harp and thou art striking (it with) the plectrum (playing on it): the lamentation is not from us, it is thou that art making lamentation."[3]

Ḥāfiẓ is also of the opinion that only by the candle (the beloved), he can describe the story of love and the lover (the butterfly) is essentially heedless and has no interest in speaking or putting down his sentences, unless he parrot-like repeats the words of the Unseen behind the mirror and lets the truths run on his tongue.

---

1. *Mathnawī*, Book I, Verse No. 33.
2. Ibid,Verse No. 559.
3. Ibid,Verse No. 558.

"A candle might narrate this tale with its fiery tongue;
For, a burnt moth has no power left to utter anything."[1]
"O Cup-bearer, come, for, love calls aloud;
For, he who told our tale, heard it from us, too."[2]

Manifesting the beauty of the Real: The lover not only is in fervor of the beloved and wants the latter for himself, but also unconsciously and paradoxically informs every one of the beauty of the beloved.

Ḥāfiẓ also has repeatedly mentioned the role of this factor in reciting his poems.

"At the hour when Ḥāfiẓ was writing this confused verse,
The bird of his thought had fallen into the snare of ardent desire."[3]
"The rose-bush of your beauty did not in itself ravish the heart;
It was our ardour which produced that effect."[4]

Rūmī calls himself "the messenger of the sun", that is, he is like an interpreter and a medium to explain what he has seen but remains hidden from others.

Relieving the Soul and Disseminating knowledge: Sometimes the mystic in the height of his love or the gloom of separation cannot but speak of the beloved and praise and admire or even complain of Him, and if he does not do that, he will perish under the burden of separation or extreme self-conceit resulting from intuition. Rūmī states:

---

1. *The Poems of Ḥāfiẓ Shīrāzī*, trans. 'Alāiddīn Pazārgādī, Ode No. 492.
2. Ibid,Ode No. 243.
3. Ibid,Ode No. 212.
4. Ibid,Ode No. 371.

> "[Reason says], If I keep silence, I fear that that Sun will rend the veil and (display Himself) from another quarter."[1]
>
> "If I should not utter even this [little] amount, O trusted [friend], the phial, [which is] my heart, would burst from weakness [inability to contain its emotion]."[2]

It is a rule when something is filled it overflows. It is the capacity of the mystic which determines the amount and quality of the overflow of meanings, and sometimes it is done automatically simply by being inspired by the other side, like true dreams.

> "Henceforth I will bury this topic. That Drawer is drawing me [in another direction]: what can I do?"[3]

Accordingly, the poetry of the mystics is a vision rather than an artifact and it is given and not taken or sought after.

> "The beauty of His state cannot be set forth: what are both the worlds (temporal and spiritual)? The reflection of His mole.
>
> When I breathe a word concerning His beauteous mole, my speech would fain burst my body."[4]

When the mystic finds himself in the station of the supererogatory acts speaking on behalf of the Real, he will invariably recite:

> "Do Thou speak and do Thou hear and do Thou be! We are wholly naught notwithstanding all this hewing."[5]

Educational reasons: Sometimes the mystics to encourage and

---

1. *Mathnawī*, Book VI, Verse No. 696.
2. *Mathnawī*, Book V, Verse No. 1886.
3. *Mathnawī*, Book III, Verse No. 4454.
4. *Mathnawī*, Book II, Verse No. 191 – 2.
5. *Mathnawī*, Book VI, Verse No. 1440.

motivate others to take the mystical road and reach the goal, or to admonish and warn them of the obstacles and misfortunes of the way or to explain their findings and correct the convictions of the disciples and seekers, or to assist the unsuccessful in the journey and sometimes out of duty (on finishing the fourth journey, namely the journey with the Real among the people and attaining the position of guidance) or merely to explain their mystical experiences they speak or write. Rūmī says:

> "Since you have mounted to the roofs of Heaven, it would be futile to seek a ladder.
> After (having attained to) felicity, the way (that leads) to felicity is worthless except for the sake of helping and teaching others."[1]
> He maintains speech, poetry and odes are like a smell from that eternal beauty which is offered to those who cannot see that face.

Fervor: One of the wonders of the mystics' states is the possibility of gathering the opposites; for example, the same fervor of the beloved which makes them close their mouth and keep silent sometimes makes them speak eloquently.

> "To utter words (concerning Him) is to shut the window (through which He reveals Himself): the very act of expression is the concealment (of Him)."[2]
> Sometimes in order to divert others from looking at the face of the beloved they speak of His works and attributes, and in this way maintain their exclusive relationship with Him.
> "Sing, like the nightingales, in the presence of the

1. *Mathnawī*, Book III, Verse No. 1403 – 4.
2. *Mathnawī*, Book VI, Verse No. 699.

Rose, in order that you may divert them from the scent of the Rose,
So that their ears will be engaged in [listening to] the song, and their attention will not fly to the face of the Rose."[1]

The Linguistic Forms of the Mystics

The narrowness of the conventional expression, phrases and word order makes the mystics to construct and use symbolic, negative, allegorical, paradoxical and ecstatic [extravagant] (uncommon or against the appearances of religion and reason) and also to coin terms, sometimes complicated, which are briefly discussed one by one here:

Negative expressions: The experience of an exalted, sublime and transcendent being makes the use of common linguistic forms that are mixed with deficiency, similitude and inadequacy impossible or difficult for the mystic, so that sometimes for this reason he speaks only of what He is not, namely of His negative attributes.

"All that you may think of is liable to pass away; he that doesn't come into thought is God."[2]

"The Divine Essence is free from where, how, and why.
Let His glory be exalted above what men say of Him."[3]

For the mystic in his experience of the elimination of determinations or looking at certain views and scenes this language is sometimes accompanied with wonder.

Of course, the mystics believe this language which deals only with transcendence is defective and hold that it should be supplemented by the language of immanence along with certain

1. *Mathnawī*, Book VI, Verse No. 700 -1.
2. *Mathnawī*, Book II, Verse No. 3112.
3. *The Mystic Rose Garden*, Verse No. 111.

restrictions. In the school of Ibn 'Arabī the negative language is the language of philosophers and rationalists[1] and also the people of transcendent revelation.

Shabistarī writes:

"In applying meanings, look to their final intent,
And regard all the attributes of each.
Use them in comparisons in the manner proper thereto,
Carefully abstain from applying them otherwise."[2]

Paradoxical expression: The mystics believe the domain of intuition is beyond the intellect and it is trans-rational, and

---

1. Mawlānā says: "In the presence of the drunken Turk the minstrel began [to sing of] the mysteries of *Alast* under the veil of melody –
I know not whether Thou art a moon or an idol, I know not what Thou desirest of me...
Tis marvelous that Thou art not separate from me, [and yet] I don't know where I am, and where Thou art." *Mathnawī*, Book VI, Verse No. 703, 704, and 705.
"When [the refrain] "I don't know" passed beyond bounds, our Turk was amazed and his heart became sick of this ditty." *Mathnawī*, Book VI, Verse No. 709.
"Tell of that which you know, O crazy fool: don't draw out [repeat continually] 'I don't know, I don't know.'" *Mathnawī*, Book VI, Verse No. 714.
"Wherefore is this long palaver [chewing of words]? 'Because' said the minstrel, 'my object is recondite'.
Before [know] you deny [all else], affirmation [of God] evades [you]: I denied [everything] in order that you might get a scent of [perceive the means of attaining to] affirmation.
I play the tune of negation: when you die, death will declare the mystery." *Mathnawī*, Book VI, Verse No. 720 – 722.
"Your agony is not finished till you die: you cannot reach the roof without completing the ladder." *Mathnawī*, Book VI, Verse No. 724.
"Not such a death that you will go into a grave, [but] a death consisting of [spiritual] transformation, so that you will go into a light." *Mathnawī*, Book VI, Verse No. 739.
2. *The Mystic Rose Garden*, Verse No. 741- 742.

though they do not believe it is against reason, they find it above the logic of reason, in the sense that when it reports its achievements it has to use simultaneously both negative and affirmative statements, such as the world exists and does not exist, and the acts are both our actions and not our actions. Ibn 'Arabī believes an explanation and justification of such experiences by the intellect would be impossible and useless. He declares questions such as the way the Real indicates His existence, the pervasiveness and manifestation of the Real in the universe (expanded existence), the development of the soul after death, the renewal of creation, and the secret of destiny essentially cannot be grasped by the intellect.

Symbolic language: It is the use of symbols, figurative language, metaphors, metonymies and allegory [analogy] to indicate a meaning or intention. Rūmī says:

> "When I speak of "lip," 'tis the lip [shore] of the Sea;
> when I say "not," the intended meaning is "except"."[1]

Symbol is leaving form for meaning, and it is a means which as a signifier explains an ambiguous signified. The language of symbol is mimetic, but mimesis along with sanctity. Symbol is not an ordinary metaphor or an intellectual (horizontal) and one dimensional attempt which results from the process of conceptualization and mental comparison, but it is "a sublime (vertical) calling to a rank higher than [intellectual] perception that guides the mind to an inner meaning treasured beneath apparent speech. The ambiguity of symbol usually makes it many-sided in meaning and multi-dimensional, which is accompanied with emotion, feeling of exaltation and sanctity."

Mystical symbols are both initiating and informing and evoking aesthetic response and feeling. Such symbolic hints in religious

---

1. *Mathnawī*, Book I, Verse No. 1759.

and mystical texts have artistic, aesthetic and mimetic functions. The prime requirements of the study of symbols are:

1. Belief in a hierarchical order with existential ranks in being;

2. The existence of similarity and parallel and ontological and intellectual resemblance among the ranks and degrees of existence.

Symbols are passages from the little world to the big world and from the unseen to the seen world. The reason that symbolism is the distinctive feature of the religious and mystical language is that it calls to the world of meaning and the unseen, for the sensible world is the shadow of the unseen world. One of the important functions of symbol, which relates to its ambiguity, is hiding the secrets from the uninitiated for the purpose of cautiousness and secrecy. The other function of symbol is increasing endurance and tolerance and accepting the different imports of one truth, for the language of the mystics though united is not one, and every mystic according to his spiritual state and station speaks in a language and uses symbols that are proper to his situation. As Rūzbahān states the mystics speak in three different languages of sobriety, steadfastness and intoxication.

Mystical symbols sometimes by referring to an imaginary beloved intend a sublime and divine meaning, as the attributes of God's kindness and the manifestation of these attributes, named by the mystics the manifestation of beauty, are called "the Face" (for it is the source of intimacy, friendship and loveliness) and the attributes of the might of God and their manifestation, which they name the manifestation of the sublime, are described in the image of "a curling lock" (since it hides the face and is the cause of veiling).

"The epiphany is now in beauty, now in majesty,
Cheek and curl are the similitudes of those verities.
The attributes of 'The Truth' are mercy and vengeance,

Cheek and curl of fair ones are types of these two."[1]

Shabistarī contends he can understand the speech of the people of the heart who knows all that exists in the world of objects is a shadow and an image of the unseen world, and since the unseen world cannot be completely compared to the seen world, through the principle of "abstraction" and by rejecting the defective aspects and considering the side of perfection one can understand the symbols and hints of the mystics' discourse more or less.

"Whatsoever is seen in this visible world,
Is as a reflection from the sun of that world."[2]
"When these words are heard by the sensual ear,
At first they denote objects of sense.
The spiritual world is infinite,
How can finite words attain to it?
How can the mysteries beheld in ecstatic vision
Be interpreted by spoken words?
When mystics treat these mysteries,
They interpret them by types.
For objects of sense are as shadows of that world,
And this world is as an infant, and that as the nurse."[3]
"Although perfect analogies are unattainable,
Nevertheless continue steadfast in seeking them."[4]
"In applying meanings, look to their final intent,
And regard all the attributes of each.
Use them in comparisons in manner proper thereto,
Carefully abstain from applying them otherwise."[5]

---

1. *The Mystic Rose Garden*, Verse No. 721- 722.
2. Ibid,Verse No. 719.
3. Ibid,Verse No. 723-727.
4. Ibid,Verse No. 732.
5. *The Mystic Rose Garden*, Verse No. 741- 742.

The important point in mystical symbols and metaphors (as quoted from Shabistarī) is their many-sidedness. For example, the image of "wine", which is used by mystics to refer to divine love, stresses the difference between the way of love and reason and opening the secrets in the state of drunkenness and intoxication of love and also forgetting the self and selfishness. The image of curling lock, as was said, also refers to the manifestation of the glory of the Real; the twisting and bending of the lock speaks of the opposition and difference among the Names in the visible world; the ringlets of the curling lock refer to the ranks of diversity; and the restiveness of the curling lock indicates the change and alteration of the chain of beings, which turn into a different kind and truth every moment.

Analogy: Another linguistic form which is deliberately used by the mystics is analogy and the comparison of the intelligible and the sensible. Although analogy in a way brings the addressee closer to the intended goal, it may distance him from it in other ways. Nevertheless, in the mystics' language it is used with an emphasis on the sublime nature and sanctity of the object of comparison.

The main difference between the mystics' analogies and other analogies is that they imitate higher worlds. They employ the analogies used in the holy Qur'an, comparing the Exalted Real to light or the light of God to a lamp and a lantern. Considering verses like 'The loftiest description belongs to Allah'[1](16: 60) and 'Clear is Allah of whatever they allege [about Him], - [all] except Allah's exclusive servants'[2](37:159–160) they try to maintain a balance between transcendence and immanence to find some examples that

1. "وَلِلَّـهِ الْمَثَلُ الْأَعْلَى".
2. "سُبْحَانَ اللَّـهِ عَمَّا يَصِفُونَ إِلَّا عِبَادَ اللَّـهِ الْمُخْلَصِينَ".

explain the relationship of God and the world, the oneness of existence, etc. Therefore, they have exploited the relationship of light and the sun, the wave and the sea, the soul and the body, the image and the mirror, etc. for this purpose, though at the end they have admitted all these analogies are defective. Rūmī recites in this regard:

> "Thou art as the spirit; we are like hand and foot: the closing and opening of the hand is due to the spirit.
> Thou art as the reason, we are like this tongue: this tongue hath its (power of) expression from the reason.
> Thou art like the joy, and we are the laughter, for we are the result of (Thy) blessed joy."[1]

And finally,

> "O Thou art beyond my conception and utterance, dust be on the head of me and my similes! (it shows that it is beyond his ability to express and understand Him)"[2]

Technical terms: The farther they get from the time when mystical questions were discussed in the first centuries, the mystics become more aware of the necessity of introducing certain terms which help them to show the difference between their intentions and the common words used by people and also the terms used by theologians and philosophers. Gradually in practical and theoretical mysticism certain terms were introduced and treatises were written on this subject.

The vogue of introducing such technical and semi-philosophical terms in theoretical mysticism was in its height in the school of Ibn 'Arabī and especially by his disciple and follower Ṣadr al-Dīn Qūnawī and his students. Introducing such terms prevented

---

1. *Mathnawī*, Book V, Verse No. 3313 – 3315.
2. Ibid, Verse No. 3318.

displaying the secrets and knowledge to common people directly, which sometimes lead to their misunderstanding, and also added to the philosophical accuracy of the wayfarers, which was often ignored on the pretext that knowledge is a veil and sometimes ended with false interpretation of the mystical experiences. Some of these terms are the permanent archetype, the breath of the Merciful, the expanded being, objectification, manifestation, perfect man, uniqueness, and oneness in theoretical mysticism, and colouring, steadfastness, sobriety, vanishing, camouflage, separation, and unity of unity in practical mysticism.

The mystics on the basis of "what cannot be attained entirely cannot be left entirely" determined to establish their own language and according to Rūmī they desperately attempted to initiate a new movement in language to come even a little closer to truth.

> "Although this intellect is too weak to declare (what thou art), one must weakly make a movement [attempt] in that [direction]."[1]
>
> "If you cannot drink (all) the flood-rain of the clouds, (yet) how can you give up water-drinking?
> If thou will not communicate the mystery, (at least) refresh (our) apprehensions with the husk thereof.
> [My] spoken words are [only] a husk in relation to thee, but they are a good kernel for other understandings."[2]
>
> "The *Abdāl* have certain mystical expressions of which the doctrines [of external religion] are ignorant."[3]

Extravagant Speeches: Extravagant speech as a term is a speech which at least in appearance is opposite to the religious text and

1. *Mathnawī*, Book V, Verse No. 16.
2. Ibid,Verse No. 18 – 20.
3. *Mathnawī*, Book I, Verse No. 3409.

religious law or explicit reason and is uttered at the time when the spiritual state or ecstasy is prevailing and is said unwittingly and unconsciously, and sometime its appearance betrays selfishness. Such a speech is counted among the pitfalls of the people of knowledge. Ibn ʻArabī holds that such a state shows the mystic has no control over himself and his states and believes the verifying mystics put forward no such speeches. Examples of extravagant speech are the claim of Ḥallāj "I am the Real" or "I am the one I love, and the one I love is I" or what is reported from Abā Yazīd, "I am the Exalted, how great is my state," or Abū Saʻīd al-Kharrāz "I knew Allah in His combination of the opposites" or Junayd "the colour of water is the colour of its vessel." In short, extravagant speech is understood to be a speech uttered at the time of intoxication and drunkenness, sometimes in imitation of the unseen caller, and in most cases as a result of the experience of unity.

Since both extravagant speech and the appearances of traditions are instances of language and are open to interpretation and different readings, it is said "it is neither accepted nor rejected, nor trusted nor blamed." It is not rejected for it may be a symbol of a lofty meaning which in reality is true. Nor is it accepted for it may be against religious law or reason and the reason, nor is it used for error may occur in its interpretation. Finally the mystic is not reproached on his extravagant speeches since they are uttered involuntarily.

The great mystics contend elaborating on extravagant speeches when they are uttered is an error, and it is like displaying the secrets without the permission of God. Nevertheless they also maintain uttering such speeches at the time of spiritual ecstasy is not a fault, for the mystic has no control over them and, therefore, he is not responsible.[1]

---

1. Shabistarī says,

"Verily 'I am The Truth' is a revelation of the absolute mystery,

The nature of ecstatic utterances: A few views have been offered on the reality of ecstatic utterances which are discussed and critiqued here.

Rhetorical ecstatic utterances: According to this view, the ecstatic statements are common utterances which also can be expressed through ordinary words, but the form of ecstatic utterance gives them a rhetorical or literary tinge by which the mystics make their speech more effective and emphatic and make the addresses more contemplative.

Objection: The truth is that the expressions of the mystics, especially those statements including affirmation and negation like "dark light", at least in some cases, reject this view.

Bad writing: It means since such explanations are an expression of the mystical experiences of the mystics and evidently

←

Who except 'The Truth', can say 'I am The Truth'?
All the atoms of the world, like Manṣūr,
You can take to be drunken or heavy with wine;
Continually are they singing this song of praise,
Continually dwelling on this mystic verity." *The Mystic Rose Garden*, Verses No. 437– 439.

"Every man whose heart is pure from doubt,
Knows for a surety that there is no being but 'One'." *The Mystic Rose Garden*, Verse No. 446

"Every man who as a void is empty of the self,
Re-echoes within him the cry 'I am The Truth'." *The Mystic Rose Garden*, Verse No. 450.

"Of a truth there is no other existence than 'The Truth',
Whether you say 'He is the Truth', or 'I am the Truth'." *The Mystic Rose Garden*, Verse No. 466.

"The saying 'I am the Truth' was lawful for the bush,
Why is it unlawful in the mouth of a good man?" *The Mystic Rose Garden*, Verse No. 445.

dependent on their knowledge and particular culture, they may be the result of bad writing or our error in application and expression, as a sensory experience could be reported falsely.

Objection: Perhaps this view is true for rare and unique ecstatic utterances, but it is not applicable to the ecstatic speeches or ideas which are unanimously endorsed by many mystics from a special group or different sects, groups and cultures, such as the ecstatic statements on the annihilation of individuality or the union of the soul with God.

The Plurality of instances: In paradoxical statements, including ecstatic speeches which both affirm and negate at the same time, if the negation is related to one instance and the affirmation to another instance, there would be no logical problem in the statement, and each of the two would apply to its special case.

Objection: This view is applicable only to some cases, for there are some ecstatic speeches with the same instances.

Plurality of meanings (ambiguity): Although in appearance the two propositions “A is B” and “A is not B” cannot be both true, A may have two different meanings, in one it is B and in the other it is not B. For example, nonexistent (nothing) may have a meaning which is not incompatible with the existence or being of possible beings.

Objection: Walter Terence Stace in his critique of this view writes: first the mystics emphasize that the mystical experiences cannot be grasped or digested by the intellect. Second, as an example, in the ecstatic utterances on the Oneness of existence and the oneness of God and the universe, we do not meet with two different meanings for God or the universe.

Stace following his critique of the mentioned views writes: since I am not aware of any other theory which the critics may use to find a rational and logical explanation for ecstatic speeches, I conclude that ecstatic speeches, in fact, have no rational justification and the contradiction we see in them cannot be solved in a logical way, for they rise from mystical experiences which in themselves are contradictory and are opposite to reason.

Stace's conclusion concerns both the language of mysticism and the relationship between the intellect and mysticism (intuition). Before this some points were quoted from Ibn 'Arabī on the intuitive knowledge being trans-rational and having no rational explanation; however, after him a group of mystics attempted to bring together the intellect and intuition (the school of Qūnawī, for example, especially in the views of Ibn Turkeh and Qayṣarī). They claimed these two sources of knowledge are compatible. Among philosophers Ṣadr al-Muta'allihīn and the followers of Transcendent philosophy also believed in rationalizing many of the mystics' claims and knowledge and they have taken important steps in this field. On the language of mysticism, considering the different views offered on the ecstatic speeches of the mystics, various approaches have been followed. Some of the ecstatic utterances, despite their uncouth and unfamiliar appearance, can be explained perfectly well on the basis of the principles of theoretical mysticism, and they refer to ideas which have rational justification. Some of such utterances result from inaccurate expression or bad writing and application; some others, however, which are both affirming and negating, can be explained away by referring to their different meanings, separate aspects or diverse instances. Evidently those which cannot be explained away at all can be put aside and interpreted as the effusion of the wayfarer's self in the process of intuition or due to his flawed intuition, as Sayyid Ḥaydar Āmulī contends the idea of incarnation and union is the result of such imperfect intuition and confusing the Real and His aspect with the manifestations.

Interpretation

The reason we discuss interpretation at the end of this section on mystical epistemology is that the mystics count the holy text of the divine discourse as one of the sources of their knowledge and inspired learning, and since some of their knowledge is not indicated by the exterior of the Qur'an and traditions, they claim such approaches are the result of interpretation rather than the explanation of the surface [exterior] of the holy Qur'an.

Different definitions have been given of *ta'wīl* or interpretation, whose linguistic root in Arabic is *awwal* or return:

1. Going beyond the form or appearance to reach the meaning: as implied in the interpretation of dream in *sūra* Yūsuf, 'Before the meals you are served come to you I will inform you of its interpretation.'[1] (12:37)

2. The truth and instance applied in a special point: as it is said the interpretation of the divine book will be revealed on the Day of Judgment (see 7:53).

3. The secret or the cause of an act or an issue: as in the story of Mūsā (A.S.) and the man gifted with inner knowledge (Khiḍr), which is narrated in the holy Qur'an (See 18:78).[2]

4. The end and destination: as we read on righteous deeds in (4: 59) 'That is better and more favorable in outcome'.[3] (4:59)

The above definitions are common in the element of "returning to the origin and truth", whether this truth is the meaning of a dream, the secret hidden in a subject, the ultimate end of an activity, or the final and eventual instance of a matter. The first and the second

1. 'قَالَ لَا يَأْتِيكُمَا طَعَامٌ تُرْزَقَانِهِ إِلَّا نَبَّأْتُكُمَا بِتَأْوِيلِهِ قَبْلَ أَنْ يَأْتِيَكُمَا.'

2. 'I will inform you about the interpretation of that over which you could not maintain patience.' (18:78). 'سَأُنَبِّئُكَ بِتَأْوِيلِ مَا لَمْ تَسْتَطِعْ عَلَيْهِ صَبْرًا.'

3. 'ذَٰلِكَ خَيْرٌ وَأَحْسَنُ تَأْوِيلًا.'

functions are more related to the question of the interpretation of the Qur'an in the verse 'No one knows its interpretation except Allah and those firmly grounded in knowledge.'[1](3:7) In short, interpretation could be defined as the process of revealing the secret, the inner and hidden meaning, or the instance and application of an event or a subject in the verses of the holy Qur'an. Interpretation in this sense comes in contrast to exegesis or commentary (meaning finding the surface meanings of the verses).

Sometimes interpretation is defined in the special sense of esoteric exegesis. Of course, here we do not mean the external demonstration of esoteric exegesis and its different trends, but a kind of language which the mystics find in the holy Qur'an as a sacred text and the incarnation and manifestation of the divine discourse and through the science of interpretation they try to find out the meanings of this language. In any case, the mystics understand this similarity in language between religion and mysticism stemming from the substantial unity of the meanings hidden beyond the verses and their own findings; to put it in other words, the Prophetic experience and mystical experience in origin and language are similar, though they may count the Prophetic experience much higher and more inaccessible to others.

The way the mystics view religion in general and the holy Qur'an in particular (as the divine speech) is both teleological and instrumental. It is teleological because they consider the religious texts as the source of sacred knowledge and reveals the "truth" and it is instrumental since they consider the religious orders and ethics (religious law) an assurance to preserving the truth and maintaining it in the soul of the mystics. Thus, religious law contains the truth in its interior and in its exterior it safeguards

1. "وَمَا يَعْلَمُ تَأْوِيلَهُ إِلَّا اللَّهُ وَالرَّاسِخُونَ فِي الْعِلْمِ."

and protects it, for divine knowledge without observing devotion and appearances cannot live, and like an unripe almond which without its shell spoils and decays the truth also without such reservations will fade away.

Most mystics believe devotions and a lifestyle based on religion, which of course can take different shapes, are necessary conditions to follow the mystical order and reach the truth. In short, the mystics turn to the Qur'an as a source of knowledge and inspirations that besides intuition and illumination teaches and guides them to the inner and hidden side of the world of being.

It was mentioned already that one dominant feature of the language of mysticism is its symbolism. The mystics believe the main feature of the language of the divine verses is also symbolic and allegorical, and as the wayfarer must interpret those revelations which are symbolic, he should also find his way into the inner side and the truth of the Qur'an through "interpretation".

Unlike what is commonly understood, they contend interpretation is not just diverting the word from its apparent meaning to find a probable meaning, that is, interpretation does not necessarily end in finding "figures" or speaking of the implied omitted agent, but rather sometimes it suggests new instances. For example, about the holy verse, 'There is not a thing but celebrates His praise, but you do not understand their glorification'[1](17: 44), on the basis of their observations and hearing the speech of water and mud, they hold it is true glorification and a kind of verbal language rather than a language indicating a spiritual state.

> "The speech of water, the speech of earth, and the speech of mud are apprehended by the senses of them

1. 'وَإِن مِّن شَيْءٍ إِلَّا يُسَبِّحُ بِحَمْدِهِ وَلَـٰكِن لَّا تَفْقَهُونَ تَسْبِيحَهُمْ.'

that have hearts [the mystics]."[1]

They argue that, first, interpreting the glorification of the inanimate as indicating a spiritual state is against the apparent meaning of the verse and, second, it has nothing to do with the second part of the verse, 'but you do not understand their glorification,' whereas the verbal language which is audible to the inner ear and is heard in spiritual revelations is not so. The same happens in many other verses, such as 'He is the First and the Last, the Manifest and the Hidden'[2](57: 3) or 'Whichever way you turn, there is the face of Allah'[3](2: 115). In short, interpretation is a kind of initiation in the holy Qur'an to profit by its interiors, which is primarily dependent on a kind of homogeneity, that is, it depends on purifying the inner and cleansing the soul.[4]

Accordingly, although an exoteric explanation of the Qur'an can be given by a non-Muslim, interpreting and penetrating its interior is not so, for the essence of the science of interpretation is the hidden inspirations and understanding the book through the divine light which is shed in the heart of the person. Interpretation which is "the revelation of the hidden" and deciphering the secrets of the revealed divine speech, in a way is opposite to gradual revelation and it is supplementary. That is, if gradual revelation is coming down from the truth and the preserved tablet and the hidden world to the soul and the world of words, interpretation is going back to the truth hidden beyond the words of the divine discourse. Therefore, a distinction should be made between the Qur'an as a concrete example and an image and

1. *Mathnawī*, Book I, Verse No. 3279.

2. 'هُوَ الْأَوَّلُ وَالْآخِرُ وَالظَّاهِرُ وَالْبَاطِنُ.'

3. 'فَأَيْنَمَا تُوَلُّوا فَثَمَّ وَجْهُ اللَّـهِ.'

4. "This is indeed a noble Qur'an, in a guarded Book – no one touches it except the pure ones." (56: 77-79). 'إِنَّهُ لَقُرْآنٌ كَرِيمٌ، فِي كِتَابٍ مَكْنُونٍ، لَا يَمَسُّهُ إِلَّا الْمُطَهَّرُونَ.'

as a figurative language. To explain, in figurative language there is more or less a degree of generalization and abstraction where both sides (the tenor and the vehicle) can be explained and understood through other ways. But in allegorical language (symbol) the analogy is not merely a possible explanation of the described subject. In other words, it is not a meaning that once and for all is clarified, but one side of it is always ambiguous waiting for elucidation, for symbolic and allegorical perception affects a kind of change in the known objects and turns them into manifestations, and if this exaltation or transcendence did not exist, moving from one stage to another would have been impossible. Interpretation is indeed approaching a higher stage where words are an image or symbol of it. Accordingly, they believe there is a deep relationship between interpretation and its ontological foundation, namely the question of manifestation in the phenomenal beings.

The mystics claim that traditions like the tradition of the seven interiors of the holy Qur'an by the Prophet(S), the tradition of the four aspects of each verse (the exterior, the interior, the limit, and the opening) by Imām 'Alī (A.S.) or the tradition of the four origins of the Qur'anic subjects (expressions, admonishes, subtleties, truths) by Imām Ṣādiq(A.S.) confirm the validity of their way of interpretation and the study of the meanings and interiors of the Qur'an. On the other hand, the belief in the interpretability of the holy Qur'an is based on the following convictions:

- The linear chain of the corresponding worlds which are the example of the other.
- Divine discourse is the image of the truth of the world in the form of words and is the incarnation of the unseen in the visible world.
- Man who himself possesses interiors (subtleties or degrees),

according to his inner journey, can grasp the secrets of the correspondence of the existential worlds and the interiors of the divine discourse.

The Importance of Interpretation for the Mystics

In Islamic philosophy and Mysticism interpretation is important because through the divine discourse it creates a passage way in existence and through tradition it acquires "enlightened intelligence" which itself is the result of the fusion of intuition and tradition. This enlightened intelligence is thought to be the means to attaining intuitions, and it has an interpretative approach to the holy texts. Unlike enlightened intelligence, the partial intelligence (which is concerned with livelihood and is instrumental) cannot grasp or understand the exalted subject and the unity of things. It perceives diversity and appearances; it is acquired and its origin is the mind. But the enlightened intelligence which is supported by intellectual revelation perceives the unity and the interior, and its place is the heart.[1]

Addressing those philosophers who interpreter the verses inaccurately Rūmī says:

> "Thou hast interpreted [and altered the meaning of] the virgin [uncorrupted] Word: interpret [alter] thyself, not the [Divine] Book."[2]
>
> Because interpretation [alteration of the meaning] is a

1. In this regard Mawlānā says, "Intelligence consists of two intelligences; the former is the acquired one which you learn, like a boy at school." *Mathnawī*, Book IV, Verse No. 1960.
   "The other intelligence is the gift of God: its fountain is in the midst of the soul." *Mathnawī*, Book IV, Verse No. 1964.
2. *Mathnawī*, Book I, Verse No. 1080.

> rejection of the gift, since he [the interpreter] regards
> that real [original] meaning as faulty."[1]

Here, it is proper to ask when one should interpret himself and when one should interpret the remembrance and holy text. A brief answer and the view of the mystics is that until man acquires the enlightened intelligence and a level of intuition he must "interpret himself"[2], in the sense that man should eventually attempt to know his origin and himself, and ascribe the problems of the text to his own defects until he acquires the enlightened intelligence and can "interpret the text" and in consequence ascend to higher horizons.

> "The view that it is faulty arises from the weakness of
> his understanding: Universal Reason is the kernel, and
> our reason is like the rind.
> Alter yourself, not the Traditions [of the Prophet]:
> abuse your [dull] brain, not the rose-garden [the true
> sense which you cannot apprehend]."[3]

Some important points on this subject are mentioned below:

1. The relationship between interpretation as understood by the mystics and interpretation which is used as an equivalent for hermeneutics is that hermeneutic interpretation in some movements is the result of extracting and deducing the meaning intended by the author from the text and in some others it is the way the text is understood by the addresses or reader (irrespective of the aim and intention of the author) in light of his previous knowledge and the historical-cultural and spiritual condition and

---

1. *Mathnawī*, Book I, Verse No. 3742.
2. Mawlānā says, "Thou interpretest the Qur'an according to thy desire: by thee the sublime meaning is degraded perverted." *Mathnawī*, Book I, Verse No. 1081.
3. *Mathnawī*, Book I, Verse No. 3743 – 4.

context of the author. Therefore, this interpretation is thought to be relative and according to the interpreter's and the reader's expectations and presuppositions it leads to different and sometimes contradictory conclusions. The interpretation of the mystics, however, though according to the degree, position and station of the mystics may differ, nevertheless since these interpretations are different versions of the same truth, they have no fundamental contradiction (that is, their expressions are not one but united). This interpretation comprises a kind of intuition rather than estimation or conjecture. Moreover, hermeneutic interpretation is a skill related to acquired knowledge and is purely mental, but in the mystics' interpretation the meaning is understood mainly in the context of their presential intuition which depends on their inner preparation and purgation of the soul to reflect the flashes of the discourse.

To explain, there are two main approaches in interpreting a text: 1. Semantic approach, 2. Hermeneutic approach. In the former, the meaning is secured by the intention of the speaker or writer and understanding the text is equal to finding out his intention. In this approach assent has priority and the main effort of the addressee is directed at understanding the real intention of the speaker. However, in the second approach conception has primacy and meaning is that which is understood by the addressee, though the real intention of the speaker may never be known. In this approach the atmosphere of the discourse is purely symbolic, so everybody would have his own understanding of the text according to his previous knowledge, personality and mentality.

It seems, however, the mystics' approach is a combination of these two aspects, that is, the mystics contend every man (whether a mystic or a layman) understands the dimensions and aspects of the divine discourse according to the level of his knowledge and thought or intuition, and because God Himself knows what the meaning of this discourse is understood by every person, it can be said He has also intended that meaning, that is, He has allowed for derivative and secondary interpretations. Of course, this does not mean these interpretations are baseless or meaningless; indeed all that is said on hermeneutics is this very point, namely interpreting the self or interpreting the text.

2. The difference between the interpretation of the mystics and subjective commentary, and the difference between seeking sympathy in the text and interpretation and explanation should be also taken into consideration. That is:

a. The mystics' belief in the Interpretability of the verses does not mean every meaning of the verses suggested is correct. Indeed a distinction is made between true and false interpretations in the works of the mystics, and also the principles and rules of interpretation have been explained.

b. Sometimes the mystics in their works use the verses of the Qur'an only to find sympathy, rather than suggesting any meaning of the verse, which may happen in any other text. Finding an echo of one's state in the verses, proverbs or holy text is one thing, and ascribing meanings to those texts is something else, which needs special care and scientific caution.

c. One important distinction between interpretation and subjective commentary is that interpretation is affected throughout the text and treats its surface but has no contradiction with it, whereas subjective commentary is not committed to such stipulation and its suggested meaning may be completely incompatible with the appearance of the verse.

Questions

1. Compare the "knowledge of the intellect", "knowledge of the states", "knowledge of the secrets", and "knowledge of specification" in the school of Ibn 'Arabī.
2. Discuss the mystical experience from the two perspectives of comparative mysticism and Islamic mysticism.
3. Explain the relationship among the esoteric, religious and mystical experiences.
4. Explain the different views offered on the nature of the mystical experience, compare them with each other and discuss each of them.
5. Explain, compare and evaluate the views offered on the reality of the mystical experience, such as the emotional view, the similarity with the sensory perception view, the inextricability of the experience and interpretation and delusion view.
6. Discuss the two objections to the mystical experience, namely "the inaccuracy of some intuitions" and "an ineffable issue is unknowable" and critique each of them.
7. Compare the universal or external and spiritual or internal mysticism from the viewpoint of Stace.
8. Compare the two stages of annihilation and subsistence.
9. Compare the stations of "gathering", "separation", and "gathering of gathering".
10. Compare the terms "intuition", "revelation", and "mystical contemplation".
11. Explain the reasons of the mystics' secrecy.
12. Explain why mystical experiences are indescribable.
13. Explain why the mystics speak of their experiences.
14. Explain the verbal or linguistic forms of the mystics.
15. Discuss the religious foundations of the interpretability of the holy Qur'an.
16. Discuss the relationship between interpretation and hermeneutics.

Chapter Two: Ontology in the Mystical Viewpoint

Primacy of Existence

There is no doubt that the term "existence" is the most important term in theoretical mysticism (meaning the school of Ibn 'Arabī). In other words, the mystical worldview is founded on the principles of existence, God and oneness. The way these three concepts are related will be discussed later, but it should be mentioned first that the mystics who have known Reality and its manifestations intuitively, in the classifications of the well-known schools, are placed among the believers in the primacy of existence. Ibn 'Arabī and his followers without any systematic investigation of the questions related to the primacy of existence argue that besides existence, which is equal and identified with the divine essence, there is nothing real or true. Therefore, whatsoever is rooted in plurality (such as quiddity) and can be captured by the mind and put in the mould of concepts is at variance with that one Reality.

Mystics, especially the followers of Ibn 'Arabī, speak of their external and inner mystical experience in terms of "being" or "existence" and to explain experiences such as diversity in unity and unity in diversity they use expressions such as the collapse of things in the absolute existence or the delivery of existence from the bounds (or the falling of the additions). It seems as in the world of concepts existence is self-evident and in the common intuitive knowledge it is clear to all, in the special intuitive knowledge (mystical vision) finding the essence of the Real is also the most essential issue, for which the mystics use the word "existence" as the most appropriate term. Shabistarī writes:

"He that knows 'The Truth' and to whom Unity is revealed,
Sees the light of the very Being at the first glance."[1]
"But the knower is he that knows the Very Being,
He that witnesses the Absolute Being."[2]

The Two Meanings of Existence in Mysticism

For mystics existence has two meanings, real and arbitrary. The former is absolutely one and the latter is graded and accepts gradation. Moreover, one is self-dependent and the other is relational or even it is the very relation. One is neither a substance nor an accident and is above both of them; the other is secondary and accidental.

Qayṣarī in his explanation of these two meanings states: existence is sometimes used to indicate the emergence, realization or manifestation of a thing which existed in other worlds and stages. In this sense existence is accidental (which is added to quiddities and entities, and it is by this addition that we know beings exist). It is in this sense that beings are predicated as a common meaning and in a graded way (gradation in the sense of appearance in different ranks and manifestations). The other existence, however, which is the real existence or the very reality of existence and the sustainer and the prop of all the ranks of

1. *The Mystic Rose Garden*, Verse No. 84.
2. Ibid, Verse No. 397.

creation, is neither a substance nor an accident but rather it is the sustainer of both. This existence is the existence of the Real Who is the essence and origin of all beings.

From the viewpoint of Ibn 'Arabī, existence is not equal to permanence (*thubūt*). Ibn 'Arabī differentiates between the thing-ness of permanence and the thing-ness of existence. For him the permanent archetypes are fixed but they do not exist. The domain of permanence is related to the divine terms and attributes, which have no existence outside the essence of the Real. Moreover, for him the term "being" does not mean existence, but it means the existence of the world and the very addition and relation which were mentioned.

The Considerations of Existence and Absolute Existence

Existence in theoretical mysticism has certain divisions including:

1. Absolute existence/ limited existence,
2. Universal existence/ determined and particular existence, and
3. Unconditional existence/ existence with no condition, existence conditioned by something.

The mystics believe these divisions return to the divisions and ways of intuitions rather than the kinds of beings and plurality in existence. The mystics in their intuition have found determined beings whose existence on the one hand is accidental, relational and arbitrary and, on the other hand, is something infinite and undetermined and pervades all that is called being. Beyond these two they believe in an absolute, unconditional, unknowable and inaccessible existence which is admitted, according to some, on the ground of reason (the necessity of the existence of a real dividable object for all divisions) and, according to others, intuitively (witnessing the dark light). The existence which they see spiritually is not only the highest degree of existence but also the only degree of existence.

To explain further, like any concept, quiddity and reality that is measured by something, when existence is also measured by a certain quality or determination it may be qualified with four aspects:

1. Existence conditioned by something (determined) [restricted existence],

2. Existence conditioned by 'No' (undetermined, absolute qualified by absoluteness) [absolute existence],

3. Unconditioned existence (a division, meaning qualified by neither determination nor indetermination), and

3. Unconditioned existence (a divider which divides the previous divisions, and in itself it is neither determined nor absolute, neither unqualified by determination nor indetermination) [absolute existence].

When the term absolute linguistically and grammatically is prefixed to a term as an adjunct it gives a general and wide meaning to the governed noun, a meaning that is qualified by no attribute or epithet, but it can be described by different attributes, like the "absolute object" in the Arabic language and syntax, which includes causative object, adverbial object, unrestricted object and also other restricted objects. Therefore, if the term absolute in Arabic follows a word, it is counted an adjective and would act as a kind of qualification. For example, in the unrestricted object the unrestricted adjective is the object, that is, the object is qualified by absoluteness. Accordingly, in existence "absolute existence" also has a wide range meaning that includes absolute existence and restricted existents as well.

It has been a matter of disagreement among mystics and philosophers which of the aspects of existence is the essence of the Real and which ones are His act and creation.

The Properties and Precepts of Existence in the School of Ibn 'Arabī

The Properties and essentials of existence (the reality of existence) in the school of Ibn 'Arabī are as follows:

1. Existence cannot be defined. It is perceived neither by universal intuitive knowledge that leads to the conception of the self-evident notion of existence in acquired knowledge, nor by particular intuitive knowledge which was discussed earlier.
2. Real existence is neither a verbal meaning nor common meaning, for it has no more than one instance However, relational existence, among different manifestations, is a common meaning.
3. All perfections return to the reality of existence.
4. There is no gradation in existence, but there is gradation in manifestation.
5. Existence and light are coequal.
6. Existence and unity are coequal.
7. Existence and necessity are coequal.

Theoretical mysticism shares the first and the third properties of existence with transcendental philosophy and peripatetic philosophy, and it has the fifth and sixth properties in common with transcendental philosophy. Other properties, however, separate it from philosophical systems.

Concerning the last two questions which lead us to the question of oneness of existence, it should be noted that unlike philosophers the mystics hold that existence is not divided into the necessary and the possible, but it is essentially associated with necessity and necessity itself is due to the reality of existence rather than any individual being. Of course, for philosophers certain kinds of necessity, namely necessity by others or necessity conditioned by a predicate can be attributed to every being. But the meaning intended by the mystics is necessity by essence and even eternal necessity rather than necessity by others. Although this view is grounded on intuition, some mystics have demonstrated it in different ways which are mentioned in their books and have been studied and critiqued so far. Indeed establishing this view is equal to demonstrating the oneness of existence, that is, denying the existence of possible beings and diversity and restricting existence to the essence of the Exalted Real.

Oneness of Existence

The two main questions in theoretical mysticism are the oneness of God (knowledge of Allah) and knowing the monotheist (the perfect man). The first issue itself is divided into two fundamental questions:

1. Establishing the unity (the personal unity of existence),
2. Explaining diversity (the question of manifestation).

Understanding the mystical ontology is possible only in the light of these two questions. Essentially the tendency of mystical worldview to unity is inseparable from its tendency to existence and unity is counted as the particular attribute of existence and these two are inseparable. This issue will be discussed in the section of "Oneness of existence".

No doubt man in his daily experiences observes diverse beings and also abstracts certain unities from different and various things, such as unity of individual, species and geneses. It can be said that the most common feature of diverse things is their being and existence.

One of the questions which has always engaged the human mind is the origin of unity and diversity and which one is real and which is unreal. In other words, is there a hidden unity behind the visible diversity and are these diverse beings the manifestations of that unity? This unity in its real aspects could be described as ultimate, subjective, formal, material or of some other kinds. In the recorded history of philosophy perhaps the pre-Socratic philosophers, especially the Eleatics, were the first who believed in the existence of a unique substance behind things, and among them Parmenides contended that the unique and permanent Being is the origin and truth hidden behind the diverse and changing things. Of course, all religions, divine and other religions, have referred to such unity, albeit divine religions put more emphasis on the unity of the agent and purpose (oneness of God, essence and worship) but some oriental cults stressed the substantial unity of the entire world, and the mystical experience implied in religions could be the source of such emphases.

The mystics believe in the primacy and oneness of existence and the arbitrary nature of diversity, and call this doctrine "the personal unity of existence" and in short "the oneness of existence". The oneness of existence assumed by the Muslim mystics is an expression rooted in their intuition and mystical experience; moreover, it is an interpretation of the religious principle of unity (the unity of the most elite) and a philosophical and ontological theory of reality. This theory calls for attributing the apparent, arbitrary and illusory diversity to the one real existence behind the diverse beings.

The Meaning of Oneness of Existence

To understand correctly the meaning of the oneness of existence which is of prior importance to its conceptual and demonstrative discussions, first this theory should be distinguished from its alternative and rival theories, such as:

1. The difference of existence. This is the school of peripatetic philosophers and theologians who believe in the diversity of beings and the difference in kind and structure between the existence of things and the existence of the Exulted Necessary existence on the one hand and their difference with each other on the other. In this school the external contains the real diversity and the mind contains the abstract unity (the concept of existence).

2. The graded unity of existence. It is the formal viewpoint of transcendental philosophy which admits to the diversity of existents but denies any diversity in the origin of existence and maintains that all beings are of one kind. It contends all existents, both necessary and possible, are the different degrees of the gradation of one reality, and entertains a kind of diversity in unity and unity in diversity (both in a real way).

3. Unity of existence and existent and negation of diversity. It is the view of some Sufis who believe diversity is a chimera and is false. They negate plurality altogether and hold no reality, in existence or manifestation, for diverse beings.

4. Pantheism. All Pantheists believe either the world and God are two realities united in one reality, or God is the sum of the beings of the universe, or God is disseminated and incarnated in the corners and sides of the universe. In any case, all the three views speak from the stand of diversity and in the terminology of the mystics the dualism in existence.[1] This group in Islamic culture is known as the believers in incarnation and oneness. The fundamental belief of all theists is founded on the objectivity of God and the world and denying their separation. They do not

1. In the criticism of this view, Shabistarī says,

"Incarnation and Communion are impossible here,
For duality in unity is clearly absurd." *The Mystic Rose Garden*, Verse No. 454.

believe in creation and believe God is not the creator of things but is the very things themselves. They contend He is everything—in the sense He is the sum of existence—and all things are God. Accordingly they deny the transcendence of God and that the Real has no essence or identity. This view first is incompatible with theism which is founded on a personal and unique God and his distinction from the world. Second, it is founded on the belief in diversity and the plurality of beings—as existential constituents of one being.

The Personal Unity of Existence

Although prior to Ibn 'Arabī some other mystics had used expressions indicating the unity of the reality of existence and the arbitrariness of diversity, introducing the theory of the personal unity of existence, adding to it the theory of manifestation as a supplement, explaining its foundations and elements and properties, and finally establishing it rationally are the achievements of the school of Ibn 'Arabī and the commentators of this school, namely Qūnawī and his followers. Ibn 'Arabī does not mention the term "oneness of existence" in his work except for one time, but there are many expressions and references in his books and treatises in reference to the content of this theory. Compared to some rival theories explained earlier, oneness of existence means restricting existence to one being but at the same time it is a kind of unity in diversity and diversity in unity, albeit different from the formal stance of transcendent philosophy which refers unity to the origin of existence and diversity to the degrees and individuals of existence. Rather, it is one reality, namely the highest degree of existence, which is also the only degree of existence manifested in the appearance and images of the diverse being. Therefore, the diverse beings not only are not chimeras or false representations but also they represent the real, and indeed the criterion of their originality and reality is their being representations. Of course, the Real in the position of His essence and hidden unseen identity remains unknown and imperceptible, but in the position of His manifestation is associated with things and diverse being and permeates them. This permeation, however, is not like the flow of water in a plant or blood in a body so that there should be incarnation and the world is not the outward form of the Real or united or with His essence or equal to His essence so that there should be union, but the world is like an image reflected in the mirror that shows the Real though it is not the Real. Accordingly, since diverse beings are the manifestations and appearances of the Real, they are not false or illusions. In other words, if they are considered by themselves, they are no more than illusions, but if they are looked at as signs and mirrors, they will reflect the Real.

According to this view, unity and existence are inseparable. Unity is the attribute of existence and existence accompanies unity. However, the oneness of the Real is not a numerical oneness to be incompatible with diversity. Rather it is absolute oneness that includes diverse manifestations, and diverse beings, which in their essence are only a show and manifestation, and they show only one thing.

In short, comparing the theory of oneness of existence with other views, one can say the oneness of existence unlike the theory of difference in existence essentially does not concern diversity in reality. It neither considers quiddities as real (primacy of quiddity) to think their diversity exists in reality, nor admits the diversity of beings and species (difference) nor even the degrees of existence (gradation), nor like pantheists deny the transcendent state of the essence, nor like the believers in incarnation and unity believe in the dualism in existence. Moreover, unlike some Sufis it does not take diverse beings as false or mere illusions; rather it stresses the real unity of existence (being) and the diverse appearances and manifestations (representations) of this Reality.

According to this view, the Real has two aspects:

1. A hidden aspect which is an eternal and unknowable secret (absolute Unseen),

2. An apparent and manifest aspect (Seen), which is accessible to man's knowledge.

Thus, as it will be said, transcendence and immanence come together in the theory of oneness of being and they come together, whereas the formal stance of philosophers is pure transcendence and the standpoint of all theists and believers in incarnation and unity is pure immanence. Moreover, on the basis of the oneness of existence, although God is present in things He is different from them, and although He is outside them He is not separate from them. According to the Commander of the believers (A.S.) "He is within things without mixing, and outside of them without separation," or "He is with all things but not by the way of association, and different from everything with no separation."

Symbols of Oneness of Existence

According to Ibn 'Arabī's description of the oneness of Being, there seems to be a kind of "He is not He" logic in the speeches and expressions of the mystics, that is, apparently some incompatible or even opposite properties are attributed to the Real and the creatures, such as:

- The world is both imaginary and real.
- The Real is the creatures in one respect and He is not the creatures in another respect.

- God is both the very things and He is other than them.
- God is both transcendent and immanent.
- God is with the world but the world is not with God.
- God is both manifest and is hidden in everything.

However, in the light of what was mentioned and will be also discussed on the subject of manifestation, the meaning of these expressions becomes clear. Ibn 'Arabī believes the deepest secret of the mystical way is to understand the world is imaginary and at the same time real.

The universe is imaginary but it is truly the Real,
He who knows this knows the secrets of the way.

In order to explain that "the imaginary world represents the Real", Ibn 'Arabī employs different symbols and expressions, such as dream (true vision), the image in the mirror, the relationship between one and numbers, and also the relationship between shadow and object, and to illustrate the question further we refer to some of them in the following.

The symbol of vision and its interpretation. Ibn 'Arabī holds that the world is not existence but an illusory thing which can be called imagination. However, this does not mean it is vain or absurd, but to the contrary it reflects a degree of reality. On the basis of the Prophetic tradition, "People are sleeping, and when they die they wake up," he states the world is a dream but the common people don't know it is a dream, and this ignorance means ignoring the symbolic substance of the world. But this dream is a true dream and not false like confused dreams. Moreover, as the truth of every symbol can be understood through explanation and interpretation, the world can also be understood by interpreting the dream in a correct way.

If the absolute is the reality of the Real, the universe and other than the Real is no more than a fancy or illusion, but an external rather than a mental illusion. In other words, other than the Real is a particular image of the manifestation of that reality, and this representation of the Real is the secret of the world of creation which makes the world a great gathering of signs and symbols for the mystic. Therefore, despite the formal difference between sleeping and wakefulness, everything is a symbol. According to Ibn 'Arabī, the mentioned *ḥadīth* teaches us the way of understanding interpretation, or death which he calls annihilation and voluntary death. He argues that it is to the degree of the level of insight and through scaling the mystical ranks and moving from this world to the other that a person gains a more precise and correct understanding of the world. Ibn 'Arabī believes his mysticism and theosophy is no more than a theoretical explanation of the world of being as seen through the eye of the awakened man (the mystic) and the perfect man (of divine vision who looks at the world from above).

The symbol of the image in the mirror. Ibn 'Arabī holds that the mirror is the best symbol that shows the personal unity of existence and the divine manifestation and its relationship with the world, for although the mirror (meaning the image in the mirror) is real, but it has no portion of reality. The image in the mirror has no essence other than what it reflects. Neither should it be imagined that the image and the mirror are united nor the image is incarnated in the mirror. In other words, the image is manifested in the mirror, but it has no real existence, that is, it is neither in the mirror nor in the space between the mirror and the spectator. Moreover, the mirror itself is not the issue in question, and as the mirror *per se* it is not visible. Ibn 'Arabī holds that you cannot see the mirror while you are looking at the image reflected in it, for the images will act as a barrier between the eye and the mirror (a hint at the annihilation of the bodies of this world when looking at their meanings, which is divine manifestation). Shabistarī writes:

"Set a mirror over against you,
Look on it and see that other person.
Again see what that reflection is,
It is not this nor that, then what is that reflection?"[1]

The Analogy of one and the Numbers. Ibn 'Arabī in elaborating on the relationship of the Real and the creatures stresses the analogy of the relationship of one and the numbers. In this regard it should be known that one is of two kinds:

a. The numerical one, which stands opposite to other numbers and is parallel to them, and

b. The real one, which is not a number and is not repeatable, but without losing its status it produces other numbers *ad infinitum*, and indeed numbers are nothing other than the multiplied one.

These two kinds of one exist in one reality, and one in this respect is an example of the existence of the Real, since the Real both exists in the rank of His hidden identity and by His appearance and manifestation creates different ranks in a way that every rank is nothing other than the manifestation of the one in respect of belonging and adding to a special concept. Shabistarī says in this regard:

"All these varied forms arise only from your fancy,
They are but one point revolving quickly in a circle."[2]
"That Unity is exposed to view in this plurality,
Like as when you count one it becomes many."[3]
"The world of command and that of creatures are here one;

1. *The Mystic Rose Garden*, Verses No. 456-7
2. *The Mystic Rose Garden*, Verse No. 15.
3. Ibid,Verse No. 137.

One becomes many and many becomes few."[1]

Among other expressions which are used in the form of metaphor, symbol, and analogy by Ibn 'Arabī and his followers are the following examples:

- The relationship of the sea and the waves or the sea and its manifestations in the form of aquatic phenomena like vapor, ice and cloud.
- Comparing the reflection of light on glass and the appearance of different colours and spectrums with unity and diversity.
- The relationship of shadow and its subject.
- The figure of A in the form of the letters or breath in different verbal forms.
- The relationship of the soul and body.

Establishing the Theory of Oneness of Existence

The belief of the mystics in the oneness of existence is based on spiritual revelation and intuition. To see one being with no qualification, to see one light in all manifestations and appearances, to see the reflection of the countenance of the cupbearer in all forms, to find the one in all diverse beings, to see one kind of beauty in different mirrors, and to observe the absolute in the limited forms—which are expressed in different ways—are the mystics' main approaches to "oneness of existence".

Ibn 'Arabī states that he whose eyes are opened by God will see Him in everything or equal to everything. Moreover, "it is through the lights that one can see the Real in the form and reality of everything as it is", and he who finds the Real through this revelation and with such knowledge is of the intimate people. Of course, the intuition of the mystics is of different levels, and as it

1. Ibid,Verse No. 14.

was explained in the last chapter Ibn 'Arabī maintains the intuition of the people of the unity of unity is above the intuition of the people of unity and separation.

Furthermore, the mystics believe the interpretation and the inner meaning of some verses of the holy Qur'an and the purport of certain traditions refer to this point. Some of these verses are:

- He is the First and the Last, the Manifest and the Hidden.[1]
- Have you not regarded how your Lord spreads the twilight? (Had He wished He would have made it still.)[2]
- Everything is to perish except His Face.[3]
- Whichever way you turn, there is the face of Allah![4]
- You did not throw when you threw, rather it was Allah who threw.[5]

Now we may ask whether besides intuition and narration the intellect can also find its way to the oneness of being. Ibn 'Arabī claims because of the following reasons the intellect has no way to understand these issues. First, the structure of the reason's intellection is founded on those concepts and essences which are rooted in diversity rather than unity. Second, the knowledge of the intellect is a negative knowledge and it cannot have a positive understanding of the Real. Third, the intellect and rational demonstration are based on the law of non-contradiction and the law of excluded middle, whereas the intuitive knowledge (at least in some cases) is based on the possibility of two contraries and issuing two negative and positive judgments simultaneously on

---

1. 'هُوَ الْأَوَّلُ وَالْآخِرُ وَالظَّاهِرُ وَالْبَاطِنُ' (57: 3).
2. 'أَلَمْ تَرَ إِلَىٰ رَبِّكَ كَيْفَ مَدَّ الظِّلَّ وَلَوْ شَاءَ لَجَعَلَهُ سَاكِنًا' (25: 45).
3. 'كُلُّ شَيْءٍ هَالِكٌ إِلَّا وَجْهَهُ' (28: 88).
4. 'فَأَيْنَمَا تُوَلُّوا فَثَمَّ وَجْهُ اللَّهِ' (2: 115).
5. 'مَا رَمَيْتَ إِذْ رَمَيْتَ وَلَٰكِنَّ اللَّهَ رَمَىٰ' (8: 17).

one and the same subject, such as the sameness and otherness of the Real's Names in relation to the Real, crediting and discrediting the servant with the deed at the same time, attributing the act to God and to the servant at the same time, and confirming and denying the attributes of the Real.

Ibn 'Arabī on the basis of Abū Sa'īd al-Kharrāz's saying, "I knew Allah in His gathering of the contraries," states "the mystics who have found the Real discern by their heart that God brings together the contraries."

Ibn 'Arabī holds that mysticism and divine command is founded on "He is not He" and believes a person who does not know Him as such essentially he has not understood the divine command. This is the speech of revelation that 'You did not throw when you threw,' where the intellect and theoretical discussions are at loss.

Another example is that the light of all lights and the manifest that makes these lights is by essence hidden and remains dark, and this absolute darkness that precedes all manifestations is the very station of essence, which in the station of intuition is called dark light (the disappearance of light because of excessive light).

Thus Ibn 'Arabī stands against philosophy which is founded on "He is He" and owes its rationality to denying contradiction and all its ambition is directed to obliterating bewilderment. Indeed for the philosopher the simultaneous belief in "the Real is the creatures" and "the Real is not the creatures" is impossible and absurd. Moreover, the inferences of the intellect are based on the principle of causality, whereas in the realm of truths the unity of cause and effect is the rule. So, the intellect is like a fetter, it is strapped and straps others, but the heart which abounds with change, alteration and fluctuation is tied to no particular thing and can always have access to a trans-rational mode.

However, the followers of Ibn 'Arabī, such as Ibn Turkeh, Sayyid

Ḥaydar Āmulī, Qayṣarī and Jāmī have endeavored to bring together mysticism (intuition) and demonstration (intellect) and believe the oneness of existence may be understood and discussed rationally and for this purpose they have written treatises and offered many arguments. However, most of these arguments suffer from logical weakness and confusion of intellectual subjects.

Ṣadr al-Muta'allihīn, among these theosophists, who dealt with the question on the basis of his philosophical principles, argued about what seems to be unreasonable or irrational in two different ways. He was of the opinion that although common intellect cannot understand this question, the "improved intellect" and that "illuminated by the light of revelation" can have some understanding of that great secret and without reducing or confining that sublime meaning to the tight garment of conventional concepts it can explain the question well. Ṣadr al-Muta'allihīn himself on the oneness of existence declares that knowing the unreality of the possible beings and the eternal annihilation of the unreal entities is of the kind of innate knowledge and the bounty and mercy of God by whose guidance he could find his way through celestial argument to the personal unity of existence. However, the reality of the encompassing being is known only to those who are firm in knowledge.

Of the two arguments of Ṣadr al-Muta'allihīn, the infinitude of the existence of the Real and the return of the causal dependence to manifestation, here, we consider the first argument and leave the other to the discussion of manifestation. In brief, the argument of infinitude is that, as demonstrated in the argument of the truthful, the existence of the Exalted Real is infinite and of simple reality, and the infinite existence does not allow for another existence besides or along itself; otherwise, that other would limit the infinite existence. Therefore, besides the existence of the infinite Real there is no other existence. To explain, plurality and diversity are the result of limitation, and when a thing is infinite, it would admit neither duality nor repetition. On the other hand, on the basis of this argument no perfection is outside the compass of the existence of the simple Reality, though it is not confined to any perfection ("the Simple Reality is everything, but it is none of them.")

Therefore, since the Exalted Real (the Necessary being of the simple Reality) is an infinite being, and the infinite does not allow for "others", the existence of the Real does not admit any existence for others and, therefore, existence is just confined to the Real. In this argument, as Mullā Ṣadrā indicates, if things predicated of the simple Reality and vice versa are predicated of what belongs to Him or predicated of the Reality and Subtlety it would be compatible with the gradation of existence. However, if they are predicated of Him qua Him or as the apparent predicated of the Revealer (that is, every perfection is He and there is no perfection or existence besides Him) it would lead to the personal unity of existence. Mullā Ṣadrā himself has used the second meaning in the argument.

Of course, the import of this argument is seen in the works of 'Aṭṭār and Rūmī before Ṣadrā al-Muta'allihīn.

Mawlānā writes:

> "Before the infinite all that is finite is naught: everything except the Face of God is passing away."[1]

Manifestation

Having demonstrated the oneness of existence, to explain away the contradiction between observing the multitudes on the one

---

1. *Mathnawī*, Book II, Verse No. 3321.

hand and restricting existence to the Exulted Real on the other, we have to either consider the question of oneness as illogical, self-contradictory and incapable of a rational solution; think of the multitudes and possible beings as merely illusory, unreal and imaginary and as a result take our knowledge for double ignorance; return and reduce the oneness of existence to the oneness of intuition;[1] or finally profess a kind of theory that besides admitting to the oneness of existence holds that multitudes are arbitrary and unreal things and one should return them to the one existence of the Real, and despite establishing a kind of diversity denies their otherness and plurality.

Ibn 'Arabī chooses the last option by introducing the term "manifestation" (in its particular meaning), and on the basis of his mystical experience of "witnessing the manifestations of the Real in others" announces that oneness is the attribute of existence and diversity is the attribute of manifestation. He, thus, neither considers knowledge as double ignorance, nor the universe as false and mere illusion, nor the universe of any existence.

Some scholars contend that manifestation plays an essential role

---

1. Shabistarī says:

"The whole world is merely an imaginary thing,
It is like one point whirled round in a circle." *The Mystic Rose Garden*, Verse No. 709.

"Every man whose heart is pure from doubt,
Knows for a surety that there is no being but 'One'." *The Mystic Rose Garden*, Verse No. 446.

" 'I', ' We,' ' Thou ' and ' He ' are all one thing,
For in Unity there is no distinction of persons." *The Mystic Rose Garden*, Verse No. 449.

"The existence of creatures and plurality is but a semblance,
And not everything that seems to be really is." *The Mystic Rose Garden*, Verse No.455.

in the views of Ibn 'Arabī and maintain "all his thoughts concerning the structure of the existence of the world are founded on this ground, so that no part of his worldview can be understood without referring it to this fundamental and central concept, and in short it can be said the theory of manifestation is the quintessence and core of his philosophy."

Unlike the theory of the oneness of existence, which is but implicitly hinted at in the works of Ibn 'Arabī, he refers to manifestation and its different dimensions openly many times, and we rarely find any of his discussions in his works without a reference to this term. In different sections we will see how the followers of the school of Ibn 'Arabī explain away diversity in the following three levels on the basis of the theory of manifestation. They state:

1. Diversity of Names and attributes is the result of the manifestation and appearance of the Essence to the Essence (the most holy emanation),
2. Diversity emerging in the fixed archetypes is the result of the most holy manifestation, and
3. Diversity of the external entities and the multitudinous of creatures are the result of the holy manifestation.

The Meaning of Manifestation

By manifestation, the appearance of the absolute essence of the Real and His perfections once determined by certain determinations (of the essence, Names or Acts) to Himself or to others in a way that leads to no separation, turning away, incarnation or union, is meant.

In other words, manifestation is the process in which the essence of the Real—Who His essence is absolutely unknowable—shows itself in the limited and diverse beings. Thus, as it was mentioned already, the theory of manifestation besides the belief in the absolute oneness of existence is a supplement to the theory of the oneness of existence and explains away the diversity of the visible beings.

This doctrine in regard of the relation of God and the world corresponds neither with the temporal creation (the theologians' creation *ex nihilo*)—for creation *ex nihilo* calls for the separation in the existence of God and the world and also the temporality of the process of creation—nor with the causality and emanation of the philosophers—which are founded on the duality (existential or graded) of the cause and effect—nor with incarnation and union or pantheism—which depend on the existence of two things, one of them penetrating the other or both reduced to a third thing—nor with transmigration, incarnation or embodiment introduced by some sects and cults, in which the atemporal and immaterial plane of existence is reduced to or resolved in the material and historical aspect at a certain period and eventually leads to immanence and incarnation.

Ibn 'Arabī following his critique of the views of causality, emanation, atemporal *creatio ex nihilo*, incarnation and union chooses the term manifestation as the basis of his thought system.

Synonymous or related terms of manifestation in theoretical mysticism are revealing, revelation, determination, relation, illumination, emanation, command, relation, etc., and in this respect it stands against terms such as concealment, hiddenness, covering up, turning away, covering, and wrapping.

As was mentioned the symbol Ibn 'Arabī uses for manifestation is mirror (the image in the mirror) where a real and original being is revealed in an unreal and secondary thing without falling into incarnation, union, descent or withdrawal.

Demonstrating Manifestation

Although Ibn 'Arabī believes the reception of the Real's

manifestation is an experiential science (rather than acquired or speculative one) and the knowledge of the divine manifestations is one of the sciences of the secrets and are confined to mystics, and the reason he chooses the term manifestation instead of philosophical causality he maintains is primarily beholding the divine lights all over the world, it seems narration-based evidence is also a good source for choosing this term by the mystics. Besides verse 35 of *Nūr*, the verse 'When his Lord disclosed Himself to the mountain He leveled it, and Moses fell down swooning',(7: 143) also indicates the appearance of God in a particular way to the Mountain and the destruction of that mountain and the swooning of Mūsā (A.S.) because of that manifestation. Some speeches of Imām 'Alī (A.S.) in *Nahj al-Balāgha* [1], etc. are also helpful in this concern.

Although according to Ibn 'Arabī manifestation is demonstrated intuitively, and he himself did not try to prove it rationally, his followers made some attempts to explain away manifestation rationally, through the question of the oneness of existence for example. The most successful of these attempts seems to be that of Ṣadr al-Muta'allihīn in his discussion of causality in *Asfār*.

Mullā Ṣadrā following his accustomed practice where he initially starts the arguments according to the well-known views but at the end separates his own special way from them and expresses his own particular view, in dealing with causality in *Asfār*, he also begins with the conventional concept of causality and argues on the basis of the gradation of existence of the complete cause and effect.

On the relation of cause and effect conventional philosophy holds that the cause is the origin of existence of the effect, supposedly one thing gives another thing a third thing, which is existence. So, there is a giver and a taker and something given and

1. See *Nahj al-Balāgha*, Sermons 108 and 147.

naturally there is a relation between the giver and the taker like all other relations that exist between two things. However, on the basis of Mullā Ṣadrā's existential analysis of causality, first the relation of cause and effect is considered to be of the kind of illuminationist relation, that is, a relation that makes the other instead of being dependent on two independent sides (only one side is real and original). Second, the meaning of the effect returns to be a relational existence, that is, its existence is not attributed to the cause, but an existence equal to relation to the cause. Third, the criteria of independence of the effect on the cause is also not an essential possibility but a possibility of dependence, that is, the existence of the effect is the very dependence and need of a cause rather than an essence which needs a cause. Therefore, the effect by essence is equal to dependence and want. In other words, the effect has no essence and in itself has no existence or attribute, and that which we call the essence of the effect is an essence by definition only, but in the external it is not separate from the cause and it is only one of the aspects of the cause. Moreover, since the revealed is in one way the revealer Himself (the rule of the unity of the revealed and the revealer) this argument culminates in the personal unity of existence.

It can be said that for Mullā Ṣadrā the relational existence of the effect is a literal existence in comparison with literal meaning which is opposite to nominal meaning, and as a result things and all other than Him are neither parallel to the Necessary being nor in the same line with Him, and they are neither within Him nor outside Him. Accordingly Mullā Ṣadrā at the end of this argument writes:

> Thus what we posited as the main subject, that is, in existence there is cause and effect, when looked at carefully and mystically we conclude that of those

two only the cause is real and the effect is one of its sides, and causality (in what is known as creative cause) and the impact of the cause on the effect return indeed to the development of the cause into the effect's mode and appropriating an aspect that does not lead to the separation of that determination or aspect from the cause.[1]

Two Objections to the Oneness of Existence and Manifestation

Some objections have been made to the questions of the oneness of existence, manifestation and appearance, restring being to the Real, and the arbitrariness and unreality of everything other than Him. Here we discuss two of these objections.

Attributing imperfection to the Real. It is argued that the mystics understand things as the manifestations and appearance of the Real, and on the basis of the rule of the unity of the manifest and the revealer as mentioned by Ibn 'Arabī in his sayings, such as "Glorified is He Who manifested things though they are no other than Him" or in some ecstatic mystical utterances, the attributes of the possible beings would be also attributed to the Exalted Real, and the Real would be described with the imperfections and the attributes of possibility, which is against reason and narration.

To answer, it is true that in mysticism the world is described as the manifestation of the beauty and grandeur of the Real, but this does not mean the essence of the Exalted Real is qualified with all the attributes of things; rather it means He is their creator and revealer, as the soul is the knower of the form of its creatures but not necessarily qualified with their qualities. The important point is that it is the Real manifest which is united with things and not

1. Mullā Ṣadrā , *Asfār*, vol. 2, 292, 300 and 301.

the essence of the Real. In Ibn 'Arabī's gnosis when the Real and the creature are sometimes claimed to be one and sometimes different, by the Real, in the discussion of objectivity or concrete existence, the created Real (the expanded existence or the breath of the Merciful) is meant, and where they are known to be different and separate by the Real the essence of the One, which is free from the creatures, is intended. For the essence is neither witnessed by the mystic nor understood by the philosopher; therefore, it could be neither judged nor predicated of things. So, it is this act of the Real (the breath of the Merciful) and His manifestation which are united with things and one with them, and despite the separation of His identity and their identity He is not different from them, and although he assumes all determinations, He retains His absoluteness. To conclude, this objection applies to the theory of pantheism and the view of union and incarnation, but it cannot be made to the theory of the oneness of existence.

Rūmī compares the Real to the light of the sun or the moon, which although shines on and illuminates everything, high or low, it does not take their qualities and retains its identity, and at the end at the evening when the light of the sun joins its origin, it is as it was pure and unpolluted by the attributes of imperfection and lowliness.

> "The light of the sun heard [the call] *Return!* And came back in haste to its source.
> No disgrace remained with it from the ash pits, no colour remained with it from the rose-gardens."[1]
> "How should the light of the moon ever become defiled, though its light strikes on everything good and evil?
> Pure of all [defilements] it returns to the moon, even as

1. *Mathnawī*, Book V, Verse No. 1262-3.

> the light of the spirit and reason [returns] unto God.
> The quality of purity is an endowment [settled] on the light of the moon, though its radiance is [falling] on the defilements of the way.
> Malignity does not accrue to the light of the moon from those defilements of the way or from pollution."[1]

The negation of the two contraries or law of the excluded middle. It is said that since there is no border between existence and nonexistence, "manifestation" should be qualified with one of the two, and since it is not nonexistent (or attributed with nonexistence) it should, therefore, be of the category of existence. As a result, plurality of manifestation should return to plurality of existence, and this is incompatible with the personal unity of existence.

To answer, to decide on a thing (including whether it exists or not) it depends on an essence which can be considered independently. But as the literal meaning cannot be the subject of any judgment or predication and it takes its meaning and in consequence its terms from independent indicators (such as noun and verb), it cannot be said whether the diverse beings of the world exist or not. Instead it can be said that they are the determinations of the Real's Act and divine manifestations, like the soul's creations, such as the human's imaginings, which are neither the soul nor other than it but one of its inseparable aspects. Therefore, in the mystics' divisions—existence, manifestation and nonexistence—on the one side there is nonexistence and on the other side existence and its manifestation. In other words, manifestation has no meaning or identity other than an attribute, an aspect, an act or

1. Ibid,Verse No. 1258 – 1261.

determination, as the images in the mirror, the shadows and waves are neither mere nonexistence (for diversity has no place in nonexistence) nor is their existence independent from the owner of the form, the stake, the light or the sea.

Questions

1. Explain the meanings of existence in mysticism according to Qayṣarī.
2. Is existence equal to permanent reality for Ibn 'Arabī? Explain.
3. Explain and discuss the divisions of existence from Ibn 'Arabī's point of view.
4. Explain the properties of existence in the school of Ibn 'Arabī.
5. Compare and contrast the concept of "oneness of existence" from the perspective of Transcendent philosophy, Peripatetic philosophy, and Mysticism.
6. Explain Ibn 'Arabī's theory of "oneness of existence" and compare and contrast it with the theory of the Peripatetic school and Pantheism.
7. What are the symbols and expressions Ibn 'Arabī uses to show that the imaginal world represents the Real? Discuss.
8. Discuss the reasons Ibn 'Arabī mentions for the intellect's inability to grasp the question of "oneness of existence".
9. Discuss one of Mullā Ṣadrā's arguments for "oneness of existence".
10. Discuss the role of Manifestation in the School of Ibn 'Arabī.
11. How do the followers of the School of Ibn 'Arabī explain away diversity on the basis of the theory of Manifestation?
12. Explain the concept of Manifestation.
13. Explain the synonymous or related terms of Manifestation.
14. Compare and contrast the view of conventional philosophy on

the analysis of causal relation and Mullā Ṣadrā's existential analysis of the question of causality.

15. Discuss the way Mullā Ṣadrā establishes Manifestation.
16. Explain and answer two objections made to "oneness of existence" and Manifestation.

Chapter Three: Theologyin Theoretical Mysticism

There is no separate discussion on the existence of God or the Necessary Being in theoretical mysticism, for with the intuitive knowledge and inner experiences such a discussion would seem useless and unnecessary. Indeed the main way of knowing God that leads to the highest degrees of certainty, as stated in some religious texts, is to know the Real by His Real essence—as 'Alī in his Morning supplication states, "O You Who guides to Your essence by Your essence"—and to find Him by seeing His light in all the existence, which is the way of the Truthful, or through self-knowledge, which is a kind of intuitive knowledge and results from purifying, cleansing and watching the self. Otherwise, God Who is the light of the whole world and its illumination would remain hidden, first, because of the excessive manifestation and, second, because of the constant presence, like a sound that is always heard or a sun that never sets would never be heard or seen. On the way of the intellect and reasoning in knowing the Real Shabistarī writes:

"That road is long and hard, leave it,
Like Moses for a season cast away that staff."[1]
"Nay more, as he sees by illumination that pure Light,

1. *The Mystic Rose Garden*, Verse No. 82.

He sees God first in everything that he sees."[1]
"To him, whom God doesn't guide into the road,
Nothing will be disclosed by the use of logic."[2]
"He is a Fool ! For he seeks the blazing sun
By the dim light of a torch in the desert.
If the sun always tarried in one position,
And if his shining was all after one manner,
Nobody would know that these beams are from him,
There would be no distinction between kernel and husk.
Know the whole world is a beam of the light of 'The Truth'
Yet 'The Truth' within it is concealed from manifestation.
And since the light of 'The Truth' alters not nor varies,
And is void of change and transitoriness."[3]
"Reason cannot endure the light of that face,
Go and seek another eye so you can see Him."[4]

Therefore, the existence of God, which is thought to be the aim of philosophy and wisdom, is the beginning of mysticism and is one of the essential dogmas of the mystics. The knowledge of God through the external world and worldly signs is a lower degree of knowledge and is particular to the veiled rather than the mystics and the truthful. In other words, for the mystic and in his position proving the existence of the Real as a posteriori (reaching the cause via the effect) is a kind of veil and covering rather than unveiling and enlightening. In mysticism the arguments are

1. Ibid, Verse No. 85.
2. Ibid,Verse No. 87.
3. Ibid,Verses No. 95-99.
4. Ibid,Verse No. 103.

understood to take man even farther from the Exalted Creator, for He is so close to man that any medium between Him and mankind will be a veil. In his well-known analogy in the tale of the archer and the treasure Rūmī states:

> "O you who have provided yourself with bow and arrows, the prey is near and you have shot far.
> The farther one shoots, the farther away and more separated is he from a treasure like this.
> The philosopher killed [exhausted] himself with thinking: let him run on [in vain], for his back is turned towards the treasure.
> Let him run on: the more he runs, the more remote does he become from the object of his heart's desire.
> That [Divine] King said, "[those who] have striven in [for] Us"; He did not say, "[those who] have striven away from Us," O restless one."[1]

Ḥāfiẓ also in this regard says that having a world-observing eye (that which sees the particulars and the multitudes) is an obstacle to see the Real directly. He holds that the best way to know God is self-knowledge:

> "To see your face one needs to have soul-seeing eyes,
> But how can my world-seeing eye attain such a rank?"[2]

Next to knowing the essence by the essence, which is the main way of the mystics in their knowledge of the Real, is "the way of the soul", namely knowing the soul and God through self-knowledge. In this way, through observing the soul or contemplating it every person, according to his capacity, understands some aspects of the Real's Names, attributes and acts

1. *Mathnawī*, Book VI, Verse No. 2354 – 2358.
2. *The Poems of Ḥāfiẓ Shīrāzī*, trans. 'Alāiddīn Pazārgādī, Ode No. 52.

(though not His essence). As it will be explained, man is seen as the mirror reflecting all the Names of the Real and his knowledge of the self is an opening to the knowledge of God, like the sunbeam, for he is like the sunbeam which has no light of its own and takes its light from the sun. The highest level of this knowledge is above the knowledge of certainty, and it is attained in the level of the essence of certitude and real certainty by appropriating the character traits of Allah.

In the following section we first discuss the principles of mystical theology and its levels, then the mystics' ways of knowing Allah, and finally the way that the mystics hold necessary in knowing Allah, namely the way of self-knowledge that leads to theology.

The Principles of Mystical Theology

1. The impossibility of knowing the Essence in depth

Ibn 'Arabī argues that the cornerstone of every discussion of the Exalted Real is the impossibility of an intellectual understanding and intuitive perception of the essence of the Real. He maintains, this point has been decreed to us both through religious prohibition—"Do not reflect on the essence of Allah,"—and reason, for rationally perception and knowledge are founded on the relationship between the perceiver and the perceived, whereas the absolute Sufficient, meaning the essence, has no relationship whatsoever with the others. That which is related to others is the essence in its being modified by the Names and attributes (rather than essence qua essence); in other words, the world reflects His Names and attributes rather than His essence. Moreover, in the station of the essence there is no determination, whereas the mystic himself is a determination and being known is another determination. We will see that this point is explained both in the discussion of self-knowledge and the knowledge of God.

2. The levels of the scholars in their knowledge of God

Ibn 'Arabī argues that people in the permitted domain of the knowledge of God, namely the knowledge of God's Names, attributes and acts, are either of the following groups:

- People of *ḥadīth* or people in general who take their knowledge from narration and traditions; for example, they grasp God's absolute power or comprehensive knowledge from the Qur'anic verses or traditions.
- Theosophists, philosophers, or theologians who know God by the natural signs and the external world, or the spiritual signs and the inner world. For example, from the creation of the world or its possibility they understand the eternality of God and His necessity, from the order of the world they infer the knowledge of the Real, or by contemplating the attributes and qualities of the soul they know the attributes of the Creator.
- The mystics and saints who know Allah through God-fearing. This way is restricted to those who can unveil and find the truth through purifying the self.

Unveiling leads to the knowledge of the Real's attributes within things once their thingness is denied and the veil of their imagined identity is lifted, so that the soul of the mystic is exposed to the light and illumination of the Real that shines through things. This way grants the knower the highest level of perception.

3. The Ways of Theology

The ways to know God comprises the following divisions:

a. Horizontal, spiritual and the way of the Truthful

In this division if we consider the different ways of finding and knowing God in regard of the traveller (the human subject), destination (God and the object of knowledge), and the way (the method of knowledge), in the first category the three parts are separate from each other, in the second the traveller and the way are one but the destination is separate, in the third the way and the destination are one but the traveller is separate, and finally in the fourth all the three parts are one.

In the first category, the external or horizontal knowledge, by contemplating and reflecting on the greater world and external signs of the subject is led to the divine attributes and acts. In the second category, the internal or spiritual knowledge [or knowledge of the soul], through the little world, which is an example of the universal world and a manifestation of all divine perfections, that is by contemplating the human form which is created in the likeness of the divine perfections (the face of the Merciful) one knows the Creator. Ibn 'Arabī maintains that this is "the best Proof" among other proofs and ways and even on the basis of narration he proves the preference of this way to the previous one. In the third category, which is the knowledge of the truthful, no distinction is made between the way and destination and according to Mullā Ṣadrā in this way the essence somehow guides to the essence.

In the domain of acquired knowledge it was Ibn Sina who for the first time suggested the possibility of such a method and offered an argument as an instance of the way of the truthful.

As it will be seen, Ibn 'Arabī holds that travelling this path by relying on theoretical method and acquired knowledge is impossible. In *al-Futūḥāt* he writes: that some thinkers maintain that the knowledge of God precedes the knowledge of the soul and its origin (the way of the truthful) does not apply to understanding the creatures and their knowledge, and it is true only in regard of the knowledge of the Real. By this he means although in respect of existence (in the world of permanence) the knowledge of the Real precedes the knowledge of the creature, and even the knowledge of the creature is only a reflection of the knowledge of the Real, in the world of concepts and ideas (the world of the mind) the knowledge of the Real demands a sign that is either in the horizons or in the souls, and evidently the knowledge of the sign precedes the knowledge of "the owner of the sign".Ibn 'Arabī, according to the different explanations he offers on the relations of the knowledge of the soul and the knowledge of God, believes that the knowledge of the soul is mainly of the second kind (the unity of the way and the traveller), but sometimes according to one special explanation he states it is of the fourth kind.

The fourth kind (the union of the three elements) can be found only in the way of the mystics, which will be explained in our account of identity in the relationship between the two kinds of knowledge and the station of annihilation.

b. Observing the Soul and the Real

In this division Ibn 'Arabī discusses the kinds of knowledge by signs (via horizons and souls) as follows: in the world of mysticism there are two views (each considering one station).

1. Seeing the soul precedes that of the Real: the mystic in this station first knows himself (or the world) and then God, which is epitomized in the saying: "I have seen nothing unless I saw Allah after it."

2. Seeing the Real precedes that of the soul: in this station the mystic more than anything else sees God and the absolute existence. The expression of his present state is that "I see nothing unless I see Allah before it."[1]

---

1. Shabesteri in this regard recites,
"He that knows 'The Truth', and to whom Unity is revealed,
At the first glance sees the light of the very Being." *The Mystic Rose Garden*, Verse No. 84.

For Ibn 'Arabī the second view is more perfect though the mystic at the beginning of the way should experience the first, too.

c. The Two spiritual ways of knowing Allah

In another division in *Fuṣūṣ* it is argued that one may attain the knowledge of God via self-knowledge in two ways: first to know Him in that "You are," and second in that "He is." The first way is the method of reasoning where the person finds his way to God through the creature (one's soul), that is, man initially knows the qualities of his nature and disposition and then knows the Real by negating any imperfection from Him or attributing all perfections to Him. Philosophers and theologians represent this kind of self-knowledge and knowledge of God, which for Ibn 'Arabī comprises a lower level of knowledge.

The second kind of the knowledge of the Real is feasible also through the soul, but here the stress is not on "you" (the soul) but on "Him" (the Real). This way is knowledge through the direct manifestation of the essence of the Real to the soul. This method has certain stages which will be explained in other chapters.

4. The characteristics of the way and destination in the way of self-knowledge

From what has been said it becomes clear that the knowledge of the self in some of its meanings substitutes the way of intellectual knowledge. Nevertheless, it must be noted which soul or which aspect of the soul can be the way to reach God. Moreover, which station is the destination, goal and ultimate end of the way of self-knowledge? Is it unity, divinity, oneness or the station of the essence?

To answer the first question it should be said that Ibn 'Arabī like other mystics believes the human soul has certain levels and degrees, and each of them has its own properties. Speaking of the three souls, the five levels of the soul, the seven subtleties of man, etc. is an example of his awareness of the degrees and inner folds of the soul, but according to another division we can say the soul has two main domains: 1. The essence, 2. Attributes and faculties. Of course, we should place the three or five levels of the soul or most of the seven subtleties within the second domain.

The first domain of the soul is undetermined, unnamed and free from any qualification and station. It has no name or description, and he who attains the station of the intimate will know his essence in depth and will be free from all determinations and descriptive definition. However, this knowledge is neither absolute nor final, for the soul in its depth is like a shoreless ocean. Ibn 'Arabī states, "The knowledge of the soul for the knowers of the soul is a shoreless ocean which has no end, and the knowledge of God, which follows the knowledge of the soul, is the same. Therefore, the knowledge of God has no end and the mystic always calls "*O My Lord! Increase my knowledge*", and God increases his knowledge of the soul and in consequence his knowledge of God."

To conclude, it can be said that each level of the levels of the soul, according to its capacity, can be the mirror of the divine attributes, but the attributes and faculties of the soul are the mirror of the divine Names and attributes and the deep essence of the soul is the mirror of the essence of the Real.

To answer the second question, that is, the ultimate aim of the way of self-knowledge and that which the mystic finally attains at the station of knowledge and reaching the depth of the soul, some of Ibn 'Arabī's words in *al-Futūḥāt* apparently indicate that the soul that has not reached the level of "No one is like Him" and is unaware and unconscious of the station of its indeterminacy will neither know the essence of "no one is like Him" of the Real nor see in the station of its indeterminacy and uniqueness the undetermined and unique essence of the Real. Nevertheless, as it was discussed earlier, the essence qua essence which has no manifestation or determination, is knowable and visible, and admits intention and union in existence; so the destination and end of the way of self- knowledge is also the station of oneness, namely the essence that is determined by the Names and Attributes.

5. The Relation of the Soul and God

In the discourse of Ibn 'Arabī and the mystics of his school, the relationship between the soul and God is compared to that of the form and the owner of the form and sometimes spoken of as the relation of identity. Ibn 'Arabī stresses the first relation so much that unlike other theosophists and philosophers who think of reason and rational soul as man's distinction, he speaks of "the divine form" as his main distinction. On the second relation he states: the mystic indeed knows his soul but his soul is no other than the identity of the Real. We will see that according to these two relations and on the basis of the mentioned tradition, there are two interpretations and explanations of the relationship between self-knowledge and the knowledge of Allah, in one the former is the origin of the latter and in the other the two are identical.

According to what is said, evidently the knowledge of the soul in some of its meanings can replace the way of intellectual knowledge.

6. Different explanations of the relationship between self-knowledge and theology

Having mentioned the Prophetic tradition "he who knows himself knows his God": Ibn 'Arabī in "*Faṣṣ Muḥammadī*" of *Fuṣūṣ al-Ḥikam* states:

> You can infer from this *ḥadīth* the impossibility of knowing the self and knowing God and also the inability to attain such knowledge; in other words, the *ḥadīth* intends to say it is impossible (like saying if you go back to the past you can see your grandfather). However, you may also infer from it the possibility of knowledge. Therefore, the first interpretation indicates that as you cannot know your soul in its deep reality, you cannot know God as He is, and the second denotes that you should know it and through it you may know God.

Ibn 'Arabī thinks of the *ḥadīth* "He who knows himself knows his God" as the key solution to some mystical difficult questions and believes self-knowledge is an important factor to enforce some subtle points of the divine knowledge and the Names and attributes of the Real and to bring close to mind for the addressee the intuitive truths and mystical terms. He gives different accounts and explanations of it, some of these explanations speak of similarity and even identity in knowledge but some others indicate the impossibility of knowledge. We can see in summary Ibn 'Arabī's different theoretical and epistemological accounts of the *ḥadīth* in the following outline.

1. Explanation indicating the impossibility of knowledge
2. Explanations indicating the possibility of knowledge through
    a. Contradiction and opposition (between the attributes of the soul and God
    b. Similarity and likeness (between the soul and God in respect
        i. Mankind: similarity in
            1. Comprehensiveness and succession
            2. Attributes: such as the gathering and creation of diversity or gathering transcendence and immanence

3. Acts: such as the breath of the Merciful and renewal of creation
4. Two-sided relationship: dependence

ii. Human individual (perfect man): the form of the Merciful and comprehensiveness

iii. The human archetype

c. Identity and unity (the soul and God)

The last eight accounts are founded on the idea that the significance of the ḥadīth is to show a way to a deeper knowledge of God. Before discussing these accounts it is necessary to note that the absolute Real is absolutely unknowable. Accordingly, unless He appears in the attribute of God or Lord there is no way to know Him. Now the question is that how can He be known in His determination? Ibn 'Arabī maintains that the way to know the Real is to know ourselves. However, our endeavor to know the Real in His absolute form would be useless. We must return to the depth of our souls and perceive the Real in his manifestations. In his interpretation of the holy verse 'Soon We shall show them Our signs in the horizons and in their own souls...'[1](41:53), Ibn 'Arabī states that both the great world and the little world are the signs of the Real and the manifestations of His divine Names, that is, not only our souls but also all things surrounding us are the different forms of the manifestation of the Real. In this respect, there is no essential difference among these things in their concrete being, but in regard of knowledge there is a fundamental difference among them, for the things in our surrounding (horizontal signs) are things which we see from outside. We cannot penetrate them and experience from inside the act of the divine manifestation which is permeating them, but rather we can only through "self-

1. 'سَنُرِيهِمْ آيَاتِنَا فِي الْآفَاقِ وَفِي أَنفُسِهِمْ.'

consciousness" probe ourselves and from inside experience the divine manifestation. It is in this sense that self-knowledge is considered as the first step to theology. Thus, in Izutsu's words, the human soul is like an opening to the world of the Real's manifestation from within, so that something of the nature of manifestation, according to its capacity, can understand manifestation and its origin.

To recapitulate, if we may think of self-knowledge as a positive step (rather than a negative step or one of admitting impotence and impossibility) to the knowledge of the Real and call it an "indication", in every indication there is a signifier and a signified. Now the indication denotes the difference of the signifier and the signified, or their similitude or their identity. In the first case (the difference between the signifier and the signified and their dissimilarity) this difference or dissimilarity is suggested without considering the "relation" between the signifier and the signified, and this is the "explanation of dependence".

In the second case (similarity) either the signifier is mankind and the signified is the Exalted Real, the human individual (perfect man) or the archetype of man. In the first case (the signifier is mankind) mankind either because of their comprehensiveness (the manifestation of all divine Names) and divine form indicate the Real or because of their attributes or acts indicate the attribute or the acts of the Real.

In the second state (where human individual is the indicator rather than mankind or species of man) the perfect man is suggested either because of his comprehensiveness and his actual divine form or because he is the successor and the Caliph.

In any case, it can be said that in theoretical mysticism some of the arguments for the oneness of existence are also used in proving the existence of the Real and in many of the works of theoretical mysticism both issues are considered simultaneously, in the sense that whenever it is demonstrated a priori or on the basis of the argument of the truthful that all existence is necessary in being and existence everywhere and in every rank is none but necessary (with all the perfections of the Necessary being) the existence of the Necessary being and His oneness along with the oneness of existence are demonstrated simultaneously. Therefore, it can be said that the mystical view in one respect is a kind of theology (*khudāshināsī* or theology) and its concerns with God and existence are interconnected and inseparable.

Of course, as it will be explained later, in some other ways of demonstrating the oneness of existence, such as the way of Mullā Ṣadrā, the existence of the Exalted Real and His infinitude is considered as the primary issue, which Ṣadr al-Muta'allihīn in turn proves in his philosophy on the basis of the argument of the truthful. But in general considering what was said on "the subject of theoretical mysticism"—which is the essence of the Real in respect of His attributes and acts—and also the fact that "the existence of the subject of a kind of knowledge" is neither discussed nor proved in it but instead its properties and precepts are discussed, theoretical mysticism also has no separate discussion on this subject, and considering the nature of the knowledge of the mystics, which is intuitive knowledge, there is no need indeed for such a discussion.

What follows in this chapter is certain questions, such as the personality or impersonality of the God of the mystics, transcendence and immanence, unity of Allah and its meaning for the mystics, divine Names, the two meanings of Allah and Lord, divine knowledge, the will and Mercy of the Real, and finally divine creation which links this chapter to the following chapter.

The God of the Mystics: A Person or an Object?

One of the important questions of every theological order is that is God considered as a person and like a human or a thing or neither in this order. In other words, is He absolutely transcendent or immanent or both? Is He absolute or restricted and determined or beyond these two? Is the relation between Him and the world of difference or union or something else?

Since most of the mystical sects are affiliated to one of the religions, we will start our discussion with the God of religions. Although the God of religions is evidently not a person or a human individual, in a sense He is human like for in the holy scriptures He is qualified with attributes or acts which human beings often have, such as mercy, kindness, anger, revenge, hearing and seeing, and hence the God of religions is different from the God of philosophers and some theologians who only think of transcendence. The God of religions answers to the desire of man to have a live and emotional relationship with their Lord and cherished God, a God Who cares for him, comes to his help and protects him, listens to him and answers him, pities him and forgives him, and at the same time does justice to the oppressed and shows his anger to the wicked and punishes them, etc.

For the mystics, the God of philosophers (or at least many philosophers) is a God separate from the world, sublime and, therefore, indifferent to and unmindful of the lower world and has nothing to do with the world of possibility and human life, and in short He is more like an object than like a human being. Of course, for the mystics an immanent human-like God not only questions the essential attributes of the Real's transcendence and Exaltation, it gives leash to human imagination and fancy in the question of knowing God and restricting His reality, and in consequence it ends with error.

In Islamic mysticism the mystics' God is the God of religion and they maintain that divine Names and attributes mentioned in the holy Qur'an are also the attributes of the Real in their order. Of course, the God of the mystics is expected to be like the God of religions, a divine Creator possessed with awareness, will, affection, mercy, benevolence and such other attributes which make Him the proper subject of praise, worship, prayer of man with whom He speaks and for whom He cares. Certainly, all these attributes coincide with His transcendence, sanctity and purity from having a similitude or any combination, change or other attributes of deficiency. In sum this God is not only like a person or a human but He is, to be more exact and considering His transcendence, is trans-human, though the Real is always "He" and is not "It".

Speaking ontologically the God of the mystics has an essence that is the most hidden (existence unconditioned by the object of division), Names and attributes which are in the level of oneness (existence conditioned by things, namely conditioned by Names), and an act or shadow (unconditioned existence in the types of division) which are the very manifestations; therefore, He can combine both transcendence and immanence. Accordingly, as it has been indicated in chapter two, the consideration of existence can be divided as follows:

- Existence unconditioned by the object of division (the essence of the Real)
    - Conditioned by nothing: oneness
    - Conditioned by things
        - Conditioned by Names: uniqueness
        - Conditioned by determination: the world of manifestations and diversity
    - Unconditioned existence in the types of division: the Ever-expanding existence (in Transcendental Philosophy)

We will see that because the God of the mystics is unconditioned by the object of division He can gather both transcendence and immanence, and He has both human-like attributes and is above determinations and constraints.

Transcendence and Immanence

As it was mentioned before, the Real has two different aspects and domains: 1. A hidden aspect, and 2. A manifest aspect. In the first sense and aspect, the Real will be a sealed mystery forever and His secret will not be revealed even with the deepest revelations and intuitions. Therefore, the Real will be the subject of human knowledge only when He is determined and manifested in different attributes and forms (such as Allah, the Living) or He is manifested in His acts (such as providing or creating) or is apparent in immaterial manifestations.

Accordingly, the questions on theology discussed by the mystics concern the Names and attributes which result from the primary divine manifestations. These questions in the first step relate to the determination of the portion of the hidden and manifest aspects, or transcendence and immanence. Evidently these two terms for Ibn 'Arabī and theologians have two different functions, for transcendence and immanence in theology are two opposite and irreconcilable dogmas, one indicating the transcendence and uniqueness of the Real and His unknowability and incomparability (for the Mutazilites and the philosophers) and the other denoting the likeness of God and the creatures (for the Karamites, the believers in incarnation and some of the Asharites. In any case, in traditional theology these two terms replace each other and are rivals of and opposite to each other, whereas in the view of Ibn 'Arabī unless they are associated and combined with each other they would be incomplete and incorrect, for each of them alone represents one aspect of one reality, that is, transcendence shows the plane of the Real's absoluteness and immanence indicates His determination and restriction. Therefore, these two meanings are compatible with and complete each other.

Ibn 'Arabī states: although the Exalted Real is free from any kind of limitation, the transcendence of the philosophers and some theologians itself is a kind of limitation and restriction, and with the incorporeal attributes they ascribe to the Real and at the end they compare the Real to a being such as an angel, whereas the Real Who is unconditioned is neither qualified by the attributes of the world of creatures nor the attributes of the heavenly kingdom and omnipotence. He is with the two worlds and is not out of them. Exalting God above any of the planes of existence and its manifestations is tantamount to establishing limits and boundaries for the infinite Real.

He further adds that confining the attributes of the Real to those of transcendence (such as Glory and Sanctity) restricts the Real as much as confining His attributes to those of immanence. Therefore, he believes most of the people who profess transcendence are in fact entangled in immanence that is presented in the garb of transcendence (in other words, he holds, describing the Real as absolute is a kind of restriction).

Therefore, "the Exalted Real" is not incompatible with "the manifest Real", and in other words, as it was discussed in the question of the oneness of existence, the world in one respect is the manifestation of the Real, and therefore, it is the Real, and on the other hand since the Real is the manifest in determinations and determinations are unreal, the world is not the Real and is separate from Him. In other words, because the world is separate from the Real "it is all from Him", and because it is not separate from the Real "all of it is Him". "All of it is from Him" is a transcendent view and "all of it is Him" is an immanent view. Ibn 'Arabī argues that the perfect man has two eyes, that is, he sees the Real and unity (transcendentally) and he also sees the diversity and manifestations (immanently). The intellect tends to transcendence (accordingly the philosophers' knowledge of the Real is a negative knowledge), but the imagination is inclined to immanence. It is unveiling, however, which combines the two planes and has both eyes.[1] Shabistarī writes in this regard:

"From blindness arose the doctrine of 'Assimilation',
From one-eyedness that of God's remoteness."[2]

Ibn 'Arabī holds that the view of the perfect mystics and the true foundation of religion and heavenly book are the "union of union" (in contrast to union and separation) and also "the Qur'an" (in contrast to separation). To explain, the station of union is to witness all the manifestations in the single existence of the Real which brings to the mystics a taste for transcendence (that leads to unveiling). The station of separation is observing the essence of the Real and the creatures, without dissolving the diversified determinations in the essence of the Real, which sometimes leads to certain mystical utterances with immanent or incarnational tendency. The station of union, on the other hand, is to see the Real in the creatures (unity in diversity) and to see the creatures

1. Mawlānā says,

"Now thou become the Sun, and now the Sea; now the mountain of Qāf, and now the Anqā.

In essence thou art neither this nor that, O thou art greater than [all] imaginations and more than [all] more!..

Both the *muwaḥḥid* [who asserts the transcendence of God] and the *mushabbih* [who asserts His immanence] are bewildered by thee, O thou who, without having image [external appearance], art [appearing] in so many forms." *Mathnawī*, Book II, Verse No. 54, 55, and 57.

2. *The Mystic Rose Garden*, Verse No. 105.

in the Real (diversity in unity) and calls for combining and mixing transcendence and immanence, which is the Muḥammadan taste and the logic of the holy Qur'an.

Ibn 'Arabī states: the best introducer of the Exalted Real is His speech, the holy Qur'an, where immanence and transcendence come along and even within each other. Ibn 'Arabī contends the best example in this regard is the verse 'Nothing is like Him, and He is the All-hearing, the All-seeing'.[1](42:11)To explain, in the combination of the two phrases evidently the first part of the verse, "there is nothing like Him", indicates transcendence (if we take the word "like" as redundant) and the second part of the verse, "He is the all-Hearing and the all-Seeing", that speaks of attributes such as hearing and seeing and are also shared by the creatures, is a kind of immanence. However, in each of the two phrases both immanence and transcendence can be seen, that is, if the word "like" in "like Him" is not taken as redundant, although this phrase proves there is a likeness and similitude for the Real, namely comparability (There is nothing like Him), since the existence of anything similar to His likeness is negated, even more substantially the existence of anything like Him is negated, that is, God is above having an equal. Moreover, although in the second part of the verse ("He is the all-Hearing and the all-Seeing") the Exalted Real is described as hearing and seeing (two attributes of immanence), nevertheless hearing and seeing (because of using the word "He" and a nominal phrase indicating restriction) are restricted to the Exalted Real and are denied to others (transcendence).

This question can also be related to the attributes of the divine beauty and grandeur, since the holy Qur'an gathers all the Real's

1. 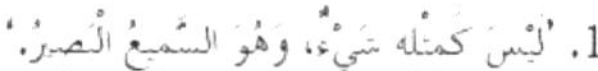

attributes of beauty and grandeur. The attributes of the first kind indicate qualities of immanence and those of the second indicate Names and attributes of the transcendence of the Exalted Real, as the mystics maintain God is described in the Qur'an as the Owner of grandeur and glory.

To sum up, it can be said that the God of the mystics is neither like an object nor is human like. He is trans-human, that is, besides His presence and appearance in different manifestations, He has such qualities that make the mystic call Him "you", "He", or "I", and appreciate Him as human-like and look at Him as living, present, and affectionate, and even feel He is closer to him than himself, and recite like Rūmī:

***

Nevertheless he knows He is above all and in His reality He is inaccessible and transcendent, and thus he succeeds in gathering transcendence and imminence.

The Characteristics of Mystical Theology

According to the mystics' understanding of the Exalted Real (especially in the school of Ibn 'Arabī), mystical theology has certain characteristics; it is, for example, affirmative, monotheistic, nominal, diversified and interactive with the existence of the world and man. Some of these features are discussed in the following:

1. Affirmation. For Ibn 'Arabī rational and philosophical theology is negative theology and is based on pure transcendence, for the intellect only knows what God is not (being incorporeal and immaterial, atemporal and eternal, invisible, immobile, etc.), whereas divine religions and also complete unveiling open the door of the affirmative theology for man. Speaking of the bewilderment of the people of reason in relation to the Real and His attributes Ibn 'Arabī writes in *al-Futūḥāt*: for the philosophers theology is the knowledge of a few negative issues called the attributes of transcendence. On the glimmers and lights that appear to the mystic he also writes: we believe the gleams are the lights of the essence and the magnificence of Allah's face which appear to the eye (with no need of the corporeal eye). This kind of perception is affirmative rather than negative.[1] On another occasion having explained that the true knowledge of the manifestation of the Real in all forms is God-given he states: since evidential knowledge (rational knowledge) pertains only to negative attributes and attributes of transcendence, it denies such a fact, but the knowledge of the unveiling (the knowledge that pertains to affirmative issues) confirms it.

2. Unity. For Ibn 'Arabī the main attribute of the "Real" and the essential attribute of "existence" is "oneness", and as it was explained in the discussions of ontology, the oneness of the Real is no other than the oneness of existence. This unity and oneness of the Real nevertheless shows itself in three aspects: 1. Unity of the essence, 2. Unity of attributes, and 3. Unity of acts. We explained the first in our discussions of ontology, for the monotheism of the mystics and what they understand by "There is no God but Allah" is not only "He is the only worshiped God" and "He is the only Cause", but also "Nothing exists except Allah" and "There is no one except Him".

The mystics maintain the true monotheist is one who through real certainty witnesses the annihilation of the essence of the world and the restriction of existence to the Real, and refrains from ascribing any act, attribute or essence to other than the Real.

1. Ibn 'Arabī, *Al-Futūḥāt al-Makkiyyah*, vol. 2, 132 and 491.

He reaches the station of "shaking off relations"[1] to become finally through real certainty one and single. Moreover, in respect of annihilation and subsistence of acts he refrains from action and assumes the action of the Creator, in regard of the annihilation and subsistence of attributes he loses his attributes and subsists by the attributes of the Real, and finally through the annihilation of essence he is released from his essence and subsists by the existence of the Real. In some of his verses Rūmī describes this meaning of unity, which is not only to know the Real as One or to see Him as One, but also to become one with Him—as Kāshifī says, "Unless He burns I and we and you, there will be no absolute unity or pure unity"—and also the way it occurs, that is, love and affection:

> "What is [the meaning of] to learn the knowledge of God's unity? To consume yourself in the presence of the One.
> If you wish to shine like day, burn up your night-like self-existence.
> Melt away your existence, as cooper [melts away] in the elixir, in the being of Him who fosters [and sustains] existence."[2]
> "As the stone that is entirely turned into pure ruby: it is filled with the qualities of the sun.
> That stony nature does not remain in it: back and front, it is filled with sunniness."[3]

---

1. In the meaning of oneness of God Shabistarī recites,
 "They have brought you news from the tavern
 That unification [the oneness of God] is shaking off relations." *The Mystic Rose Garden*, Verse 840.
2. *Mathnawī*, Book I, Verse No. 3009, 3010, and 3011.
3. *Mathnawī*, Book V, Verse No. 2025-6.

> "Strive that thy stony nature may be diminished, so that thy stone may become resplendent with the qualities of the ruby."[1]
>
> "Thou must unite the [scattered] parts by means of love, to the end that thou mayst become sweet as Samarcand and Damascus."[2]
>
> "Love is that flame which, when it blazes up, consumes everything else but the Beloved."[3]

It is important to note that the unity of the mystics ontologically is the oneness of existence and intuitively it is the oneness of vision. As it was discussed in the first chapter, these two dimensions are inextricable and for Ibn 'Arabī one can see the whole world as the Real because the whole world is the Real ("There is no other than Him in the house") for there is no difference between the essence of the Real and His manifestation (according to the rule of the unity of the creature and the Creator or revealer and manifest) and the face of the Real is Real in one respect, as there is no essential difference between ontological manifestation and intuitive manifestation, and on the basis of the oneness of "witnessing and existence", for him, finding and being are inseparable, for it is in the process of the experience of the oneness of existence that the mystic seeks to taste the very existence (God).

3. Being Nominal. Islamic mysticism is founded on the science of the Names, and mystical theology is in fact based on the science of the Names rather than on knowing the essence, for knowledge is dependent on manifestation, whereas the essence in the rank of oneness has no manifestation (the rule of "There is no

---

1. Ibid, Verse No. 2039.
2. *Mathnawī*, Book IV, Verse No. 3289.
3. *Mathnawī*, Book V, Verse No. 588.

manifestation in the Oneness"). The God of the mystics is manifested in the form of the Names and attributes throughout the world and He is also manifested in the mystic's heart in the form of different lights. In our discussion of the divine Names we will explain this point in detail.

4. Diversity. Ibn 'Arabī introduces two rules under the titles of "The God created in dogma" and "The Manifestation in forms" which indicates certain dimensions of mystical theology and also some functions of the theory of manifestation in theoretical and also practical mysticism. It can be said that the first rule concerns the individual diversities present in divine manifestations and the second rule indicates the diversity in the kinds of these manifestations. According to these two rules the understanding of each individual of God is proportioned to: 1. His disposition and capacity according to the permanent entity, 2. His relation to a particular Name among the Names and the manifestation of that Name in him.

According to Ibn 'Arabī, every Name has an external manifestation and that Name is the God of that manifestation, and every individual in every state has his particular God in that state. In other words, the God of every individual in all conditions and states is the manifestation of God in the form of the Name which fulfills his demand in those conditions and his disposition demands the manifestation of that Name. Accordingly, God in every moment has a special manifestation, and He doesn't have the same manifestation for one individual in two different moments. Moreover, the worshipped God and Lord of every individual (the absolute essence) knowingly or unknowingly is not the Real, but He is the determined Real, and the determination in question is dependent on the disposition (the condition of the receiver) and the manifestation of the Names (the condition of the agent). Ibn 'Arabī on the basis of the Real's acceptance of the different forms and shapes, which is a constitutional reality, advances his religious view on the necessity of refraining from excommunicating the followers of different sects or suspecting them of disbelief and atheism.

5. Interaction and mutual relationship. Ibn 'Arabī argues that in the process of the Names' demand for manifestation and the manifestations' call for that which manifested them there is a two-sided transaction between God and the creatures, which in the stage following creation can be called the two-sided mirror (reflection). God for Ibn 'Arabī is not only an agent of the world (manifesting it), but also in one respect He is affected by it, that is, the substance of the world is the face of the Real (the breath of the Merciful or Ever-expanding Existence) Whose manifestations are the forms of the world or the figures on that substance. Accordingly, the changes in the world are nothing other than the diverse divine manifestations, and God's acceptance of the attributes of immanence is done through accepting these forms and changing the forms, to the extent that Ibn 'Arabī describes God as the lender and the borrower.

6. Simultaneous opposition (inducing confusion). As it was mentioned already, for Ibn 'Arabī the Real, from the perspective of man, is imperceptible unless through "simultaneous contrary". Ibn 'Arabī as evidence quotes Abū Sa'īd al-Kharrāz, a third-century Sufi Master, who says, "God is known only through combining the contraries." This logic, which is understood as the logic of "He is not He" (in contrast to the logic of He is He), speaks of the comprehensiveness of the Real and His encompassing all the manifestations of beauty and grandeur and His exterior and interior (so that the act of those manifestations can be attributed and denied to them, which is indicated by the holy verse 'You did not throw when you threw'.[1] (8:17) Moreover, it also indicates the superficial nature of the oppositions present in the realm of the possible beings compared to the divine plane, and the termination of these apparently opposite issues, such as good and evil, material and immaterial, manifest and hidden, actual and potential, one and many, and their return to one thing (as showed in the holy verse 'Our command is but a single [word]'[2])(54: 50). Ibn 'Arabī explaining al-Kharrāz's speech, on the apparent opposition (between the manifest and the hidden) writes:

> He is the first and the last, and He is the Manifest and the Hidden. He is the very identity of what is the manifest and He is the hidden despite His manifestation. No one can see Him except Himself.... He is the manifest only to Himself and He is hidden only in relation to Himself.... The origin is one though the properties are different. There is no way to ignore this, for every man finds it in himself and it is the face of the Real.

Man's perceptive act in relation to such reality (the simultaneous realization of the opposites) once it is seen is called "bewilderment".

Divine Names

As it was mentioned, in theoretical mysticism the station of the essence is unknowable and beyond thinking and witnessing, and it has no relation with the others. Indeed that which the mystics succeed to know is the determinations of the absolute essence, which are first presented in the plane of oneness in the form of the divine Names. In the descending arc the divine Names are the source of those manifestations that result in the emergence of

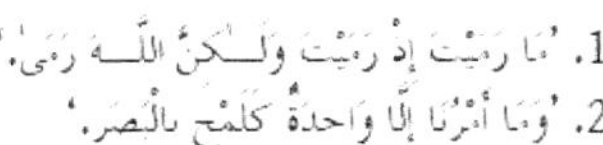
1. 'مَا رَمَيْتَ إِذْ رَمَيْتَ وَلَـٰكِنَّ اللَّـهَ رَمَىٰ.'
2. 'وَمَا أَمْرُنَا إِلَّا وَاحِدَةٌ كَلَمْحٍ بِالْبَصَرِ.'

things and phenomena, and in the ascending arc they are the origin of the illuminations and manifestations that appear in the heart of the mystic and acquaint him with the Real. Thus, the divine Names in mysticism both in regard of ontology, theology, cosmology, epistemology and mystical wayfaring are of essential importance. It can be even said that theoretical mysticism is based on the science of the theory of the Names. The double function of the Names in the plane of existence is to manifest the phenomena in the ascending arc and completing them in returning to their origin in the ascending arc. In the realm of knowledge, the epistemological relationship of man and God is made possible through intuitive knowledge and the manifestation of the Names.

Divine Names and Ontology

In theoretical mysticism Name refers to the determined essence of the Real. For the mystics, like theologians, the Name of the Real finds meaning and is realized only when the essence of the Real is qualified by one of the attributes. They use different terms in reference to the attributes, such as the properties of the Real's essence, relations, directions, additions, meanings, aspects, determinations, and the manifestations of the essence. According to al-Qayṣarī, the essence of the Real by assuming one of its attributes or in respect of one of its manifestations or one of its relations is called a Name. The spoken Names (the expression of the Name) are in fact the Names of the Real's Names, that is, they are arbitrary signs of the constitutional signs of the essence.

In sum, whenever the unknowable essence of the Real (meaning the absolute existence and unconditioned by the object of division) is considered in respect of one of its determinations of perfection or its relationship with the acts and the world of creation, it will be qualified by the Names, and on the basis of this determination it becomes manifest and knowable.

In consequence, in the mystical perspective the Names come in a later rank of the essence and, according to Ibn 'Arabī, as the essence of the Real is independent of the world and its manifestations, it is also independent of its Names, for the Names are the relations of the Real with the world and this relation is for the creatures and to their benefit. Therefore, that which needs the Names is not the Real but the world. The station of the essence (unconditioned existence) and also the determination of the unique essence, that is, the rank of uniqueness (existence conditioned by nothing), where none of the Names and attributes are manifested, supersede the determinations of the Names that occur in the stage of oneness and through the primary manifestation or the most holy emanation (the manifestation of the essence to the essence).

In the Oneness all the Names are included and united with the non-compound existence and there is no concrete diversity in this station and still there is no manifestation. The mystics believe this station, which Ibn 'Arabī calls divinity, is the origin of the diverse concrete beings and external manifestations. According to Ibn 'Arabī, "That which is disposed to create all that is other than the Exalted Allah is divinity in its properties, relations and additions, and it is this divinity that demands the emergence of the creatures. "The mystics believe the first station or Uniqueness is neither the origin nor is it related to any of the manifestation or determinations. Ibn 'Arabī's view in this respect is that the rank of the Names is equal to the rank of the emergence of relations and connections, for relations do not exist in the rank of Uniqueness. He states, "No manifestation is there in Uniqueness, for manifestation calls for duality, and because manifestation is necessary, duality would be necessary, too."

The Identity and the Large Number of the Names and Attributes with the Essence

From the viewpoint of the mystics neither the divine Names are meanings superadded to the essence as the Asharites believe, nor are they certain states as the Mutazilites claim, nor the essence substitutes the attributes as some other Mutazilites argue. It is rather the unity of attributes which reigns in all ranks, whether in the rank of Oneness or those which follow, that is, the essence and the attributes, on the one hand, and the attributes with each other, on the other, are one and the same.

To explain further, Ibn ʻArabī and his followers consider the attributers as identical with the essence in one respect and as different in another respect. The attributes of the essence are certain meanings, aspects, relations and additions, and in this respect they are identified with the essence, for besides the essence there is no existent. On the other hand, they are different from the essence, for the attributes conceptually are different from each other and from the essence, and it is only in practice and in reality and being that they are equal to the essence.

Ibn ʻArabī in his treatise *Kashf al-Maʻnā* ("Revealing the Meaning") writes: His speech is His knowledge and His knowledge is His essence. Therefore, it is in respect of the essence that He is called by the Names. In *al-Futūḥāt* he also states: the knowledge, life, power and other attributes of the Real are relations and additions. They are not certain entities added to the essence, for in that case the essence would be imperfect, and that which is made perfect by an addition is imperfect in its essence.

Al-Qayṣarī in his introduction to the Commentary on *Fuṣūṣ al-Ḥikam* argues that the ontological aspect of the question of the identity of the attributes and the essence can be discussed in two stages:

1. In the stage of oneness where two unities may be suggested:
   a. The identity of the attributes and the essence, and
   b. The identity of the attributes with each other.

Having explained that the diversity of the Names is due to the diversity of the attributes and the diversity of the attributes is because of the hidden levels of the attributes (the keys of the hidden), he adds: the attributes and the hidden keys exist in the hidden existence of the Real in the form of intelligible meanings rather than real beings, and essentially they do not come under the title of "existent".

2. In the stage of action, where all the Names of action refer to the absolute manifestation of the Real and the breath of the Merciful, he also believes the attribute and the essence are united. Denying that the attributes are additions to the essence he argues that since it is through the attributes that the Exalted Real is Allah (in reference to the station of divinity), were the attributes superadded to the essence, divinity would be the effect of the attributes. In that case, if the attributes were identical with Allah, the thing (divinity) would be its cause, and if it were different from Him, Allah would be the effect of a cause which is not identical with Him, which is absurd, for the cause precedes the effect.

The Unity of the Name and the Named or Their Difference

Since the Names have a two-fold interpretation, a Name can be considered as identical with the essence (the Named) and also different from it. According to Ibn 'Arabī, the divine Names are one with the Named, for all the Names in their reference to the Real are no other than the Named (the essence); therefore, they are the essence in respect of the different relations which result in the manifestation (the realities of the relations). On the other hand, the Names are different from the Named (the essence) when they are considered independent and separate from the essence of the subject they indicate.

In many of his works Ibn ʻArabī, on the basis of the rule "The reality is one but the properties are different," which indicates the possibility of the oneness of the defined essence and the appearance of its diverse and different properties as attributes, argues that the Exalted Real and His Names are the most obvious instances of this rule and in *al-Futūḥāt* referring to this point, states:

> Allah and God, the Merciful and the King
> Are truths sharing one essence.
> Reality is one but the properties differ,
> So the body and the soul and the sphere appeared.

He believes that the Names are many but the Named is one. Nevertheless they are not one in meaning; otherwise the diversity of the divine Names would be meaningless. Therefore, the intelligibility of the Names rests on considering the relations, and as a result the meanings of the Names are not one.

In Faṣṣ of Ismael of *Fuṣūṣ al-Ḥikam* Ibn ʻArabī states that "know that the subject of the Name Allah is one in essence but all [universal] in meaning," that is, the divine Named in respect of the essence is one, non-compound and indivisible, but in respect of divinity (the station of Oneness) has infinite relations, as the number one has infinite relations with other numbers and with half and third and other sums, and, therefore, it is both one and all.

Ibn ʻArabī in his review of the different views on the identity or difference of the Name and the Named concludes: those who own the difference between the Name and the Named have looked indeed at the expressions and meanings of the Names (the names of the Names), but those who profess the identity of the Name and the Named consider the ancient Names, which are the very

Oneness in all respects. Ibn 'Arabī holds that not only is the essence named by all the Names and is one with them in existence, but also each Name is defined by other Names and in practice it is one with them, that is, every Name (like the essence) is in one respect equal and in another respect different from the other Names and comprises the realities of the other Names. It is in this context that the general rule suggested by Ibn Qasī, a Sufi Master of the sixth century A.H., becomes meaningful, that is, "Every divine Name is defined by all other Names." In other words, every divine Name in regard of the essence it indicates and its oneness with it is characterized and identified by other Names. It owns them all, for every Name in respect of the essence is one with the Named, and it differs only in respect of its special meaning.

The Divine Names and the World

The world is the sum of the divine Names that are concretely realized (the manifestation and the demonstration of the divine Names) and in this respect every being indicates the essence of the Real. Since the essence of the Real is manifested only through the medium of the Names, the Names are called the keys of the hidden or the hidden keys and treasures in the descending arc, as they are the gates or ways to approach God in the ascending arc. According to this two-fold aspect of the divine Names, the unity of the Names is because of the essence and their diversity manifest the phenomena in the world of diversity.

The dependence of the creatures on the Real is mediated through the Names and in the rank of the Names, that is, the Real creates the world in the level of the Names rather than that of the essence (in which level He is independent of the worlds and has no relation with anything). According to Ibn 'Arabī, for every reality of the realities of existence there is a Name, which is particular to it, and that Name is the Lord of that reality and that reality is the worshipper of that Name and is under its obligation and care. Moreover, it is likely that in the one and the same thing there are several aspects and realities, and each of those aspects demands one of the divine Names, so that even in a single substance there are many realities, each of them demanding one Name. For example, the reality of its creation demands the Name "the Powerful", its properties demand "the Knowing", its being particular demands "the Willing", and its manifestation demands "the Seeing". These aspects are secondary realities, which are difficult to know, and finding them through unveiling is even more difficult. Shabistarī states in this regard:

"His limit and portion are appointed to each by 'The Truth',
Each arises from and returns to one Name.
In that name each creature has its being,
To that name it is forever giving praise;
At its beginning each proceeds from that source,
At its return that is its door of departure."[1]

The Relations among the Names

There are different relations among the Names. Since some of the diverse beings are the manifestation of different divine Names, the mystics have divided the relations of the Names and also the effect of a few Names in their manifestation in the possible beings into different kinds, including:

1. The Cooperation of the Names: When a Name cannot induce a certain property or effect which fits its aim, this will be done with the help and intervention of some other Names. For example, the

1. *The Mystic Rose Garden*, Verses No. 289-291.

Provider shows its manifestation with the help of the Names the Knowing, the Contriver, etc. These helping Names are called the aides and servants of that Name, and in this division one of the Names is the principal Name and the others are secondary.

2. The Marriage of the Names: The combination of the divine Names leads to their mutual effects and the emergence of a being that is their comprehensive united form. Moreover, the created being will possess a property that is different from the property of each separate Name. In this division all the contributing Names are principal Names.

3. The Confrontation of the Names: The Mystics explain away the phenomena's constitutional or religious differences, conflicts and oppositions by the conflict, opposition or hostility of the Names. This hostility, nevertheless, is believed to be commendable, for it works in the way of establishing the best order. This conflict indeed results from the different demands of the divine Names in their manifestation; for example, the demands of the two Names the Life-giver and the Death-Giver or the Guide and the Misguider are different.

4. The Preference of the Names: Some of the Names are great, such as the Bountiful, and some are greater, such as Allah; some in regard of inclusiveness encompass the beings, such as the Knowing, and some are encompassed, such as the Life giving; some are followed by other Names, such as the Powerful, and some are followers, such as the Providing; etc. Likewise, these relations exist among the manifestations of these Names, and the different degrees of the Names causes the difference in the degrees of their manifestations, too. Finally, the manifestation of the comprehensive Name or the Greatest Name is also the greatest divine manifestation, who is believed to be the pole, the axis and the mediator of the world and is called, as it will be explained, the Perfect Man.

This order of Names where every higher Name comprises all other lower Names extends to the world of manifestations where every greater manifestation contains other manifestations, and because the divine Names are the best Names, the order of the world of manifestations, which is the shadow of the world of Names, is the best order. Moreover, since the manifestation of the Names in the stage of the Real's oneness is the result of the love of the essence and the Names, the manifestation of the world's phenomena is also due to the love of the Names and Actions for the manifestation of the Names. This demand for manifestation in different ranks is called the love movement.

Particular Names

The mystics also consider the manifestations, works and acts of God in their indication of the Named and the perfections of the essence as Names, and in order to distinguish them from Names rooted in attributes they call them particular Names, and in this designation the divine signs are also Names. These Names, unlike the universal Names which are limited, are infinite, for the divine manifestations and the relations the Real can have with the world are endless. Ibn 'Arabī in *Faṣṣ of Seth* in *Fuṣūṣ al-Ḥikam* writes: the Names of God are infinite and they are known by the works and actions He does; those works and actions are also endless, though the Names refer eventually to finite principles, namely the principal Names.

In *al-Futūḥāt* he also divides the Names into special (particular) Names and Names of counting (universal) he maintains the highest knowledge of the people of Allah is to know that the divine Names, like the possible beings, are infinite, and to every possible being that is defined in a certain way one of these Names belongs, which distinguishes it from other possible beings.

To conclude the discussion on the divine Names and the world, it is important to note that essentially the view of the mystic of the world is a bird view, that is, it is mediated through the divine Names and is based on one's awareness of the permanent entities. This divine view is subsequent to reaching the station of intimacy of supererogatory acts, when according to the experience of the mystics and the import of the divine tradition, the eye and the ear and all the mystic's faculties of perception and movement become divine and God-like. Thus, the mystic's understanding of the world and his mental categories and his mind's classification of his findings change. In other words, a view that is based on the knowledge of the Names and witnessing the manifestation of the Real's Names in and their permeation of the world makes the conventional, formal, philosophical, or theological divisions lose their colour in the mystic's eye, such as dividing the world of possible beings into substance and accident, mobile and immobile, animate and inanimate, speaking and speechless, light and dark, good and evil, etc.

The Division of the Divine Names in Mysticism

As it was explained, the divine Name is the Real's essence accompanied by a special attribute or determination; therefore, the Names are divided only through the attributes or their manifestation or the accessories and effects of these manifestations. The mystics divide the divine Names in some respects in the way the philosophers and theologians divide them, such as dividing the attributes into positive and negative and dividing the positive attributes into real, relational and real along with a relation. But in some cases, they have introduced some other divisions, especially on the basis of the degrees and precedence of the Names, the way their perfections or manifestations are displayed, the way they are known or the requirements of their manifestations. The following are some of these divisions.

1. Names of Transcendence and Immanence: Ibn ‘Arabī in the introduction of *Kashf al-Ma‘nā ‘an Sirr-e Asmā Allah al-Ḥusnā* (“The Revelation of the Meaning of Secret of the Best Names of Allah”) divides the divine Names into the proper Name (particular Name), such as Allah, and attribute, such as the Merciful and the Gracious. He further divides the latter into two parts, the first indicating the attributes of transcendence (particular to God and His Exaltation), such as the Single and the One, and the second denoting the attributes of acts and are shared by others, such as the Creator and the Provider.

2. The Greatest Name, the Pillars, and the Principal Names: According to the precedence and degrees of the Names, the greatest of the Names of God is called the greatest Name, and there are two groups of Names which are counted as the root and origin of the other Names and encompass all of them that we explain respectively.

a. The Greatest Name: Most of the mystics hold that the Greatest Name is the Name Allah (the reality of the Name Allah rather than its verbal expression or the name of the Name), for Allah represents the rank of Oneness and encompasses all other Names. Allah is believed to be the Name of the essence that is characterized by all the Names and attributes (the all-comprehensive Name). The properties of the Name Allah are possessed by one who (in practical mysticism and the ascending arc) owns the manifestation of and is annihilated in this Name. Ibn ‘Arabī believes the two Names ‘Allah’ and the ‘Merciful’ are the most comprehensive Names in the hierarchy of the inclusive divine Names.

b. The Four Pillars. The four Names encompassed by the all-comprehensive Names Allah and the Merciful and encompass all the manifestations and things are the First, the Last, the Manifest, and the Hidden. Al-Kāshānī contends these Names are the Hearing, the Seer, the Powerful and the Speaker.

The Seven Principal Names. The mystics argue that there are seven Names titled the principal divine Names and the seven leading Names which encompass and precede all other Names. Al-Kāshānī in *Iṣṭilāḥāt al-Ṣūfiyya* ("The Sufi's Terminology") states that the leading and principal Names are the Living, the Knowing, the Willing, the Powerful, the Hearing, the Seer and the Speaker; however, in *Laṭā'if al-A'lām* ("The Witty Remark of the Masters") following Ibn 'Arabī in his *Inshā al-Dawā'ir* ("Constituting the Circles") he suggests that the main principal Names are the Living, the Knowing, the Willing, the Speaking, the Powerful, the Bountiful, and the Just. In another place he contends that the Names of the essence are the hidden Names, and they are the Speaking, the Hearing, the Seeing, and the Powerful, which he calls the keys of the Hidden. Al-Kāshānī states that the origin of all the hidden Names is the divine Oneness and their prime origin is the first manifestation, which is the manifestation of the essence in the essence. Some others believe that the Name "the Living" is the principal Name that encompasses other Names.

3. Names Particular to God and Names Taught to Others. Another division which Ibn 'Arabī introduces in his works, including *Kashf al-Ma'nā* ("The Revelation of Meaning") is dividing the divine Names into those particular to God, that is, those confined to the knowledge of the Real and people have no knowledge of them, and those which are taught to the servants of God and are general. Some of the latter Names, however, are made known to all people, such as the Seer and the Hearing, whereas some others are confined to the chosen friends of God, such as the Greatest divine Name.

Those Names which are taught to the people are in turn divided into two kinds: those whose reality and properties are revealed in the form of manifestations, and others whose properties are revealed but their realities are confined to God and are hidden. People in relation to the latter kind are also divided into two groups: some know the origin of the mentioned manifestations and the Names they belong, and some do not know. This division can be put briefly in the following diagram:

- Divine Names
  - Confined to God
  - Taught to others
    - To the elite
    - To all people
- Revealed in their reality and properties
- Revealed in their properties but hidden in their reality
  - Known in regard of their originating Name
  - Unknown in regard of their originating Name

4. Names of Beauty and Grandeur. In the terminology of theoretical mysticism, the Names of grandeur are Names which indicate the greatness and glory of the Real and His transcendence, or hide the Real or deny the people certain blessings or perfection, such as the Haughty, the Almighty, and the Avenger. In practical mysticism such Names refer to those Names whose manifestation causes contraction and fear in the wayfarer, for they indicate the anger and might of the Real.

The Names of beauty, however, in theoretical mysticism are those Names which reveal the Real and give the people one of the perfections or blessings, such as the Beneficent, the Provider, the Subtle. In practical mysticism they refer to those Names whose manifestation induces intimacy and joy in the wayfarer, for they indicate the kindness and Mercy of the Real.

However, from the viewpoint of Ibn 'Arabī, the mentioned opposition is only a seeming one and not real, for there is beauty inside grandeur and grandeur inside beauty. On this question, which he thinks is one of the most astounding secrets, he says: there is grandeur in beauty because in every instance of beauty, especially the absolute beauty, there is such a coercion that leaves no space for others, as the shining of the sun leaves no space for the stars to show themselves. On the other hand, there is beauty in grandeur, for if the grandeur of God means His hiddenness behind the veil of phenomena, the phenomena being the manifestation of the Name the Beautiful and indicating the best divine Names are themselves beautiful and display beauty.

Jīlī in *al-Insān al-Kāmil* ("The Perfect Man") speaks of the Name or attribute of perfection, which is shared by beauty and grandeur, that is, it has one face to grandeur and another to beauty, such as Lordship that in respect of power indicates grandeur and in respect of nurturing the world denotes beauty.

5. The Names of essence, attributes, acts. Another division introduced by Ibn Fanārī in *Miṣbāḥ al-Uns* ("The Light of Intimacy") and al-Qayṣarī in his commentary on *Fuṣūṣ al-Ḥikam* following al-Qūnawī and Ibn 'Arabī is to divide the Names into Names of essence, Names of attributes, and Names of acts. To illustrate, when the Names manifest the essence they are called the Names of the essence, such as Allah and the Lord; when they indicate one of the attributes and perfections of the essence they are called the Names of attribute, such as the Living, the Thankful, and the Powerful; and when they reveal one of the acts of the Real they are called the Names of act, like the Originator, the Restorer, and the Guardian. Although all the Names indicate the essence of the Real in one way or another, this indication is sometimes direct and sometimes indirect. Of course, one Name may have different aspects, like the Name the Lord, but it is called by the Name of that aspect which it reveals more.

6. Names with Incessant or Terminated Manifestation. The Name of the act discussed in the last section in respect of its manifestation and the dominance of its manifestation in a phenomenon or in a certain period in this world is divided into three kinds:

a. It is incessant on both sides, and its manifestation and rule are eternal (meaning it has no beginning and no end). The sovereignty of such Names is everlasting, like the Names that rule over the immaterial beings (the holy spirits, heavenly souls and all originators which are trans-temporal).

b. It is terminated on one side, that is, its manifestation has a beginning but no end. The domain of these Names have a beginning but it is eternal; such Names are those which rule over the other world, for the other world has a beginning—the end of this world—but no end.

c. It is terminated on both sides, that is, its manifestation has both a beginning and an end, and the command of these Names is impermanent; such Names are the Names that rule over the material beings and moving bodies.

The Divine Names in Respect of Meaning

It has been explained that the divine Names in one respect are divided into Names of transcendence and immanence, and the function of the latter is shared by the Real and the people and these names apply to both of them, such as hearing, seeing, and speaking. These Names are also called declarative Names, which are mentioned in the holy Book, and also some attributes like describing the Real as having a hand and face.

It is important to find out, however, if there is any justification, from the perspective of the mystics and in regard of meaning, for using such attributes of immanence. In other words, are these Names equivocal terms (between the Real and the people) or they are univocal? Moreover, is the mystics' approach to the Real's attributes based on transcendence, immanence or something different? On this Al-Qayṣarī in his commentary on *Fuṣūṣ al-Ḥikam* writes: "They are predicated of the people and the essence in a common meaning but in different grades." To explain, predicating such attributes of the Real and the possible beings is neither equivocal nor unequivocal (sharing the attributes unequivocally and in the same degree), but it is graded. Therefore, the predication of knowledge and knowing to God and the possible beings, in regard of meaning, is unequivocal, though in one rank knowledge is accidental and in another substantial, in one level it is possible and in another it is one with the essence of the Necessary, and even in one position it is real and in another it is figurative. These degrees of gradation, however, are not incompatible with the unity of the meaning knowledge as awareness in opposition to ignorance.

Ibn 'Arabī discusses this issue in regard of existence and meaning under the title of gathering transcendence and immanence of the Exalted Real. As it was explained, for Ibn 'Arabī as immanence restricts the essence of the Real by stressing His likeness to corporeal beings, transcendence also in another way limits His essence by comparing Him to the immaterial beings, whereas the Exalted Real is above the comparison and exaltation of the believers in immanence or transcendence. He is neither held in the narrow forms of matter nor is separate from them to be placed in immaterial forms. God is simultaneously transcendent and immanent, that is, in Action (extended existence) He appears in all forms and, at the same time, in essence He is confined by none of them.

The Fixed Names

Ibn ʻArabī on many occasions declares that the Names of Allah are set and fixed and even claims that there is consensus on this point. He mentions that not only are'nt we allowed to call God by Names that convention holds as unpleasant like the deceiver, the cheat, and the forgetful (meaning to suggest such names on the basis of verses that use expressions like these for God), but he also warns against using names which are thought to be good but are not mentioned in religion. In *al-Qaṣd* ("The Intention") he writes: "We are not allowed to call the Exalted Allah except by Names that He has called Himself by His Messengers." Moreover, in chapter 177 of *al-Futūḥāt* he states: it is not permissible for the courteous and those who observe politeness in the presence of God to attribute to Him a name by the way of derivation, though that name is a pleasant one. On another occasion he holds that the Names of Allah are fixed and limited; they are known to be one thousand and one or ninety nine Names. Of course, this restriction relates to the universal Names rather than the particular Names, which are countless and infinite.

The Relation of Man and the Divine Names

Apart from the existential and constitutional relationship of all the possible beings and phenomena and the Names, and their dependence in essence, attribute and action on the divine Names, which is called "universal dependence" on the divine Names, man as the special manifestation of the divine Names has three kinds of relationship with each Name, which are called respectively dependence, realization and assumption of traits. In the introduction of *Kashf al-Maʻnā ʻan Sirr-e Asmā Allah al-Ḥusnā* ("The Revelation of Meaning of the Secret of Allah's Best Names") on the relationship of the servant and the Names of the Real Ibn 'Arabī writes: dependence means your universal insufficiency and total need of these Names is that they indicate the essence. Realization on the other hand means your knowledge of the meaning of those Names in relation to the Real and you, and the assumption of traits is to attribute to yourself what is proper to you and to the sublime God what is proper to Him. By dependence in the discourse of Ibn 'Arabī, as it comes in form of the direct address, man's special dependence is meant, which al-Kāshānī defines as "the special dependence on the divine Names, namely the servant's knowledge of his need of and dependence on all divine Names in a way that makes him desire the effects of those Names in himself, and in proportion to every Name manifested in him to do something like thanksgiving, reward, apology, etc."

On the basis of the explanation Ibn 'Arabī gives of the three terms following each of the 99 divine Names in *Kashf al-Ma'nā*, it can be said that dependence means the universal or particular existential relation of man and the Name, that is, the existence and manifestation of the Name in man in general or in a particular man who desires to represent that Name. On the other hand, realization is the perfection or perfect meaning through which the Exalted Real is called by that Name; in other words, it is the existential aspect of this Name or attribute in the Exalted Real. Finally, the assumption of traits is the effects or states of a particular Name in man or the way to reaching its manifestation so that he may resemble the Exalted Creator.

For example, Ibn 'Arabī on the Name the Most Kind writes: dependence on the Name the Most Kind means your need of the sublime God to inform you of the hidden blessings so that you may thank Him or to warn you of His hidden guile so that you become watchful. The realization of that Name (the Most Kind as the Name of God) is that in His essence He is hidden from the perception of the perceivers and in His action He cannot be seen and, moreover, He helps the destitute in unknown ways. Finally, the assumption of traits in regard of this Name is that the servant in the stage of spiritual (hidden) remembrance and secret worship should be hidden from others and even from himself, and (like God) he must attempt to meet the need of the destitute anonymously.

The Greatest Divine Names

Following our general explanation of the theory of the divine Names and its dimensions, here, we discuss a few Names (the Names Allah, the Lord, the Merciful, and the Knowing), which are essential to the mystical view of Ibn ʻArabī and relate his theology to cosmology. We will also have a glance at some of their accessories, namely the permanent entities and the secret of destiny.

1. Allah and the Lord

The difference in meaning and existence of the two Names Allah and the Lord is one of the distinctive features of Ibn ʻArabī's thought. For him, the Lord is the Real manifested in the reality of one Name in one particular aspect and name and appropriate to certain conditions. In other words, the Name Lord in every individual person indicates that the person is always under the care and rule of that Name. Accordingly, Lord has permanence, stability and individuality, whereas Allah is the Real Who in regard of encompassing all the other Names is varied through those Names and, therefore, He is in a new state every day, that is, the Real through the Names changes and varies moment by moment. Allah is the essence comprising all attributes and indicating all the Names.

To explain, every existent in its survival is dependent essentially on His Lord, and that Name (Lord) also has no manifestation without its servant. Therefore, there is an existential relationship in the personal relation between every existent and its Lord, on the basis of which the Lord of every being demands it according to the capacity of that being, and in this respect every existent is pleasing to its Lord. Thus, man in his prayer should attend his Lord, and the best Name by which the supplicant addresses God is that which fulfills his needs.

On the Name Allah it should be said that the Real in His unity is the sum of all the Names and this unity of the sum has also some manifestations in the station of "Oneness", one being the world and the other the perfect man, which will be discussed in the next two chapters. One of the differences between Allah and the Lord is that divinity (Allah) is independent of the worlds, but Lordship is not, for there is a kind of two-sided relationship and interaction between the Lord and the servant. In other words, the servant is dependent on the Lord (demand) and the Lord also depends on the servant. The Lord in every case essentially demands something to exercise His Lordship. In other words, "divinity" represents the presence of the Names, those Names that belong to the Real in respect of being God and being worshiped. In this domain the Real is described with Greatness and praise, worship and piety, and obedience by the creatures; "Lordship", however, indicates the plane of acts, that is, those Names which belong to the Real in respect of Lordship. In this stage the Real is described as managing, directing, supplying and conducting the affairs of the creatures.

2. The Merciful

The Name "the Merciful", which for Ibn 'Arabī is like "Allah" and holds the same level and rank, is the Manifest Real; it encompasses all beings and is the existence and life that permeates all beings and, in other words, it is the presence of the Real and His all-encompassing act. From the viewpoint of Ibn 'Arabī the Merciful besides Allah is the highest and the most comprehensive Name in the hierarchy of the Names. For him Mercy, which in regard of existence and command encompasses all things, pertains to existence and its function is giving existence to things (though a relational existence) with a tinge of care and compassion from the Benefactor. Mercy is the essential attribute of the Exalted Real's essence, so that it even dominates His anger, and indeed His anger is a form of His endless Mercy.[1] Al-Kāshānī explains this precedence of God's Mercy over His anger, which is the subject of many traditions and prayers, as follows:

His Mercy is by essence... but His anger is not essential to the Real; it is rather non-existential and results from the inability of certain things to receive the perfect manifestation of the properties of existence... If Mercy does not inundate these things it is because of their inability to receive perfection and Mercy.

Therefore, "evil" is only the negative description of those things which cannot receive the Mercy (of existence) in its perfect form. Unlike what may appear, the divine Mercy does not include only the entities and things, but in the school of Ibn 'Arabī it encompasses the divine Names, the permanent entities and even itself. For the manifestation of the Name the Merciful Ibn 'Arabī mentions certain stages:

1. The Mercy of the essence: It is the first stage of the

1."Giving and grace and flavour are the fundamental substance of His coin: wrath is [only] as a speck of alloy on it.
He made the world for kindness' sake: His sun caressed the motes [in its beams].
If separation [from Him] is big with His wrath, tis for the sake of knowing the worth of union with Him." *Mathnawī*, Book II, Verses No. 2631 – 3.

manifestation of Mercy, which is the manifestation of the Real in Himself, or the manifestation of Mercy in the essence of the Real, and in the words of Ibn 'Arabī it is Mercy protected by Mercy.

2. The Mercy of the Names: It is the second stage of the manifestation of Mercy, which is the revelation of the reality of the Names and the emerging permanent entities; in regard of manifestation it is the most holy emanation.

3. The Mercy of acts: It is the stage of the manifestation of the entities (external beings). In this stage, which is the last stage of the Real's manifestation, the entities appear through the breath of the Merciful or the holy emanation.

On the other hand, Ibn 'Arabī divides the divine Mercy into two kinds:

a. Gratuitous Mercy (Universal). It is the reality of existence and conferring existence (universal manifestation), which with no difference or discrimination encompasses all things, entities and even the Names, and the Real in this regard is called "the Merciful".

b. Obligatory Mercy (particular). It is the Mercy and favor showed mainly to conscious and willful beings like as man, and it is given as recompense. It encompasses a special kind of beings, and it is in this regard that the Real is called the "Beneficent".[1] This Mercy is subordinate to the Mercy of the Merciful.

Ibn 'Arabī adds, considering the unity of acts, to consider the obligatory Mercy as recompense for human deeds indicates a superficial understanding of the subject, for the real agent and doer is always God.

On the other hand, the gratuitous Mercy is the act of conferring existence and it is not concerned with the vice or virtue of

1. 'My mercy embraces all things. Soon I shall appoint it for those who are Godwary...' (7: 156)..وَرَحْمَتِي وَسِعَتْ كُلَّ شَيْءٍ فَسَأَكْتُبُهَا لِلَّذِينَ يَتَّقُونَ

existence. In other words, this Mercy is beyond good and evil or good and bad, for everything in respect of existence is constitutionally directed by God and is pleasing to Him (constitutional beneficence) and is encompassed by His gratuitous Mercy. Nevertheless, things relatively and from a human perspective may be identified as good or bad (moral or religious vice or virtue). Things in the world happen, with no exception, according to the divine rule and Will rather than the rules defined in the religious law. Thus, no one should object to the divine determination, though in respect of the determined this is not true and one may find it unpleasant, for every reality and creature in relation to its Name and Lord is pleasing, and everything in regard of existence is obedient rather than disobedient.[1] It is only in relation to the religious law or the human perceiver—and not in themselves and as they are created by God—that human states may appear as unpleasant. Ibn 'Arabī gives as evidence the change of vice into virtue that is mentioned in the Qur'an. He explains, this change shows that these two descriptions (vice and virtue) are virtually one in nature, and the question is that of difference in decree but oneness in essence and reality.

Now does this mean the mystic essentially believes there is no good or bad, pleasant and unpleasant, or good and evil in the world? Ibn 'Arabī's answer is "No". He states, "One who does not distinguish between good and bad essentially has no perception; every man by nature understands both (good and evil), and even

1. "Since colourlessness [pure Unity] became the captive of colour [manifestation in the phenomenal world], a Moses came into conflict with a Moses.
When you attain unto the colourlessness which you [originally] possessed, Moses and Pharaoh are at peace [with each other]." *Mathnawī*, Book I, Verse No. 2467 – 8.

the Exalted Real abhors certain deeds (the vices) and likes certain others (the virtues). It is also narrated that the Messenger of God disliked some things and liked some others." Of course, since man (as it will be explained in the following chapter) is created in the likeness of the Real, and the world of existence is also similar to the Real, his practical reason and moderate nature corresponds with the reality of the world of existence and evidently agrees with the divine religious law and what is set by the Real as pleasant and unpleasant. So, all humans in a way understand the good and evil and the pleasant and unpleasant of the world. There are people of certain disposition, however, who are aware of the precedence of the pleasant over the unpleasant, and the knowledge they have of the pleasant makes them abhor the vice. We will follow this argument in our discussion on the characteristics of the world in the Mystical Cosmology.

3. The Knowing: Divine Knowledge and the Permanent Entities

One of the divine Names especially emphasized in the holy texts and religious mysticism and that has an essential role in creation, divine activity, determination and destiny is "the Knowing". As it was explained, the God of religions and the mystics is a "trans-human" God, for He has both the attributes of perfection, such as will, hearing and seeing, and these attributes in regard of time, space and existence are infinite, and there is no end for His knowledge and omnipotence. The matter of dispute among some philosophers and theologians was about whether God knew the things before their creation or not. Moreover, in case such knowledge existed, how it happened and how it can be explained. This conflict, however, for the mystics, considering what is explained in the following, is taken for granted. According to the school of Ibn 'Arabī, prior to creation (the realization of the diverse entities by the holy emanation), the Exalted Real knew the possible beings of the world, but this knowledge also existed in the level of Uniqueness and Oneness.

The mystics refer the knowledge of the Real in the level of the essence to “the permanent entities”. The permanent entities could be defined as the reflection of the divine Names and attributes in the knowledge of God in the station of Oneness. In other words, they are the concomitants of the Names and attributes realized by the most holy emanation in the plane of God’s knowledge. God in the level of the essence in His essential knowledge of His essence also knows the Names, attributes and their concomitants. The permanent entities are indeed the counterparts of the external entities.

The external entities, which Ibn ‘Arabī calls the level of “the thing-ness of existence”, are externalized in the stage of diversity and the Real’s action, whereas the permanent entities that are called also by Ibn ‘Arabī “the thing-ness of permanence”, exist in the station of Oneness and are still not externalized. So, the prior level of everything in the knowledge of the Real is in the world of the permanent entities, which is the essence that is uncreated and causeless and on the basis of which things are realized. In mysticism, the fact that things are created according to their essence and everything has its own essential features is explained by these permanent entities in the reality of the Real’s knowledge.

Jāmī compares the entities to different coloured glasses on which the light of the sun reflects and takes the special colour of the glass through which it shines. In this exact analogy, the colour of the coloured glasses indicates the variety of the Names, attributes and the manifestation of the entities in relation to the Names, which determine the capacity of each entity before its appearance. The light of the sun, on the other hand, is the divine manifestation and the holy emanation, which although at the beginning in regard of colours is absolute and undetermined, once it is coloured by the concomitants and properties of the permanent entities it becomes determined. Finally, the colourful light that reflects through the glasses is the manifestation and the relational existence of the entities. Jāmī explains this point in one of his quatrains:

The entities are different glasses all
On which the light of the sun of existence has fallen.
Each glass red, yellow or blue
Shows the sun in the same colour.

These entities, which are the result of the most holy emanation and are by "the creation of destiny" and according to the eternal and essential knowledge of the Real in the domain of the divine knowledge, determine the essential capability and the existential and growing capacities and the main features of the existents in manifestations that appear through "the creation of origination" (and based on the creation of destiny) by the command of the Real and the holy emanation. Ibn 'Arabī believes these entities "do not exist in reality but exist in effect", for they have no independent or separate existence from the essence and the attributes of the Real. Nevertheless, they determine the capacity and capability of receiving the manifestations in the external entities; the divine emanation on the basis of this silent demand of the existents (praying by the language of capacity) realizes the manifestations and gives them perfection. Mawlānā says:

"Thou didst show the delightfulness of the Being unto the not-being, [after] thou hadst caused the not-being to fall in love with thee."[1]

---

1. *Mathnawī*, Book I, Verse No. 606.

We were not, and there was no demand on our part, [yet] thy grace was hearkening to our unspoken prayer [and calling us into existence]."[1]

The Middle Nature of the Entities

The permanent entities in different respects show they have a mediatory nature and a reconciling two-sided disposition:

1. In respect of existence and non-existence. Ibn 'Arabī holds that the permanent entities do not exist, that is, they are not external realities or outside the divine essence, though they exist in the divine knowledge and accordingly, he believes, they are not nonexistent. Although this view brings him close to the fixed entities of the Mutazilites, his commentators state by holding that the entities are neither existing nor nonexistent (or, in his words, "the permanent entities have not smelled the scent of existence") he means the entities in regard of existence have no independent existence from the Real, but they do exist in the reality of the essential knowledge of the Real and they are eternal by His eternality.

2. In Respect of Action and Passiveness. That the creatures participate actively in their creation and are not merely passive is due to the effect of the permanent entities in the process of manifestation. The entities in one respect are passive and receive (the most holy emanation from the Real), and in another respect they are doers and active (in realizing the external entities). They both rule over and are examples for the course of creation and are ruled by and follow the most holy emanation, and accordingly they are considered as both created and uncreated. To explain further, the entities in regard of being the forms and concomitants

1. Ibid, Verse No. 610.

of the Real's Names and to emerge from them depend on the emanation and are passive. On the other hand, they are the conduit of the emanation to the external entities and rule over the emergence of the possible beings and determine their capabilities, capacities and features.

3. In Other Respects. The entities are ancient in regard of their existence in knowledge and also temporal in their manifestation through the most holy emanation. They are both universal (encompassing) and via the holy emanation lead to the creation of the particulars and affects them, and are particular and special. Finally, the entities, on one hand, are the entities of the possible beings and, on the other hand, are necessary by the divine necessity, for they are the concomitants of the Names in the divine knowledge.

To recapitulate, the relation of the external entities and the permanent entities is like the relation of the permanent entities and the divine Names. That is, each of them is the reflection and the manifestation of the other in a lower rank. The following diagram shows the role of the permanent entities in the order of manifestation and the mystical viewpoint:

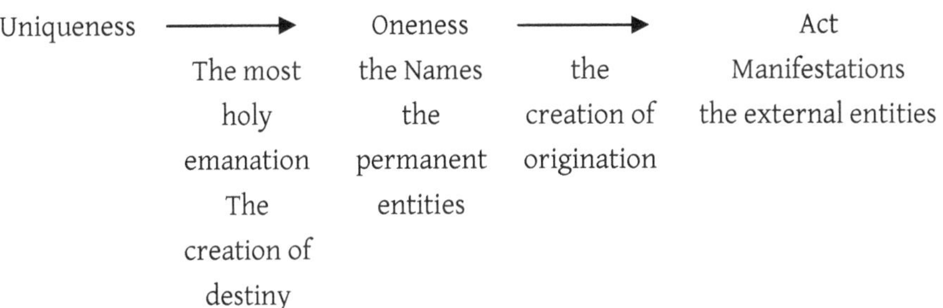

The Secret of Destiny. For Ibn 'Arabī the secret of destiny, which in the language of religion is considered as something secret and hidden, is no other than "the rule of the permanent entities" over the course creation, which is known, of course, only by a few of the perfect men. To explain, as it was discussed in the last part, the main role of the permanent entities in the manifestation of the beings of the world is its mediation and connecting the creatures (manifestations) and the Real (the Manifest) in the course of creation. Ibn 'Arabī believes the permanent entities in the divine knowledge wield infinite power, and they dominate even the Will and creativity of the Real, for the entities, according to him, do not vary or change, and this immutability even limits the activity of the Real. This stability of the entities assigns a definite station for all things in the world, that is, although the command of God and the existence He gives are one (the breath of the Merciful), the receptors, according to their permanent entities, receive them in different ways. Accordingly, the order of creation also existed in the form of permanent entities in the essential knowledge of the Real before creation, and the order of the possible beings is a shadow of that order of knowledge. Moreover, the existents because of their permanent entities enjoy perfection and a degree of existence, and the rule of the permanent entities accordingly means the absolute divine Mercy encompasses all, but the portion of every being of that divine gift is determined by its capacity and capability. Ibn 'Arabī claims this perspective is the result of acquiring "a divine vision", one which is achieved by looking at the world from above. He further explains that the secret of destiny, which is connected to the knowledge of the permanent entities and their exigencies, is confined to the Exalted Real and a few of the Prophets and Saints of God. He states, "He who knows the secret of destiny is aware of the content of theology, for by knowing the self he has the same knowledge of himself which God has given to him." Such a person knows the beginning of the creation of the individual persons and their nature and also the end of their capacity and destiny. Rūmī holds they are those people who

"Before the [creation of the] heavens they have seen Saturn; before the [existence of] seeds they have seen the bread".[1]

"Before the creation of grapes it has quaffed wines and shown the excitements [of intoxication].

In hot July they [*Pirs*] see December; in the sunbeams they see the shade.

In the heart of the grape they have seen the wine; in absolute *fana* [privation of objectivity] they have seen the object".[2]

In Ibn 'Arabī's view, one of the signs of the person who is given the secret of destiny is that he becomes the manifestation of the Name "the Manifest", and he can have a manifestation everywhere that he likes. Moreover, he is aware of the hidden capacities and demands of individual persons and things, and in consequence their beginning and end. On the other hand, he reaches the state of absolute ease and total disappointment; he accepts the excuse of people even when they do not apologize, for by knowing the permanent entities he understands their capacities and qualities and, therefore, will expect no more than what their entities demands.

4. The Disciple: the Divine Creativity and Will. The theologians, philosophers and mystics are of different opinions on the agency of the Real. There are two main principles, however, for dividing these views: 1. the knowledge of the Real, 2. the Will and intention of the Real. In regard of the former, the difference is mainly on the quality of the knowledge of the Real before creation and also His knowledge after creation; the mystics' views on this issue were discussed in the last section.

1. *Mathnawī*, Book II, Verse No. 174.
2. Ibid, Verse No. 180-2.

a. The reason of the divine Creation. In regard of the intention and will of the Real, the school of Ibn 'Arabī stresses the sufficiency of the Real (negating any purpose outside the essence) and also the movement of desire. This school suggests that any kind of intention, purpose and motivation of the Real in His action other than the essence—even if that motivation is to benefit the creatures, meet their needs or show generosity to the needy—is incompatible with the independence of the Real's essence and His infinite perfection and is essentially incompatible with the oneness of existence.

The mystics maintain creation through manifestation (or love) and hold the Real above any deficiency or want and argue that in the course of the emanation from the Exalted Real there is no cause other than His essence. They further add that on the basis of the rule "Love is the cause of manifestation" the end of creation is neither the benefit of the Creator nor showing generosity to the creatures, but it is love of His essence and essential perfections. According to 'Irāqī:

The Monarch of Love desired to pitch His tent in the wilderness. He unlocked the treasures; spread His riches in the world.... Otherwise the world slept in its nonexistence.... There where Allah existed and nothing existed besides Him.... Suddenly restless Love in order to manifest His perfection unveiled His work and driven by love He revealed Himself to the eye of the lover.

He further adds, "Although Love always saw Himself by Himself, He desired also to see His loving beauty and perfection in the mirror. He looked in the Love mirror and saw His image .... He loved His image and raised the cry of "He loves them" in the world."

b. The Divine Creation and the Question of Mediation. As it was mentioned, many-sidedness and the logic "He /not He" are two of the features of Ibn 'Arabī's viewpoint, which are also discussed in the question of direct or indirect creation. To explain, Ibn ʻArabī on the question of unification of acts suggests two rules of "eliminating the causes" and "setting the causes", the former indicating the presence of causes and mediation and the latter the absence of any cause or mediation other than the Exalted Real. In other words, the school of Ibn ʻArabī puts emphasis on the direct presence and manifestation of the Real in the world of beings and that all the acts are the Real's acts, and in short all existents and beings are just a reflection of the Real and a glance of the face of the cupbearer. On the other hand, it holds that there is an order and systematic organization in the emanation of beings from the essence of the Creator; for example, instead of the first emanated being Ibn ʻArabī speaks of the first manifestation and calls it the breath of the Merciful, the Ever-expanding existence, the creator Real, etc.

The combination of these two dimensions in the school of Ibn ʻArabī makes the discussion of "particular mode" necessary in this school.

The Particular Mode

The "particular mode" is the question which was discussed for the first time in the school of Ibn ʻArabī and it had no precedence before in philosophy. The mystics believe the existents are related to the Exalted Real in two ways:

1. **By chain of order**: In this way every being is related to the Exalted Real through a chain of causes or manifestations, and they receive the emanation from the Real through these conduits. The emanation which reaches them depends on the association and combination of those causes. This chain of productive mediums is called "the chain of making causes".

2. **By way of special mode**: This is a direct and immediate

relationship between the Exalted Real and all things where every existent and manifestation gets its special emanation directly from the Real. This way which is called special mode results from the manifestation of the divine Name, but it is a Name that is known only to God and, therefore, this mode is also hidden and particular to God. This way is called "the chin of burning the causes".[1]

Ibn 'Arabī in *al-Futūḥāt,* on the basis of his knowledge of this special mode through unveiling, compares the entire course of creation to the creation of the first being, and claims he is the first to hint at this special mode; thus, he combines the rejection of causes with positing them or, to put it in other words, acquirement with creation.

The followers of the school of Ibn 'Arabī express different views on whether this special mode is an existential matter of intuitive. Some of them believe the spiritual states of the mystic, especially union and separation are the origin of two kinds of approach to creation, namely both denying and approving mediation. Some others contend that they have given an existential interpretation of the question on the basis of the concept of the breath of the Merciful (Ever-expanding existence or pervasive manifestation)—as it will be explained—which is considered as the first actual manifestation of the Real and at the same time is universal encompassing in existence all levels and manifestations and gathering in itself both unity and diversity. To put it in other words, the entire world through the breath of the Merciful and the

1. Mawlānā says,

"He cherisheth Abraham in the fire; He turneth fear into security of spirit.
By His burning [destroying] of secondary causes I am distraught; in [my] fancies of Him I am like a sophist [sceptic or agnostic]." *Mathnawī,* Book I, Verse No. 547- 8.

pervasive manifestation of the Real is directly related to the Exalted Real, for it has no existence separate from the Ever-expanding existence and it is annihilated in this manifestation in its properties. On the other hand, although all things in regard of their determinations, priority and posteriority, and precedence, which make some the requisite or conduit for the emanation of others, are the determination of the breath of the Merciful, like different waves that are different from each other and at the same time connected with each other, they are nevertheless no more than different determinations of water. It is in this relation that the question of the first manifestation is discussed.

The First Manifestation (Emanation): the Extended Existence

Accepting in general the rule "From the One nothing emanates except the one" and on the basis of the Oneness of existence and the rule of manifestation instead of causality and emanation, the mystics believe the "one" and the first manifestation is the extended and universal existence which encompasses all things[1] and gathers in itself unity and diversity. This identification also explains the unification of acts and attributing the existents directly to God.

On the basis of the Oneness of existence the mystics argue there is no diversity in existence to look then for the reason of diversity in the world. However, in respect of the manifestations they prove God has certain attributes and relations and these very aspects, relations and attributes are the reason for the emanation of diverse beings from the Exalted Real. It is because of this one Being that the unreal and relational entities are realized. Of

1. Mawlānā says, "This world is one thought [emanating] from the Universal Intellect: the Intellect is like a king, and the ideas [are his] envoys." *Mathnawī*, Book II, Verse No. 978.

course, when the Exalted Real is considered in the unity of His essence, only one thing is emanated from Him. Ḥāfiẓ states:

> "When the splendor of your beauty once displayed itself in the mirror,
> All these images fell into the mirror of illusion."[1]
> "All these reflections of wine and colorful images which it showed,
> Where the light of the cup-bearer's face that the cup displayed."[2]

For the mystics the intellect, the soul, and other ranks of the world cannot be the first emanation or manifestation. It is, they maintain, the extended existence which represents the highest relation between God and the breath of the Merciful, and the first Intellect and other worlds are only some of its determinations.

The extended existence has certain features which put it in direct relationship with the Real, such as:

1. Existential (rather than conceptual) universality and comprehensiveness, which allows it to encompass all other manifestations.

2. Absence of any limitation or determination, so that it appears through each being in the extent of that being.

3. Being diverse in its unity and one in its diversity (due to its real shadowy oneness).

The mystics argue that it is the Ever-expanding existence, rather than the intellect or any other being, which is the first representation and even the first manifestation (the first emanated being) because every manifestation (emanated being) should be related to its Origin (source of emanation) and the first manifestation (emanation) should have the most perfect relations.

1. *The Poems of Ḥāfiẓ Shīrāzī*, trans. 'Alāiddīn Pazārgādī, Ode No. 111.
2. Ibid, Ode No. 111.

The universal extended existence has, first, a unity, which is the shadow of the divine "all-inclusive unity" and, second, like the Exalted Real it has no special determination or limitation and, therefore, it has no determined quiddity but possesses a sustaining association with all beings. Therefore, it has the most complete relation with the Exalted Real and indeed it is the very creating Real or the first manifestation (emanation).Thus, the creation of the world is no other than the appearance of a universal manifestation—called the breath of the Merciful, the Ever-expanding existence or the permeating manifestation—that embraces certain manifestations and ranks with different attributes, degrees of precedence, and priority and posteriority.

To conclude, for the mystics the Real's love of His essence and Names, and the necessity of the manifestation and reflection of these Names and attributes and also His love to see His perfection and beauty in the mirror of manifestations are the reasons of creation. In other words, if for the thinkers and philosophers it is the intelligence, knowledge and providence of God that moves Him to create the world, and for the Asharite theologians it is His Will and Power, for the mystic it is love that reveals the manifestations of the Real.

On the quality of creation, the mystics' view is that God's creation is ordered and is based on the best order of Names, and He is related to His manifestations and creatures both directly and immediately and also through causes. Therefore, neither the Asharites are right who believe the emanation of the world from God is neither ordered nor mediated, nor the Mutazilites who hold the course of the world after creation follows the chain of causes and God is only a spectator, nor the philosophers who maintain that God is related to the world only through linear causes. The other features of the creation of God, which are related to the world of manifestations, are discussed in the next chapter.

Questions

1. Compare and contrast the Gods of the philosophers and mystics.
2. Explain the features of the principles of transcendence and immanence from the viewpoints of the theologians and Ibn 'Arabī.
3. Discuss the relationship between the divine Names and the world from Ibn 'Arabī's point of view.
4. How are the Names related to each other according to the mystics' viewpoints? Discuss!
5. Compare and contrast the universal and particular Names from the perspective of the mystics.
6. Compare and contrast the known and unknown Names in regard of the origin of the Names.
7. Explain the difference in meaning and existence between the two Names "Allah" and "the Lord" in the thought of Ibn 'Arabī.
8. What are the Compassionate Mercy and essential Mercy in the viewpoint of Ibn 'Arabī?
9. Discuss the different aspects of the Mediatory and intervening nature of the permanent entities.
10. What is the meaning of "the secret of Destiny" according to Ibn 'Arabī?
11. Discuss the import of the two rules of "eliminating the causes" and "establishing the causes" in the school of Ibn 'Arabī!
12. How many ways, according to the mystics, do the beings relate to the Exalted Real? Discuss!
13. Explain the meaning of "establishing the chain of causes" and "burning the chain of cause" in the school of Ibn 'Arabī!
14. What is the mystics' interpretation of the rule "Only one emanates from the One"?
15. Why do the mystics claim the extended existence is the first manifestation (the first emanation) of God?

Chapter Four: Cosmology in Practical Criticism

It is commonly known that "when the soul changes the world changes, too", so the view of the mystic of the world is different from that of the common people, philosophers and scientists. In this chapter first we discuss the identity of the world, and then the relation of the Real and the world, the way the world was created, and the features of the world in the perspective of theoretical mysticism, and finally the order of the world in the school of Ibn 'Arabī.

The Identity of the World

The word '*ālam* (the world in Arabic) derives from '*alāma* (Arabic for sign), which is a noun indicating another thing. In the mystics' terminology all things besides Allah indicate the Real and are His sings and, therefore, they are called collectively the world. In mysticism the world has no objectivity, as sings qua signs have their meaning from the others and like the letters and words have no function other than the meaning they indicate. So, in the mysticism the world and the soul are seen in the light of the one principle of "the seeing God." So, whosoever does not see the world as a sign and means, he has not understood it even if he has studied and analyzed its phenomena and has composed many treatises. In this respect it has been said:

The entire being is an expression and You are the meaning,
The hearts are iron and You are the magnet.
Mawlānā in a reference to Shams Tabrīzī writes:
"The Reality is Allah, said the Shaykh of the Religion,
[who is] the sea of the spiritual realities of the Lord of the created beings."[1]

Ibn 'Arabī also believes the Real is the identity of the world (in respect of manifestation) and, therefore, the indication of the Real by the world is not separate, he argues, from the indication of the Real by Himself. Of course, the beings of the world are signs of the Real in relation to His Names and attributes rather than His essence, that is, by everything in the world some of the divine Names are known and made manifest, for everything is one of the manifestations of the Names:

"Know that [the world of] the created beings is like pure and limpid water in which the attributes of the Almighty are shining.

Their knowledge and their justice and their clemency are like a star of heaven [reflected] in running water."[2]

"The beauteous are the mirror of His beauty: love for them is the reflexion of the desire of which He is the [real] object."[3]

"Kings are the theatre for the manifestation of God's kingship; the learned [divines] are the mirrors for God's wisdom."[4]

"The whole sum of the pictured forms [phenomena] is a [mere] reflexion in the water of the river: when you rub your eye, [you will perceive that] all of them are really He."[5]

---

1. *Mathnawī*, Book I, Verse No. 3338.
2. *Mathnawī*, Book VI, Verse No. 3172- 3.
3. Ibid, Verse No. 3181.
4. Ibid,Verse No. 3174.
5. Ibid,Verse No. 3183.

Ibn 'Arabī sometimes states the world is no more than fancy and imagination, sometimes he maintains it is like an image in the mirror, and on some other occasions he holds it is like a shadow. For him each of these metaphors explain a certain aspect of the identity of the world: the shadow is dependent and cannot be the subject of existence or nonexistence, the image in the mirror is neither existing nor nonexistent, the possibility of multiplying a thing that is one in reality in the mirrors though at the same time it indicates oneness, and the inauthenticity of the imagination and its dependence on the imagined thing. These symbols may be explained as follows.

a. Imagination and Dream

To say the world is an imagination or a mirage could be interpreted in two ways. The imagination is sometimes counted as absurd and illusory to be rejected and ignored, and sometimes an imitation and a mirror and means of interpretation that, like a dream, must be explained and interpreted. In the first case it should be said that the world is just imaginary and illusory and has no meaning or reality. In the second case, however, the world is a two-fold thing and has two sides, one side to illusion and another to reality. It is neither totally false nor completely real. It is not real but shows the Real and is His sign and mirror, as the image in the mirror would be false and deceptive when it is considered as independent but is indicative of reality when it is considered as a reflection of the owner of the image. Ibn 'Arabī suggests the second meaning most succinctly in the following verses:

The world is imaginary though real in truth,
He who is aware of this knows the secrets of the path.

Therefore, he who knows that the world is both imaginary and real knows the secrets of the mystical way and the divine knowledge.

For Ibn 'Arabī the world is imaginary in two ways: it is symbolic or "seemingly existing" and the continual change of the mentioned symbolic images, as in a dream the both mentioned features, namely the continual change and seeming existence, exist. Shabistarī explains:

"The existence of the two worlds is as a dream,
In the moment of eternity they become naught".[1]
"How can you doubt that this is a dream?
For duality by the side of unity is a pure delusion".[2]

Ibn 'Arabī believes the perceived world is not only imaginary but also twice imaginary (imagination within imagination), for the world is revealed to man according to his perceiving faculties, senses and intellect, and when these faculties, senses and intellect, which are parts of the world, are considered as imaginary, their product, namely the world they reflect and are seen by man would be twice imaginary (as Ibn 'Arabī maintains man's dream is a dream within a dream). In "Faṣṣ of Yūsuf" he states: Know that you are the imagination itself and whatever you perceive and say they are other than Me. So, existence is imagination within imagination. By the first imagination he means the whole world of existence and by the second all the faculties of human perception. Ḥāfiẓ states:

"The world and its affairs are nothing in nothing;
I have found this point a thousand times".[3]

In any case, in Ibn 'Arabī's view the world is not existence but an illusory thing. On the basis of the Prophetic tradition "People are sleeping and when they die they wake," he asserts the world is like a dream, though not an absurd or vain dream and somehow it

1. *The Mystic Rose Garden,* Verse No. 471.
2. Ibid,Verse No. 713.
3. *The Poems of Ḥāfiẓ Shīrāzī,* trans. 'Alāiddīn Pazārgādī, Ode No. 298.

reflects the reality. What is necessary is to interpret this dream in the right way and to refer it to its original form, which is the work of the mystics. He explains that the death and waking in the tradition refer to voluntary death and annihilation. So, he can give a true explanation of the world that is awake and has reached the state of annihilation. Such a person knows that only the Real's absolute essence is real, and the universe (and all that is other than God) is an image of His manifestation or a realized imagination. In other words, the world is an external illusion rather than a mental illusion, and the assumption that the imaginary world is a representation of the Real is one of the deepest secrets of the world. Accordingly, the diverse beings of the world are only the symbols and manifestations of the Real—as it was mentioned in our discussion of the symbols of the oneness of existence—but the common people are ignorant of the illusion of the visible world.

b. Mirror

For Ibn 'Arabī the metaphor of mirror also has the two-fold structure, for the image is reflected in the mirror but it has no real existence. Moreover, the image is neither in the mirror (for there is nothing in the mirror), nor in the spectator, nor in the space between the two (for between the two there is only the reflected light). Besides, the mirror (meaning the image in the mirror) itself has no objectivity and as a mirror it is not seen.

c. Shadow

Ibn 'Arabī in "Faṣṣ of Yūsuf" compares the world to a shadow and states: know that what they call "the world" or other than the Real is only a relationship with the Real. Like the shadow to a person, the world is also the shadow of Allah, which is no other than the relating existence to the world. He also states one of the features of the shadow is its twofold character. On the one hand it is a shadow and, therefore, it exists, and on the other it does not exist, for the shadow is no other than a relation to an existing being. Finally, shadow is the absence of light, and it is always subsidiary and dependent.

Ibn 'Arabī states: the world is an image of the divine Names and, therefore, it is the shadow of the Real. On the other hand, the shadow has a sensible existence when there is light and the owner of the shadow also exists. In our argument, the pole (the owner of the shadow) is the Real (the absolute existence), its light is the manifest Name Allah, and where the shadow falls is the world of possible beings. The origin of the shadow is a mystery and it is absolutely unknown, which is indicated by the darkness of the shadow.

Al-Kāshānī in his explanation of this analogy writes: as in the sensible world the shadow is connected to the pole and is inseparable from it, the light of existence and the extensive manifestation of the Real in the entities and possible beings is also connected to the Real and can never be separated from Him. The difference of the two is that the connection in the sensible things indicates duality, whereas the connection of the light of existence or the world to the Real denotes oneness, for it is of the kind of the connection of the limited to the absolute.

d. Light

The other symbol which the mystics frequently use in their description of the world is "light", which apparently has its root in the holy Qur'an, in its description of the relation of God's light and the world (24:35), and in witnessing the divine light throughout the world. The Real is the light of the world and the world is a beam of His light. Shabistarī writes:

"Know the whole world is a beam of the light of 'The Truth',
Yet 'The Truth' within it is concealed from manifestation"[1]

---

1. *The Mystic Rose Garden*, Verse No. 98.

The different levels of command and creation, the unseen and the manifest, and the exterior and interior commonly share the light of the Real which sustains them. Ḥāfiẓ says:

"Both worlds reflect one image of the friend's face;
I have indicated it to you both openly and secretly."[1]

The identity of the one ray and the direct light and the Ever-expanding existence was discussed in the last chapter. The mystics in their interpretation of the holy verse 'Allah is the Light of the heavens and the earth...',[2](24: 35) argue that the verse does say Allah illuminates the heavens and the earth so that no one should think the relation of the Real and the world is merely a causal relationship (unless we understand, like Ibn 'Arabī, by the effect the form and the manifestation of the cause and by the cause the reality and the essence of the effect). Rather the expression "the light of the heavens and earth" is mentioned to emphasize that there is no light or existence other than that of the light of God and the heavens and earth reflect the same light. These explanations refer in one way or another to the logic "He/ He not" (paradox and the coincidence of opposites), which according to Ibn 'Arabī is the foundation of mysticism. That the Real and creatures, despite their difference, are one does not mean their absolute "identity", but despite identity they are different. This paradoxical state has been expressed through the images of imagination, shadow, light, dream and magic.

The Genesis of the World (Creation)

Creation, one of the essential concepts in the worldview of religions and especially Islam, is a key concept and has an important role in theoretical mysticism. The creational word "Be" has an existential

1. *The Poems of Ḥāfiẓ Shīrāzī*, trans. 'Alāiddīn Pazārgādī, Ode No. 365.

2. 'اَللّٰهُ نُورُ السَّمَاوَاتِ وَالْأَرْضِ.'

meaning in Ibn 'Arabī's viewpoint and equals the concept of "manifestation". If the world is nothing other than the manifestation of the Real's perfections, the concept of creation naturally indicates the same manifestation; nevertheless in the school of Ibn 'Arabī this concept is not just a figure of speech or only a synonym for manifestation. In fact, this essential reality has two aspects for Ibn 'Arabī: one is manifestation and the other is creation. In the following we discuss first some of the common aspects of the two concepts, and then explain the features of the second concept (creation).

a. Divine Love and Intention

One of the common features of the two concepts is the divine purpose and intention of manifestation and creation. In the school of Ibn 'Arabī the purpose of creation is rooted in the love and movement of desire. To explain, as it was discussed in the last chapter the mystics believe the purpose and aim of the creation of the world is neither the benefit of the Creator nor generosity to the creatures, but it is the love of the Real of His essence and perfections. They argue that on the basis of the two rules of "Loving a thing makes the love of its effects necessary" and "Love is the reason of manifestation," the eternal love of the Real makes Him reveal and manifest Himself in the forms of His perfections of Names, so that as He had seen Himself in the level of the essence He may see Himself in the mirror of the Acts. The mystics claim their finding is in agreement with the divine tradition of "The Hidden Treasure". So, according to the two rules mentioned above, beauty is the very purpose of creation and settles the debates on creation, for beauty through the medium of love leads to the manifestation of beings.

Ibn 'Arabī, on the basis of the mentioned tradition, explains the important issue of the movement of desire. He states that creation is the result of three kinds of love or necessities:

1. The love of the Real to be known, that is, to manifest His hidden perfections, which are revealed by creating the world.

2. The love of the Names to manifest their concomitants (permanent entities) in the world of the divine knowledge and also the external world.

3. The love of the permanent entities to move to the external world, that is, to see themselves in the external world as they are in the world of permanence.

The mystics state that if it was not for this love (love that is dependent on the Real's beauty and perfections), nothing would have been created through manifestation. According to Ḥāfiẓ, "Men and angels all depend on the existence of Love," for this movement of desire is one of the instances of the rule "Love depends on beauty" in the world of creation. On the other hand, God's knowledge of the world is the same as His knowledge of Himself; the world is also created on the form of God and His best Names; therefore, the world is the manifestation of God, a representation in which God sees nothing other than His beauty. According to the tradition "Allah is beautiful and likes beauty," God's love of the world is a reflection of His love for His beauty. Ḥāfiẓ states:

> "Since the beginning of time the rays of your beauty manifested themselves,
> Causing love to appear and set fire to the whole world".[1]
>
> Ibn 'Arabī concludes that whosoever loves the world from this perspective indeed loves it through the divine love.

b. Mutual Dependence

The second common feature of the two concepts of creation and

1. *The Poems of Ḥāfiẓ Shīrāzī*, trans. 'Alāiddīn Pazārgādī, Ode No. 152.

manifestation is the two-side need and mutual dependence. The question which Ibn ʻArabī raises often to distinguish the station of the essence and that of Act and the manifestation of the Names and attributes is the independence of the essence from the worlds and the reliance of Act on the manifestations in the stage of the Names and attributes. This dependence, according to him, is two-sided. That is, as it was discussed in the question of the Names and permanent entities, the (creating) Real and the creatures and the Lord and the subject are mutually dependent and in need of each other. In other words, in regard of the best Divine Names, the Names and their manifestations are realized by and give meaning to each other, and in respect of the permanent entities, the entities rule over the creation of the Real and the Real dominates the entities, where the term "two-sided subjugation" explains the meaning of "the secret of destiny".

Moreover, in relation to manifestation and creation there is also a "mutual dependence", in the sense that Allah's manifestation and creation are essentially not a single phenomenon, but on the one side all existents depend on the Real in essence, which indicates their need of and reliance on the Real in their existence, and on the other hand the Real is dependent on the world as a place of His manifestation and its possibility. Ibn ʻArabī claims that "We have given Him something by which He is manifested in us, and instead He gives us existence; so, the order is divided between Him and us." The meaning of this speech, despite its strange and rough appearance, is that were it not for the world and the creatures, the attributes and Names would not have existed (meaning manifested), for the reality of the Names, as it was explained, is no other than the relations.

However, as it was mentioned in relation to "the permanent entities' subjugation of the Real," the Real always manifests Himself in His works, and awards them according to their capacity. That capacity also derives from the Names of the Real and, therefore, at the end only the Real rules over the Real. Nevertheless, no one should think the Real needs or is dependent on others, or the dependence of the Real's Names on the manifestations means they are made perfect by "others", for according to the principle of the Oneness of existence, His act is Ever-existing existence and has only relational existence, and in itself has no reality. It is sufficient because of the sufficiency of the Real (though it is insufficient by essence). So, what Ibn 'Arabī means in the above statement is no other than what the poet says:

I manifest You and You give me existence,

You may not appear without me, and without You I have no existence.

Ḥāfiẓ also states:

> "What if the shadow of the beloved fell upon the lover?
> We were in need of her, and she was eager for us".[1]
> However, there are two aspects which, according to Ibn 'Arabī, are particular to creation (rather than manifestation).

1. The Triad

In our analysis of creation we mainly speak of the Creator and the creature. The main side is the Real in the Name the Creator; however, intuitively the Real in the act of creation comprises three aspects:

1. The absolute Real, as the manifestation and the Manifest.
2. The Will, or the Real as the Willing.
3. The command or the Real as the Commander.

These three aspects reflect the entire process of creation; in other words, creation comprises the following stages:

1. *The Poems of Ḥāfiẓ Shīrāzī*, trans. 'Alāiddīn Pazārgādī, Ode No. 206.

1. The rise of knowledge in the Real and the appearance of the permanent entities, namely the determination of the Real in the plain of divinity and Oneness;

2. The determination of the Will (on the basis of knowledge) to create the entities; and

3. The turning of the divine command (on the thesis of Will) into language (the creative word "Be!"), which leads to the creation of the world.

Ibn 'Arabī believes that knowledge in the last stage (meaning command and speech) is attained only through revelation or unveiling, whereas the intellect attains knowledge and determination in the process of creation. The philosophers ultimately interpret the speech and command of God as His will. In any case, Ibn 'Arabī holds that the creation of the world depends on the mentioned triad. Here are his words in brief:

Know that the order is dependent on singleness and the triad is no other than singleness; therefore, singleness begins with the number three and three is the first single number.... And it was due to this divine plain (single in inner triad) that the world was created. " The Exalted Real states: "And Our command is no other than to say to a thing to be and there it is." So, we find the triad of the essence, the Will and the word, and everything that is created is due to 1. The essence; 2. The will, which moves the essence to create a particular thing; and 3. The word "Be", which in harmony with the will is addressed to the thing. In parallel to the mentioned triad related to the agent, there is another triad on the side of the receiver (meaning the thing to be created): 1. the essence of the thing in the world of entities, 2. hearing the word "Be!", and 3. accepting "Be" and obedience.

Ibn 'Arabī believes that at the very moment when the word of creation (Be) is uttered, "the threefold singleness appears in the (created) thing, and it is because of this threefold singleness that the creation of that thing and its existence become possible. The three folds are its thingness, its hearing, and its obedience to the command of its Creator. So, three things in the receiver stand against three things in the agent: 1. The permanent essence of that thing in its nonexistence against the creative essence (of the Real), 2. Its listening against the originating will, and 3. Its acceptance (and obedience) against the word "Be", where the thing is dressed in existence."

It is also understood from this argument that the difference between Ibn 'Arabī's theory of creation ex nihilo and that of the theologians is that for Ibn 'Arabī nonexistence is not "absolute nonexistence", but it is relative and accidental. In other words, the forms of the things were already present to the knowledge of the Real so that they could be addressed as things and objects and ordered to be. The other distinction in regard of creation is the renewal of creation, which is discussed in the following.

2. Renewal of Creation or Constant Creation

The second particular feature of creation which Ibn 'Arabī often discusses in his argument about creation is the renewal of the world. Ibn 'Arabī in "Faṣṣ of Shu'ayb" of *Fuṣūṣ al-Ḥikam* writes "The people of the unveiling see that the Exalted Allah manifests Himself in every breath and the manifestation is never repeated." Indeed the cause of subsistence is different from that of annihilation, and at every moment subsistence and annihilation rule over the world; therefore, the manifestation in the world is not repeated. In short, "the Renewal of Creation" is the order of existence (manifestation) which is repeated *ad infinitum* and at every moment is exhibited in the form of annihilation and subsistence where, accordingly, no part of the world can be experienced in the same way in two successive moments. Shabistarī writes:

"The world is this whole, and in every twinkling of an eye,
It becomes non-existent and doesn't endure two moments'."
Then over again another world is produced,
Every moment a new heaven and a new earth".[1]

***

"Things don't remain in him for two hours,
The same moment they perish, they are born again".[2]

The other point which is inferred from the argument of Ibn 'Arabī is that this constant and everlasting change occurs in such an order and follows such definite paradigms that to the shallow minded the world appears as it was, and they have no knowledge or awareness of this momentary doffing and wearing. Ibn 'Arabī states that since what is newly created is one in nature with that is already created, the veiled become confused, for every manifestation presents a new creation and annihilates that which existed, and this is more illustrated in the example of fire. About a group of people and even about most of the people of the world states: "Rather they are in doubt about a new *creation*". Mawlānā states in this regard:

"Every moment the world is renewed, and we are unaware of it being renewed whist it remains [the same in appearance].
Life is ever arriving anew, like the stream, though in the body it has the semblance of continuity".[3]

Lāhījī in his commentary on *Gulshan-e Rāz* writes:

Know that without the existing Real the possible beings by

1. *The Mystic Rose Garden,* Verses No. 644-645.
2. Ibid, Verse No. 647.
3. *Mathnawī,* Book I, Verse No. 1144-5.

essence have no existence and will remain ever nonexistent. The existence of the possible beings is indeed no other than the appearance of the Real in their form. All things also by essence perish every moment and come to exist through the breath of the Merciful, and the existence of things is the emanation from the breath of the Merciful.... However, because of the speediness of the renewal of emanation from the Merciful one does not perceive that in every breath and in every moment a possible being is annihilated and comes again to existence, for there is no interval between its nonexistence and existence to make its nonexistence apparent, but the emanation of existence is unbroken and continuous.

The guarantee of the formal unity of the manifestations and the continuity of their identity, despite the constant renewal of the states, is the permanent entities of things, which are the paradigm of the renewal of creation and the ground of the incessant manifestations of the Real.

Ibn ʻArabī believes the continuous development of man is one of the results of this truth: "One of the most astonishing things is that man is in constant development, but because of the subtlety of the veil and the similarity of the forms he is not aware of it." To put it in al-Kāshānī's words, "In every moment everything is constantly developing, for it is continuously accepting the divine existential manifestations, which continues eternally, and in every manifestation the thing finds more capacity to accept the following manifestation." In other words, the development of things is no other than the opposite direction the Real descends to meet them. Of course, having a vivid and real experience of the renewal of creation inside and outside of man is possible only through self-knowledge.

On the basis of the knowledge of the Names every moment the

divine manifestation moves in the descending arc towards the Name "the instigator" (the breath of the Merciful or inhalation) and returns in the ascending arc towards the Name "the Inheritor" (exhalation). Mawlānā writes:

> "The form came forth from Formlessness and went
> back [thither], for '*verily unto Him are we returning*'.
> Every instant, then, thou art dying and returning:
> Muṣṭafā declared that this world is [but] a moment".[1]

Accordingly, existence has an exterior and an interior, which result from the depth of the Real's providence. The order of the world of creation is that an exterior is manifested in the seen world (creation) from the interior of the Real, and then once again it returns to hide in the unseen and the interior (return and resurrection). This corresponds with the meaning of the holy verse 'Indeed we belong to Allah, and to Him do we indeed return'(2:156) in a sense it is the question of manifestation and hiddenness, rather than creation and annihilation.

On the basis of the above argument, we may clearly see the difference between Ibn 'Arabī's theory of renewal of creation and other similar theories, such as 1. the renewal of the similar (the Asharites), 2. the flux of the world (Hisbanities), and 3. the substantial movement (Transcendental philosophy). Ibn 'Arabī himself discusses and critiques the first two theories. He states: although these two groups have to some extent understood this important theory (change in every moment), each of them has gone wrong in one point or another. The Asharites, for example, believe in the renewal of the similar in accidents and the impermanence of the accidents for even two successive moments; nevertheless, they do not know that considered deeply, the whole world is an attribute, accident or aspect of the real

1. *Mathnawī*, Book I, Verse No. 1141-2.

substance—the exalted Real—and the Ever-expanding emanation and His face. Therefore, they have not understood the renewal of creation in the entire world. In other words, they don't know that the entire world is the sum of the accidents that are changing, and these accidents are no other than the many manifestations of the Real. For Ibn 'Arabī the substance is the independent existent that manifests the essence of the Exalted Real (the Ever-expanding existence) in contradistinction to the accident which is dependent and manifests the attributes of the Exalted Real (the world and all that is other than God). In other words, everything is an accidental form of the Real which is not self-dependent, and all things are accidents that appear and disappear in one eternal and everlasting substance.

On the other hand, although the Hisbanites or the Sophists believe in the instability and mutability of the entire world and the momentary annihilation of the whole universe holding that nothing is permanent or real, nevertheless they are unaware of the unity behind the alterations and the changing forms. They do not know that behind these changes, there is an intelligible substance and an absolute Reality that accepts these forms (the Face of Allah and the Ever-expanding existence). Finally, the main difference between Ibn 'Arabī's renewal of creation and the substantial movement of Mullā Ṣadrā is that the subject of the renewal of creation and the renewal of the similar in mysticism is the relational existence (other than God), whether it is material or immaterial, whereas the subject of the substantial movement is the world of bodies and matter. In other words, the substantial movement describes the material world, but the renewal of creation explains all the levels of the world of existence.

Accordingly, for the mystics the creation of the world is not an event that occurred once and after that the world is in the state of subsistence, but rather on the basis of the infinite divine bounty and grace, it has a new creation every moment. They maintain that the meaning of the holy verse 'Every day He is engaged in some work'(55:29),[1] corresponds with this view and vision. Shabistarī states:

"Continually the overflowing bounty of 'The Truth'
Is being revealed in His continual working.
On this side the world is renewed and perfected,
On that side it is annihilated every moment".[2]

The Features of the World in the Mystical Cosmology

In the mystical view the world has certain features which indicate its absolute dependence on the Exalted Real and also explain the oneness of existence, such as:

1. It is a sign and a mirror. The world is the mirror that reflects the Real, and as a mirror naturally reflects the other, there is no perfection in the world unless it reflects the perfection of the Real. As it was mentioned, since it is impossible for other than the Real to know Him while free of any determination, and philosophically the effect is the incomplete definition of the cause, that every existent being which is one of the determinations of the Real indicates the divine perfection according to its capacity and might. As Shabistarī states:

"Know the world is a mirror from head to foot,
In every atom are a hundred blazing suns.
If you cleave the heart of one drop of water,
A hundred pure oceans emerge from it".[3]

The people of mystical wayfaring at the beginning see the Real in

---

1. 

2. *The Mystic Rose Garden*, Verse No. 673-674.

3. Ibid,Verses No. 145 - 146.

the mirror of the creatures and along with the creatures and through their veil, but as in other arguments—where in the school of Ibn 'Arabī a comparison is made among the three views, namely the views of the people of separation, unity, and unity of unity—the perfect view is attributed to the people of unity of unity who don't only see the possible beings as mirrors reflecting the beauty of the Real in different ways, but also see the Exalted Real as the mirror of the images of the possible beings (as in philosophy the complete cause is understood to be the complete definition of the effect). Thus true cosmology or knowledge of the world is possible only in the light of theology or knowledge of God. This supplementary argument (the Real as the mirror of the world) in the mysticism of Ibn 'Arabī along with the first argument in sum presents the principle of "the two-sided mirroring". Ibn 'Arabī in his discussion of the tradition "The believer is the mirror of the believer" in his works deals with this issue. This mirroring is sometimes called "the book" and knowledge is considered as the Real's genetic book written by the high Pen.

"To him, whose soul attains the beatific vision,
The universe is the book of 'The Most High Truth'.
Accidents are its vowels, and substance its consonants,
And grades of creatures its verses and pauses".[1]

2. The Best Order of the World. Ibn 'Arabī believes if the whole world is the shadow of Allah and the manifestation of the Real's Names, and if each of the Real's Names is the best Name and all are among the best divine Names, the order of the world should also be the best order. The mystics first intuitively and second on the basis of the mentioned a priori argument claim the order of the world is the best order and evil has no place in it. In the "Faṣṣ of Job" Ibn 'Arabī writes: "If the Exalted Real is the identity or essence

1. Ibid,Verses No. 201- 202.

of the world (on the basis of manifestation), the precepts and attributes of the world also belong to Him; therefore, there can be no world better or more beautiful than this world, for it is created in the form of the Merciful; it is the shadow of the order of the Real's Names and it is created by the breath of the Merciful." The mystics stress that all parts of the world are created on the basis of benevolence, virtue and beauty, and according to the holy tradition "Allah is beautiful and likes beauty" the beauty of the order of the world derives from the beauty of the Real. Shabistarī states:

"Know that God has created it,
And whatever comes from the Good is good".[1]
"Whatsoever is seen in this visible world,
Is as a reflection from the sun of that world.
The world is as a eye, curl, mole and brow,
For everything in its own place is beautiful".[2]
"If you take one atom link from its place
The entire universe falls to ruin".[3]

If to some, however, there seems to be deficiency, imperfection or something against the good or human interests in the world, indeed all that deficiency and imperfection will return to their eye rather than the world. As Ḥāfiẓ says:

"The eye of the polluted sight is far away from the beloved's face;
So, cast a chased glance at her face from a clean mirror".[4]

****

"Our *pir* (elder) said that no error was made by the pen of creation;

1. Ibid,Verse No. 870.
2. Ibid,Verses No. 719-720.
3. Ibid,Verse No. 159.
4. *The Poems of Ḥāfiẓ Shīrāzī*, trans. 'Alāiddīn Pazārgādī, Ode No. 264.

May many praises be given to his clean and error-covering vision".[1]

Of course, to change such an eye that sees diversity, appearances and the particulars into a pure eye that reveals the beauty of the world.

"I never had a care for the affairs of the world;
For, your visage adorned my world so elegantly".[2]

3. The Flow of Life and the General Consciousness. For the mystic the world and all its parts, the minerals, the plants, animals, etc. are sentient and conscious. This truth in the first place is understood intuitively. The divine verses also indicate that all things are praising and glorifying God. Ibn 'Arabī states that besides believing the true narrations we have understood this through unveiling and have heard the stones in their remembrance of God.

"The speech of water, the speech of earth, and the speech of mud are apprehended by the senses of them that have hearts [the mystics]".[3]

"All the atoms of the world, like Manṣūr,
You can take to be drunken and heavy with wine;
Continually are they singing this song of praise,
Continually dwelling on this mystic verity.
If you desire that its meaning may be clear to you,
Then read the text, 'All praise Allah'.[4]

The existential explanation of this point is founded on the oneness of existence and the divine permeation in the whole world, that is, the flow of existence (Ever-expanding existence), the manifestation of the Real and the parts of the manifestations along with the flux of its attributes of perfection. In other words, a subtle spirit of life, perception, love and other perfections of existence permeate all

---

1. Ibid, Ode No. 105.
2. *The Poems of Ḥāfiẓ Shīrāzī*, Trans. 'Alāiddīn Pazārgādī, Ode No. 22.
3. *Mathnawī*, Book I, Verse No. 3279.
4. *The Mystic Rose Garden*, Verses No. 438- 440.

parts of the world, following the flux of the Ever-expanding existence and the breath of the Merciful, and have appeared somehow in every manifestation and level. To explain further, to say that the Real encompasses the beings is like saying the divine life permeates the entire world of existence and embraces it. In short, the pulse of the whole world is beating with the everlasting life, but this beating is not recognized by most people. For them only a small part of the world is alive, that is, the existential and visible aspects of the breath of the Merciful can be easily seen by every person, but the living aspect is not perceived easily by all, and it must be seen intuitively. Ibn 'Arabī states: "There is nothing in this world unless it is alive, but this is hidden from many people in this world and will be known to all in the hereafter, for the other world is the abode of life."

The Order of the World and the Levels of Manifestation

The Planes and Levels

In the school of Ibn 'Arabī the manifestation of the breath of the Merciful, which rises from the oneness of the Real, leads to the appearance of the degrees of manifestation and the order of the world's representation.[1] The term "five planes" or "five presences" refers to certain levels of the determination of the absolute existence, two of those planes or levels—the determinations of uniqueness and oneness (the divine kingdom) which were discussed already—relate to the divine world and the rest to the world of the other than God and objects phenomena, which are:

1. The World of Almightiness (*Jabarūt*): the manifestation of divine

1. Asharites states:

"When the *Kaf* of His power breathed on the pen,
It cast thousands of pictures on the page of the not-being.
From that breath the two worlds were produced,
From that breath the soul of Adam was preceded." (*The Mystic Rose Garden*, Verses No. 4-5.).

realities and Names of transcendence in the form of immaterial and simple beings which are called (in the language of philosophy) intelligences. This plane and level (in mysticism) also includes the rational and spherical souls (in the terminology of the theosophists).

2. The World of Dominion (*Malakūt*): the manifestation of the divine Names and realities in the form of subtle immaterial beings with some material features and attributes like shape but indivisible, which is also called (in the terminology of the theosophists) the discontinuous imagination (or the macrocosmic world of imagination).

3. The World of Bodies (*Nāsūt*): which is the lowest level of manifestation and pertains to compound things that have dimensions and are divisible.

These planes and levels make one homogeneous whole, that is, things that are in a lower plane and level are forms and images of things in a higher plane. Whatsoever is in the seen world is an image of the things in the world of imagination, and all that is in the world of the intellect is an intangible reality (*raqīqa*) that reflects a certain state of the affairs of the plane of the divine Names and attributes (Divinity). However, passing through each level and observing higher levels makes the mystical "unveiling" necessary. To sum up, the hierarchical order of the world of phenomena comprises at least four planes or levels:

1. The unmanifested God: the divine essence and the infinite Being, Who is beyond our description and perception. He is the subject of negative theology (Oneness).

2. The manifested God: those aspects of Divinity that we can perceive by our mind. He is the subject of positive theology (Uniqueness).

3. The insensible aspects of the phenomena (for man): all that is other than Allah or that part of the world of creation that is unperceived by the outward senses (the hidden worlds) like the intellect and the soul.

4. The sensible aspects of the phenomena (for man): the world of the body and certain aspects of the world of creation, which are perceived by man's outward senses (the visible world), such as nature and its qualities.

The other point is that the mystics and Ibn ʻArabī himself in their description of the order of manifestation speak of different worlds and various stages, such as Cloud (*amāʾ*), Dust (*habāʾ*), the High Pen, the Throne, Mother of the Book, the Preserved Tablet, the Isthmus, the High Element, etc. Some of these correspond with the mentioned stages, some result from seeing some of the worlds divided or overlapping, and some indicate a particular world known only intuitively or through unveiling. However, here we do not intend to discuss all the views discussed in the school of Ibn ʻArabī.

The holy emanation (the creating Real and the Intellect, the high Pen, etc.) is the revelation of the breath of the Merciful and the first—and also the last—manifestation of the Real in the world of Act, for that unity is real (the real shadowy unity) and its first has no second, as in regard of the Real the most holy emanation is also the hidden aspect of the breath of the Merciful (see the diagram). Moreover, the Ever-expanding existence is like a tablet that from each part and side of it certain determinations and essences are extracted, and the five planes and other stages mentioned before are the result of a plurality-oriented view of this one Ever-expanding existence.

The mystics divide this order of manifestation into the hidden and the seen or the interior and exterior, though in a sense each part or stage is the manifestation of the previous stage and the origin and source of the following stage and it's interior. But according to one division the two planes of uniqueness and oneness are related to the unseen world or the divine world, and other worlds are related to the visible world. There is also an intermediate world between those two worlds by the name of the

Perfect Man that will be discussed in the next chapter. Ibn 'Arabī argues that "Existence is one (the Exalted Real) and it has an exterior, which is "the world", and an interior, which is "the Names". It has also a comprehensive intermediate state, which is the link between the two and is "the Perfect Man"."

Moreover, the phenomenal order of the world is divided into two descending and ascending arcs. The former indicates the movement from unity to diversity and comprises the five planes through which the Real leaves His absolute and imperceptible identity for the lower worlds (without any injury or decrease). On the other hand, according to the same degrees and worlds, the completion and development of the defective phenomena and their movement from diversity to unity occurs in the ascending arc. Thus it is said, "The ends are turning back to the beginnings). Shabistarī writes:

"Again he may be likened to a pair of compasses,
Ending in the same impression whence they began".[1]
"Verily they ask, saying, what is the end,
And the answer is the return to the beginning".[2]

Mawlānā also in regard of these two arcs and the descending movement to diversity and ascending and turning back to unity writes:

"We were simple and all one substance; we were all without head and without foot yonder.
We were one substance, like the sun; we were knotless and pure, like water.
When that goodly Light took form, it became [many in] number like the shadows of a battlement.
Rase ye the battlement with the mangonel [*manjanīq*], that difference may vanish from amidst this company

1. *The Mystic Rose Garden*, Verse No. 365.
2. Ibid,Verse No. 368.

[of shadows]."[1]

Moreover, the phenomenal order in the mystical view can be divided into two ways:

1. According to the distance from the world of unity

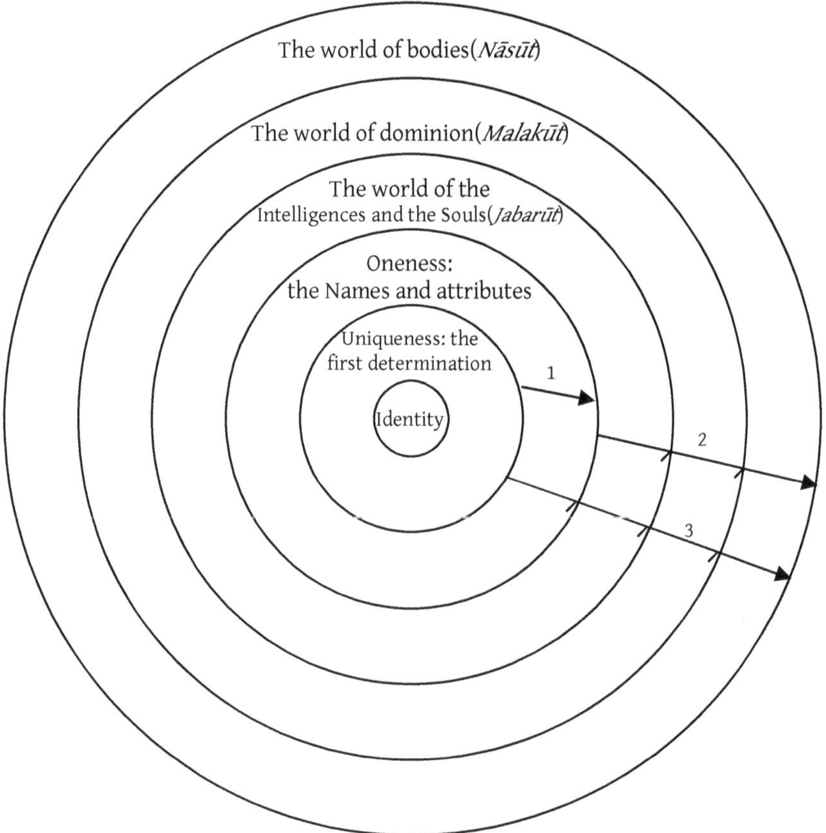

The meaning of the signs (the flashes)

1. The most holy emanation (manifestation)
2. The holy emanation (manifestation)
3. The breath of the Merciful

---

1. *Mathnawī*, Book I, Verse No. 686 – 9.

2. According to the descending and ascending arcs

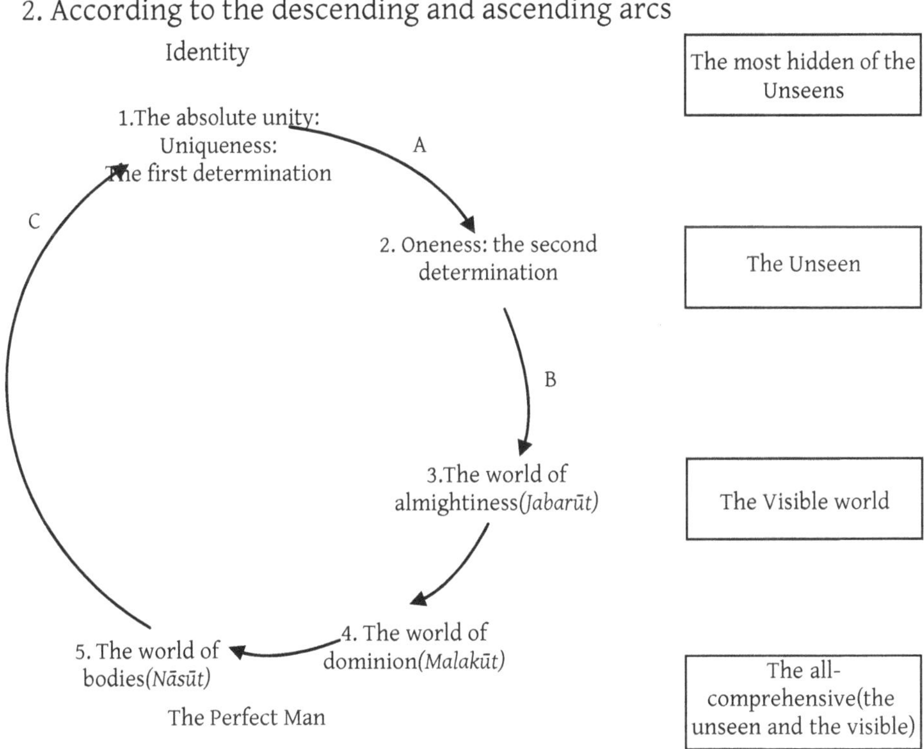

The meaning of the arcs and the stages in the diagram:

1. The descending arc: arcs A and B comprising stages 2-5
2. The ascending arc: arc C reversing the mentioned stages

Resurrection and the Return of the World

Since the world belongs to Him and is ever turning to Him it has the tendency to return to its Origin. Creation and resurrection in theoretical mysticism refer to the two descending and ascending arcs, which are so interdependent that the last point of the ascending arc touches the first point of the descending one to make the circle of existence complete.[1] Indeed in mysticism the

1. "Aḥmad is twice-born in this world: he was manifestly a hundred resurrections." *Mathnawī*, Book VI, Verse No. 751.

axis of resurrection is not man only but the whole world. Sayyid Ḥaydar Āmulī writes: for the people of the religious dogmas resurrection is the return of the soul to the disintegrated parts of the dead body once those parts are recomposed. For the people of mystical orders resurrection is the return of manifestations of some Names to the manifestations of other Names. But for the people of truth, resurrection is annihilation in the unity of acts, attributes and essence, and subsistence through the Real and turning to Him in all issues. Shabistarī writes:

> "The worlds of command and of creatures proceed from one breath,
> And the moment they come forth they go away again".[1]
> "Things revert to their proper original,
> All are one, both the visible and the invisible".[2]

Of course, the distinctive feature of man's turning back is the manifestation of the human deeds on the day of resurrection and, in other words, the display of humans' interior following the display of the interior of the world.

The mystic's interpretation of the journey of the world and man to the Day of Judgment and after is not one of annihilation and

←

"Do thou, then, become the [spiritual] resurrection and [thereby] see [experience] the resurrection: this [becoming] is the necessary condition for seeing [knowing and experiencing the real nature of] anything." *Mathnawī*, Book VI, Verse No. 756.

"They asked him [Muḥammad] concerning the Resurrection, saying, 'O [thou who art the] Resurrection, how long is the way to the Resurrection?" *Mathnawī*, Book VI, Verse No. 752.

"O beloved, if anyone says, 'Where is the Resurrection?' show thyself, saying, 'Behold, I am the Resurrection'." *Mathnawī*, Book IV, Verse No. 1480.

1. *The Mystic Rose Garden*, Verse No. 10.
2. Ibid,Verse No. 12.

creation but manifestation and hiding. Ibn 'Arabī in this regard maintains, "The rule of the world is to take back rather than annihilating or destruction. Death is also taking back. Allah says, 'If it be His will, He takes you back,' but He did not say, 'He promises you', for that which is said to exist is the Exalted Real Who appears in these manifestations, and nonexistence has absolutely no place in Him."

Essentially the Day of Judgment is not the end of the Real's manifestations, but it is the manifestation of the Real in a different way and in other Names. That is, the manifestation of the Real in the hereafter is in the Names of the Inward, the Dominant and the Restorer and in this world it is in the Name of the Manifest, the Originator, and the Creator. But on the basis of the rule "All the Names are in all" and that everything can be considered as a manifestation of all the Names of Beauty and Majesty (though the appearance of one Name in a particular phenomenon may be more dominant and eminent), resurrection is not an event that did not exist before, but indeed the other world is the inward of this world. This world and the other world coexist in the divine manifestation and correspond in the descending and ascending arcs. Accordingly, resurrection is something relative, that is, for most people it has not happened yet, but for God and the people of divine vision it coexists with this world, for the final revelation of the Real and His manifestation in the Name of the Subduer is permanent and this world and the world of dominion belong to Him forever. Nevertheless, this is not understood by the veiled people who could not go beyond the appearance of the world and have no perception of its inward. Allah states: 'They know just an outward aspect of the life of the world, but they are oblivious of the Hereafter'.[1] (30:7)

1. 'يَعْلَمُونَ ظَاهِرًا مِّنَ الْحَيَاةِ الدُّنْيَا وَهُمْ عَنِ الْآخِرَةِ هُمْ غَافِلُونَ.'

Of course, on the Day of Judgment the manifestation of the Real would be much clearer to all compared to His manifestation in this world, and thus in the holy Qur'an this day is called the Day of the Real, and the like. On this Day the Ownership and Lordship of God, the termination of the causes and the falseness of things would be displayed to all, including believers and disbelievers.

The other point to be mentioned is that according to the theory of Renewal of Creation and in the course of creation some of the inward aspects of the Real are manifested in the visible world (the creatures), but once again they lapse into the hidden and the inward and become Unseen (return). Indeed by the world's identity, which is derived from Him and is turning to Him, this manifestation and annihilation is intended; every person in every moment has a manifestation and in the following moment he is hidden, and thus he is in constant manifestation and hiddenness.

The final remark is that as the creation of the world begins with love and a movement of desire, the return of the world is also based on love and such a movement of desire in two directions: the love of the Real of His manifestations and their return to Him, and the love of the phenomena to reach absolute perfection and the ultimate goal (the essence of the Real). The entire world indeed is in search of elevation and ever demands an abode of permanence and since this search is endless and there is no termination in the divine aid, the other world and movement in it is eternal and everlasting. Mawlānā says,

> "All particles [of the phenomenal being], [whether] in movement [or] at rest, are speakers [and declare]: '*Verily, to Him we are returning*'".[1]
>
> "The returning one is he that comes back to his

1. *Mathnawī*, Book III, Verse No. 464.

[native] city, and [by fleeing] from the revolution of Time approaches the Unity".[1]

The Divisions of the Day of Judgment

The mystics on the basis of their intuition and also some verses and traditions related to the degrees, levels and stages of resurrection divide the different kinds of return to the Origin, which occur in the worlds of existence. In what follows one of these divisions, namely the comprehensive division of Sayyid Ḥaydar Āmulī, is discussed. In his treatise *Aṣrār al-Sharīʿa, Aṭwār al-Ṭarīqa wa Anwār al-Ḥaqīqa* ("The Secrets of the Religious Law, the Modes of the Mystical Order, and the Lights of the Truth") he divides resurrection into the two kinds: formal and spiritual resurrection. The former (the formal) indicates the general change that occurs in the external world and the visible worlds. The latter relates either to the change which happens in the unseen world, which he calls the spiritual horizontal resurrection, or the change resulting from the development of the wayfarer's soul and occurs inside him, which he calls spiritual resurrection.

The last kind is divided in turn into two kinds: 1. The spiritual resurrection of the people of the mystical order, which shows the journey through the stages and stations of the human soul from awakening to annihilation, and also death to each station and life in a higher station. 2. The spiritual resurrection of the people of truth, which indicates the mystic's journey through annihilation in act, attribute and essence to the three stages of subsistence, which are called the paradise of act, the paradise of attributes and the paradise of essence, to finally attain the vision of the unity of the chosen people, namely the oneness of existence, and know that in the world of existence there is nothing other than the

1. *Mathnawī*, Book I, Verse No. 3936.

existence of the Real and His Names, attributes and acts.

The mystics call this very general revelation "the great resurrection" and its two preceding stages the small resurrection and the middle resurrection. The following diagram shows the points discussed so far in brief:

Resurrection:

1. Spiritual
    - a. Inward or internal
        - i. For the people of the mystical order
        - ii. For the people of truth
    - b. Outward or external
2. Formal

Questions

1. Discuss the identity of the world from the mystic's viewpoint.
2. Explain how in mysticism the view of the world and that of the soul are incorporated in the one principle of the view of God.
3. Explain the symbolic function of shadow, light, imagination and mirror in relation to the world.
4. Compare and contrast the two concepts of manifestation and creation in the school of Ibn 'Arabī.
5. Explain divine love and purpose and the mutual dependence as the two aspects shared by manifestation and creation.
6. Explain in view of the visible world how many aspects the Real has in the act of creation.
7. Ibn 'Arabī believes the creation of the world is based on a triad. Explain.
8. According to Ibn 'Arabī, "the constant development of man" is dependent on which truth? Explain.
9. Discuss the theory of the Asharite's renewal of the similar and the Hisbanite's flux of the world on the basis of Ibn 'Arabī's view.

10. Explain the levels of the almightiness, dominion and humanity in the school of Ibn ʻArabī and discuss their relationship.
11. Explain the levels of the order of manifestation and the world of the phenomena.
12. Compare and contrast the most holy emanation and the holy emanation in the mystical view.
13. Explain the phenomenal order in the mystical view.
14. Discuss the phenomenal order of the world in view of the two descending and ascending arcs.
15. Discuss Ibn ʻArabī's interpretation of the course of the world and man until resurrection (the question of resurrection).
16. The creation and the return of the world in mysticism are based on the movement of desire. Explain.
17. Explain the divisions of resurrection according to Sayyid Ḥaydar Āmulī.
18. Compare and contrast the views of the people of the mystical order and the people of truth on the spiritual resurrection.

Chapter Five: Man in Theoretical Mysticism

In theoretical mysticism man has a special position among the creatures of the world. The mystics believe all the worlds mentioned in the five planes exists in sum in man and accordingly the perfect man (the proclaimer of God's unity) along with the question of the oneness of existence (unity) is thought to be one of the two essential principles of theoretical mysticism. In mysticism the knowledge of man as the knowledge of the soul is an introduction to "the knowledge of God", and according to the degree of people's knowledge of the soul they have different degrees of the divine knowledge.[1]

In the mysticism of Ibn 'Arabī man is studied on two levels: 1. On a constitutional level, 2. On an individual level. We discuss the terms of each in the following.

The Constitutional (Existential) Domain of Man

In this domain man is considered as "the perfect man" and "typical man" who is the most perfect manifestation of existence

---

1. Shabistarī says,
   "You are the reflection of 'The Adored of angels',
   For this cause are you worshipped by angels" (*The Mystic Rose Garden*, Verse No. 278).

who is created in the image of God. He is that little world which is the soul of the greater world; he is the comprehensive universe, the comprehensive isthmus [intermediate state], the most perfect of the Real's manifestations, the primary purpose of creation to whom the angels prostrated. This reality appears in the form of men in the world of human nature and the visible world.

Ibn 'Arabī explains the position of man (the perfect man) in the world of existence, his existential necessity, and his relation with the Real and the world of creation on the basis of the two essential theories of "manifestation" and "the knowledge of the Names". As it was discussed before, first every Name among the divine Names demands a manifestation, and each existent in the world is one of the manifestations of the Real. Moreover, the secret of the creation of the world is God's desire to be manifested and to display His essence in the form of the Names and attributes and to see His beauty and perfection in the mirror of others. Second, one of the divine Names is "the greatest Name", meaning "Allah and the Merciful", which embraces all the attributes of the Real; evidently the manifestation of this Name possesses the perfections of all other manifestations. The existence of such a manifestation becomes necessary as a mirror that manifests most accurately the perfections and attributes of the divine beauty and grandeur and an indication of all the best divine Names. The true instance of this meaning is "the perfect man" rather than other beings, which individually represent only a part of the Real's perfections.

About the perfect Man Ibn 'Arabī explains that a subject may have two kinds of vision, for it would be different to see oneself directly and to see oneself reflected in something else acting like a mirror. The Exalted Real from eternity sees and is aware of Himself, but He has another aspect, namely an essence with attributes, and since the attributes are realized only in external manifestation, the Real must see Himself in the mirror of "others". Of course, the first thing which seems to be able to represent the Real is the universe (the greater world). In other words, when the Real intended to see the reality of His Names in an all-inclusive universe that encompasses the entire order, He created the world to see His attributes reflected in the mirror of its phenomena. So, the world reflects directly the existence of the Real and unveils His secret and the hidden treasure.

However, the distinctive feature of the greater world is that each of its existents represents a particular aspect and only one or a few of God's attributes. So, the world is like a group of scattered points or like an unpolished or opaque mirror. God, therefore, created another phenomenon that like a transparent and polished mirror reflects everything as it is, that is, it reflects all the Names and attributes in a comprehensive way, so that all the dispersed things are focused in one point. This mirror is man who reflects the whole structure of the world delicately and clearly. Thus, while existents and even the angels manifest and have the capacity to reflect only some of the Names, man is the manifestation of all the Names and the greatest divine Name, and therefore he is the teacher of the angels.[1] Of course, the greatest divine Name (Allah) has three manifestations, only one of them has the absolute comprehensiveness and perfection. These three

---

1. Shabistarī says,

"Though the angels stand hard by the throne,
They don't reach the station 'I am with God'." (*The Mystic Rose Garden*, Verse No. 120)

Mawlānā in a comparison between the Prophet(S) and Gabriel says,

"If Aḥmad should display that glorious pinion [his spiritual nature], Gabriel would remain dumbfounded unto everlasting." *Mathnawī*, Book IV, Verse No. 3800.

manifestations are: 1. The world in sum in which each existent and manifestation reflects individually and in detail one of the aspects of the divine perfections, 2. The Ever-expanding existence (the breath of the Merciful) or the first manifestation, which in general and in brief comprises all the forms of the world and the perfections of the best divine Names, and 3. The perfect man who both generally and in detail represents the perfections of the Real's essence, for he is present in the descending and ascending arcs and possesses all the mentioned perfections. In short, the simultaneous detailed and general vision of the Real as unity in diversity and diversity in unity (in the perfect man) is different from the vision of the Real as pure unity in general (in the extended existence) or as pure diversity in detail (in the world). Rūmī describes this aspect of man's position as follows:

"Adam is the astrolabe of the attributes of [Divine] sublimity: the nature of Adam is the theatre for His revelations".[1]

"Since in eternity it was the will and decree of God, the Forgiver, to reveal and manifest Himself...

Therefore He made a viceroy, one having a heart, to the end that he might be a mirror for His sovereignty".[2]

The mystics believe the reason the angels prostrated to Adam and his knowledge of the divine Names is that man according to his capacity and ability reflects all the Names, and thus he is called the little world (though in meaning he is thought to be the greater world). Shabistarī writes:

"Hence you learn all the names of God,
For that you are an image reflected from 'The Named'".[3]

---

1. *Mathnawī*, Book VI, Verse No. 3138.
2. Ibid, Verse No. 2151 and 2153.
3. *The Mystic Rose Garden*, Verse No. 293.

"You are the Hearing, Seeing, Living, Speaking,
Yet you don't endure for yourself but for Him!"[1]
"Of everything in the world above or below
An exemplar is set forth in your soul and body".[2]

In his explanation of this point Mullā Ḥusayn Kāshifī writes in his book *Lubb-e Lubāb-e Mathnawī* ("The quintessence of *Mathnawī*"):

Know that man is the manifestation of the beams of the keys of the Unseen in the highest levels of manifestation, for wherever the Names the hearing, the seeing, the speaking and the powerful, which are called the keys of the unseen, appear, except in the ear, the eye, the tongue and the hand, as understood from the tradition "I would be his ear and eye, etc." would be figurative. No doubt the plane of perfection, which embraces the two planes of grandeur and beauty, is this intermediate state that is both general and detailed and the rank of the grand vicegerency is found only in this eminent kind. Man in regard of form is the last and in respect of meaning is the first, for according to the tradition "I liked to be known," the purpose of the creation of the world is the perfection of the manifestation, and the perfection of the manifestation is dependent on both the general or detailed manifestation of the reality of the unity of the essence, and the manifestation of that very united reality is no other than the elemental form of man. Thus, the accepted proposition "The beginning of thought ends in action" relates to him. It is said:

First is thought and action is last,
So do not deceive yourself.

All that exists in detail in the world is implied in general in the creation of man. So man is the general little world and the world is

1. Ibid,Verse No. 295.
2. Ibid,Verse No. 652.

the detailed great man insofar as the form is concerned. In respect of the rank, however, man is the greater world and the world is the little man, for he is the vicegerent and the vicegerent is higher than the subjects. The Commander of the Faithful (A.S.) says:

Do you think you are a little body
While you embrace the greater world?[1]

In what follows we discuss those features of the perfect Man that make him deserve the vicegerency of God.

The Features of Man

1. Comprehensiveness. The perfect Man's comprehensiveness, which gave him such titles as the comprehensive isthmus and the conclusive word, can be discussed in a few respects:

a. In respect of the Names: Except for man, all other phenomena are the manifestations of a particular Name or attribute of the Names of beauty and grandeur. Man, however, who according to the tradition is created "in the image of the Merciful," is the mirror of all the divine attributes and the manifestation of the moderation of divine beauty and majesty. This is also Ibn 'Arabī's interpretation of 'He created him by the two hands' (38:75), which discusses the creation of man by the two hands of God.

b. In respect of the levels of the world: Man is called the little world because he possesses all the features and dimensions of the creations before and after him, that is, he retains the dimensions of the mineral, vegetable, animal, imaginal and also the rational worlds.

In the language of the mystics the term "the seven subtle substances", as it will be discussed, means man potentially or actually possesses all the features of the worlds and divine manifestations and the seen and the unseen, especially that he

1. Mullā Ḥusayn Kāshifī, *Lubb-e Lubāb-e Mathnawī*, 361 and 366.

manifests these features and the two essential dimensions, meaning the body and soul, "moderately". In Ibn 'Arabī's viewpoint all the determinations of the world of being and the levels of the manifestations in the world can be understood and explained with reference to the two terms "manifestation and hiddenness" or union (the whole or unity) and separation (details). Man is the union, the sum and the inward of other worlds. Shabistarī writes:

"Of everything in the world above or below
An exemplar is set forth in your soul and body."[1]
"You are that plurality which becomes the very Unity
You are that Unity which becomes the very plurality".[2]
"You your Self is a copy made in the image of God,
Seek in your Self all that you desire to know".[3]

c. In respect of activity and passiveness: the perfect Man is both acting and lording over the world and passive (serving) in relation to the Real. In short, as Ibn 'Arabī's explains in the first Faṣṣ of *Fuṣūṣ al-Ḥikam* ("the Faṣṣ of Adam") about the attributes of Adam as "comprehensive existence" or "the microcosmic being", man is the soul of the world, the polish of the mirror of the universe, the form of the world and the pupil of its eye, and possess the station of union in three respects, which explain the existence and subsistence of the manifestations.

1. In respect of divine eminence (the plane of oneness),
2. In respect of the reality of realities, and
3. In respect of the demands of the universal nature.

This point in fact is the ground of one of the important rules in

1. *The Mystic Rose Garden*, Verse No. 652.
2. Ibid,Verse No. 322.
3. Ibid,Verse No. 435.

the school of Ibn 'Arabī in relation to the knowledge of the Real, which Jāmī explains: "You know nothing about Allah the Exalted unless through comparison with something in yourself." This correlation of the knowledge of the self and the knowledge of God that is rooted in the holy tradition "Whosoever knows himself knows his God" is discussed in the discourse of Rūmī:

Man is the Astrolabe of the Real but an astronomer is needed to know the Astrolabe.... Astrolabe is useful only for an astronomer. In the Astrolabe of his existence he witnesses the manifestation of the Real and the absolute beauty moment by moment and in every glimpse, and that beauty is never out of this mirror.

The mystics of the school of Ibn 'Arabī in other different places also refer to the unity of manifestation and hiddenness, the inward and the visible, creation and eternality, etc. in man.

2. Mediation. As it was discussed, the best divine Names essentially demand the existence of the world. Indeed by teaching Adam the Names it means each of the Names has a subtle substance in Adam's nature and disposition, so that with this treasure he becomes ready to realize all the Names of beauty and grandeur. Thus with the reality of the perfect Man the first existential determination emerges and the door for the manifestation of the other worlds is opened. Man mediates between the Real and the creatures in two ways:

a. Mediating the emanation of existence. Considering his existential position in the phenomenal order man enjoys a place between the active divine reality and the passive reality of the world. In other words, he mediates the emanation and is the creating Real. He is both a creature and the Real, that is, in respect of his sovereignty over to the creatures and his divine attributes he is the Real, and in respect of manifesting the Real he is the servant. He is higher in rank and degree than the possible being and the creatures. So, he is the intermediate state between Necessity and possibility and it is through him that the existential assistance and emanation from the Real, which is the cause of the subsistence of the universe, reaches the world. As Jīlī in *al-Insān al-Kāmil* ("The Perfect Man") states, the perfect Man witnesses all the diverse issues in his essence, for all existents, high and low, are emanated from him. Thus Ibn 'Arabī argues that when the perfect Man leaves the world, the order is transferred to the other world and this world becomes empty of perfections. Mawlānā also maintains:

> "Therefore he is the heart of the world, because by means of this heart the body attains to [its proper] art [function]".[1]
>
> "Therefore the theatre of the [Divine] rays is that iron; therefore the theatre of God is the heart, not the body".[2]

b. Mediating the giving of knowledge and Perfection. It is through the perfect Man that the Real looks at His creatures (and cares for them) and has mercy on them. So, as Ibn 'Arabī states, man is called *insān* (pupil in Arabic) for he is the pupil of the eye of the Real. Shabistarī writes:

> "Not-being is the mirror, the world the reflection, and man,
> Is as the reflected eye of the unseen Person.
> You are that reflected eye, and He the light of the eye,
> In that eye His eye sees His own eye.
> The world is a man and man is a world:
> There is no clearer explanation than this".[3]

In short, it is through man that the divine secrets and true knowledge become manifest, the first and the last are joined, and the levels of the inward and outward worlds become complete.

1. *Mathnawī*, Book II, Verse No. 836.
2. Ibid, Verse No. 838.
3. *The Mystic Rose Garden*, Verses No. 140 – 142.

3. Vicegerency and Authority. The union of man reflects the divine unity, and as the greatest divine Name includes all the other Names and modifies the demands of the Names of beauty and grandeur and in consequence influences them, the manifestation of the greatest divine Name is the vicegerent of Allah that must possess the attributes of the One he represents. By nature and qualified by divine power, this godly vicegerent can exercise his authority in the world and through him God protects his creatures. He influences the world through the divine Names, which God has taught and trusted to him. In other words, as the soul protects the body and gives life and grace to it, the perfect Man gives meaning and is the virtue of the world. Of this Shabistarī writes:

"Therefore they are all the subject to your dominion,
For that the soul of each one is hidden in you,
You are the kernel of the world in the midst thereof,
Know yourself that you are the world's soul".[1]

4. Teleology or Purposefulness. On the basis of the rule "Thought is first and last is action," every agent acts for a certain purpose; the world is also created for the emergence and manifestation of the "perfect Man". The mystics hold the tradition "Were it not for you, I would not have created the spheres" means that the appearance of man, who is the soul and perfection of the world of creation,[2] is the final purpose of the creation of other existents. Shabistarī states:

---

1. *The Mystic Rose Garden*, Verses No. 280-281.
2. In this regard Mawlānā says,
   "The thought [idea], which is first, comes last into actuality, in particular it is the thought that is eternal." Mathnawī, Book IV, Verse No. 530.
   "Although the fruit comes last into being, it is the first, because it was the object." Mathnawī, Book III, Verse No. 1129.
   "Therefore in reality the Father [Adam] was born from me, therefore in reality the tree was born from the fruit." Mathnawī, Book IV, Verse No. 529.

"The last that was made was the soul of Adam,
The two worlds were a means to his production.
There is no other final cause beyond man,
It is disclosed in man's own self".[1]
"First who is also the essence of the last!
Inner who is also the essence of the outward!"[2]

5. Free Will. One of the features of man's constitution is his freedom. The mystics' belief in the unity of acts and the necessity of attributing of all actions to God is not incompatible with attributing natural actions to certain phenomena (such as minerals and plants) and attributing voluntary actions to a particular being (man). In other words, so far as the knowledge of the Names is concerned among the existents of the world, man is the manifestation of the Name the Willing and the Free of the Exalted Real, and the reason of his free will is nothing other than the demand of the Real's will and His Name "the Willing" to be manifested. Rūmī writes:

"His [God's universal] power of choice brought [our individual] powers of choice into existence: His power of choice is like a rider [hidden] beneath the dust [which he raises]".[3]

The voluntary actions of man and his free choice, according to the holy verses 'You did not throw when you threw',[4] (8:17) and 'You do not wish unless it is wished by Allah',[5] (76: 30) are the shadow of the divine action and God's will. As a result, both man and his actions are determined by divine destiny and decree, and

1. *The Mystic Rose Garden*, Verses No. 273- 274.
2. Ibid,Verses No. 296.
3. *Mathnawī*, Book V, Verse No. 3087.
4. 'وَمَا رَمَيْتَ إِذْ رَمَيْتَ وَلَـٰكِنَّ اللَّـهَ رَمَىٰ .'
5. 'وَمَا تَشَاءُونَ إِلَّا أَن يَشَاءَ اللَّـهُ. '

he is destined to choose his way and action on the basis of divine destiny and decree in God's knowledge and reality. In other words, according to Ibn 'Arabī, he must choose and, therefore, it is absurd to think there is incompatibility between divine decree and individual will as it is absurd to assume there is any disagreement or opposition between a person and his shadow. As Mawlānā maintains, "How should the picture strive with the painter?"[1]

The unity of acts cannot be taken as evidence for determinism, for unity of acts indicates the phenomenal relation of the entire world with the Real and the sustaining association of the Real with the existents (whether determined or free) in the form of manifestation. As Mawlānā says in this regard:

> "This is the union with God, and it is not compulsion: this is the shining forth of the moon, this is not the cloud".[2]
>
> "Their freewill and compulsion is different [from that of ordinary men]: in oyster-shells drops [of rain] are pearls".[3]

Ibn 'Arabī in *al-Futūḥāt* argues that he who knows the reality of the substance of dust and its function in the world attributes the acts in one respect to God and in another to the servants, so that the praises and the beauties of the deeds are ascribed to the Real and the defects, faults and vices to the servant. As evidence he refers to (8:17): 'You did not throw when you threw'. He adds in Faṣṣ of Ilias:

> The evidence that the Real appears in the form of the entities and that the Exalted Real is the doer of all deeds and the creator of all things is the saying of God the Exalted (in *Anfāl*).... For God at the beginning

---

1. *Mathnawī*, Book I, Verse No. 608.
2. Ibid, Verse No. 1464.
3. Ibid,Verse No. 1468.

> negates the act of shooting by the Prophet(S), (you did not shoot), in the middle He confirms it ("when you shot"), and at the end He once again negates it and attributes it to Himself ("but it was Allah Who shot"). Therefore, the real shot is the Exalted Real but in the Muḥammadan form. Of course, the act of shooting can be attributed to the Prophet(S) in that he is the locus of the Real and the place of His manifestation. It is likewise in respect of all other possible beings, for each of them by nature has one way to the Real and unity... and another way to the creatures and diversity.[1]

"[The text] *thou didst not throw when thou threwest* is relative: it is negation and affirmation: both are authorized.

Thou threwest that [gravel], since it was on thy hand; thou didst not throw, for God manifested [His] power.

'O [Muḥammad], the handful is thy handful, and the throwing is from Me': on account of these two relations [both] the denial and the affirmation of it [the throwing] are right."[2]

Note. The mystics mention man's superiority to angels, the possibility of attaining the highest ranks of friendship and intimacy, creation by determination, guidance by command, and the possibility of gathering the proximity by supererogatory acts and proximity by obligatory acts as other features of man.

Besides all the mentioned features, Ibn 'Arabī holds that the main difference between the perfect Man and the Real, despite the similarity of their perfection, is the insufficiency and dependence of the world and the sufficiency of the divine essence. In other words, the supremacy of the Real is essential whereas the supremacy of man is incidental. Therefore, Ibn 'Arabī claims that

---

1. Ibn 'Arabī ,*Fuṣūṣ al-Ḥikam*, 185.
2. *Mathnawī*, Book III, Verse No. 3659, 3660, and 3665.

the perfect Man is the cause of both the manifestation of the Real and also his hiddenness. That is, to the extent of his essence, permanent entity and capacity he is the mirror that reflects the Real, but like other phenomena he is dependent and insufficient and, therefore, he is a veil (of light) that covers the Real and hinders knowing Him in depth.

The Personal (Evidential) Level of Man

Although every man as a man has realized (potentially) union in him, in the sense that on the cosmic (existential) level man is the perfect Man and the differences that exist result from the degree of the clarity of this point for humans. However, some people are so deeply aware of this point that the degree of their awareness comes close to the degree of the Real's knowledge of His Names and attributes, and it is only in such people that the human soul acts as a mirror reflecting the Real. Some others, however, virtually descend to the level of ignorance and idiocy. So, it is said that all people at the individual level are imperfect and their difference at this level is to the degree of their ability and the manifestations of the Real to them.

Ibn 'Arabī divides people at this level (individual level) into different kinds, such as the people of this world and the people of the other world; the knower, the laymen, and the ignorant; or the people of the heart (unveiling), the people of imagination, and the people of intellect.

The Existential Domains of Man

a. The Four Domains

Man as the little world is the mirror of the greater world and reflects in himself the world of existence. So, if the world of existence, as it was discussed, has four levels (the unknowable domain of God, the knowable domain of God, the insensible side of the world, and the sensible dimensions of the world),there are also four corresponding and distinguishable levels in man, namely the body, the mind, the soul and the spirit.

The first level of man is the body, whose highest part is the brain. The second level of man is the mind or the course of his consciousness, which is neither reduced to the brain nor completely dependent on it. It is experienced and felt in the three forms of sobriety, imagining, and daydreaming.

The third level is the soul, namely the immaterial substance that is essentially independent of matter and is the source of the mentioned course of consciousness though it never appears in that course. The soul is not only at the basis of the flux of the mind but also at the root of all changes and tendencies that the individual human endures. Moreover, the soul is the last stage of man's individuation and personalization and it is at this level that he develops an "I-you" relationship with the knowable God.

The fourth level is the spirit in which no trace remains of individuation or personalization. In this domain the spirit is united and becomes one with the unknowable God. Shabistarī puts these four levels in verse:

"'I' and 'you' are higher than body and soul,
For both body and soul are parts of 'me.'
The word 'I' is not limited to man,
So that you should say it means only the soul.
Straightway lift yourself above time and space,
Quit the world and be yourself a world for yourself".[1]
"You are that plurality which becomes the very Unity
You are that Unity which becomes the very plurality".[2]

---

1. *The Mystic Rose Garden*, Verses No. 309- 311.
2. Ibid,Verse No. 322.

b. The Seven Subtle Substances

As it was discussed, for the mystics man is an existent with different interiors and domains. Unlike the philosophers who claim man has at most two or three domains (body and spirit or the physical body, imaginal body, and the spirit) the mystics hold man is endowed with up to seven subtle centres or interiors. These subtle centres, for the mystic, correspond with the seven interiors of the Qur'an and also the seven interiors of the world, for all of these three are a kind of book with different layers of meaning and interpretation. They are the book of the soul,[1] the book of creation[2] (the world), and the written book or the book of divine law (the holy Qur'an). The mystics believe he who explores his inward and understands more of its subtleties will more understand the inner of the world and the Qur'an.

Besides the body, which distinguishes man from other animals by its specials features, there are seven subtle centres, which according to the mystics are as follows:

The soul: It is one of man's dimensions that is higher than and rules over the body and resists the physical instincts.

- The Intellect: it is the rational soul or its faculty, which in the domain of theory perceives the universals and in the domain of action distinguishes the good and the bad.
- The Heart: it is the source of development, change and alteration in man; it is the light that helps its owner to step in the valley of faith.
- The Spirit: it is the subtle substance and the locus of

---

1. See (17:14), '*Read your book! Today your soul suffices as your own reckoner.*' اقْرَأْ كتابَكَ كَفَى بِنَفْسِكَ الْيَوْمَ عَلَيْكَ حَسِيبًا.
2. *Say, 'If the sea were ink for the words of my Lord, the sea would be spent before the words of my Lord are spent,....* قُلْ لَوْ كانَ الْبَحْرُ مِدادًا لِكَلِماتِ رَبِّي لَنَفِدَ الْبَحْرُ قَبْلَ أَنْ تَنفَدَ كَلِماتُ رَبِّي...

knowledge, inspirations and love; it is immaterial and separate from the bodies.

- The secret inward: it is the inward of the heart and the centre of intuition, on attaining which the mystic is called the "Friend" or "Saint".
- The Hidden: it is the degree in which the wayfarer reaches the station of spiritual stability and a black light (the manifestation of the essence) is reflected on him; as a result he is totally absorbed in Allah. With the Prophets Guardianship leads to this subtle substance and results in Prophethood.
- The Most Hidden (the real subtle substance): it is attained only by the perfect Man and the Muḥammadan reality where annihilation and subsistence are experienced at all levels.

It can be said nature and body are related to the world of humanity; the soul, the intellect, the spirit and the heart belong to the world of dominion; the secret inward is related to the world of almightiness; and the hidden and the most hidden are of the world divinity. In any case, in practical mysticism the mystics deal with the different degrees and stations of individual humans, but since the necessary condition for attaining the stage of the mirror-like reflection of God is reaching the station of "Guardianship", it suffices here to explain it.

Sainthood

"Sainthood" (*wilāyat*) and its ranks enable man to reach the highest human state at an individual level, and "sainthood" is the highest degree that a mystic may attain. In *Iṣṭilāḥāt al-Ṣūfiyya* ("The Mystical Terms of the Sufis") al-Kāshānī defines sainthood as the servant's sustenance by the Real in the state of self-annihilation, which he attains through the proximity and protection of the Real, to reach the highest point of intimacy.

Sainthood commences with voluntary death, which the mystics according to the tradition "Die before you die" call the middle resurrection. It continues with a wonderful transformation of the individual's existence and his new birth to transcend the self by rejecting the world. On receiving the manifestations of acts and attributes the guardian reaches the levels of annihilation of acts and Names to be absorbed finally in the manifestation of the essence. Once he attains the station of subsistence he will reach the station of union of unity and his greater resurrection.

The saint (*walī*) is a divine Name and one of the Real's perfections and, therefore, sainthood is eternal and everlasting. This Name is the manifestation of desire and the necessary condition to be a perfect Man is the attainment of the rank of sainthood and becoming the manifestation of the Name the saint. In Ibn 'Arabī's words, to become a guardian is to transcend servitude and to reach the position of Lordship that the mystic can attain only by drowning himself completely in the Real and realizing all the divine Names.

In respect of knowledge, knowing the ultimate reality of existence and the relationship of the Real and the world, namely the unity of existence and that the diverse beings are no more than the manifestations of the Real, is the most important feature of the saint, which is attained through his annihilation and then subsistence through the Real. In other words, the state of sainthood results from the experience of annihilation and has three stages:

1. Annihilating the deeds in that of the Real (dependence),
2. Annihilating the attributes in those of the Real (acquiring the disposition of God), and
3. Annihilating the essence in the essence of the Real (verification).

Accordingly, the saint (*walī*) attains the station of "Proximity through supererogatory acts", knows the world by divine knowledge, and through subsistence and reaching the station of "Proximity through obligatory acts" as the deputy of the Real will have authority over the world.

The Kinds of Sainthood

The mystics divided sainthood in the first place into sainthood or guardianship by essence, which on the basis of the holy verse 'He is the Guardian, the All-laudable' (42:28) is confined to the essence of the Real, and sainthood by accident or that of others (which is derived from the sainthood by essence). The first kind of sainthood in turn is divided into two kinds: the universal sainthood, which according to the holy verse 'He takes care of the righteous' (7:196) is common to all believers, and the particular sainthood, which is special to the accomplished of the mystics, and it is the annihilation of the servant in the Real and then subsistence by Him. The second kind of sainthood (sainthood by accident) which is attained by acquiring divine disposition and realizing the levels of annihilation and subsistence is also divided into two kinds: the absolute and the limited sainthood (discussed in the next chapter). Hujwīrī offers another classification of the characteristics and the number of the saints as follows:

There are four thousands among them who are hidden and do not know each other or even the beauty of their state and they are always hidden from people. This is mentioned in the narration and the discourse of the saints and I myself have been certain of this. However, there are three hundreds among them who are the decision makers and the agents of the court of His Exalted Glory who are called "the chosen", forty others who are called "the substitutes", another seven who are called the "the righteous", four others who are called "the pillars", three others who are called "the chiefs", and one who is called "the pole" or "the help". These, however, do not know each other but in their affairs need each other's permission and this is related and confirmed by narrations.[1]

Sainthood, Prophethood, and Messengership

From Ibn 'Arabī's viewpoint there is a strong relationship among the above three titles. Sainthood is more universal than Prophethood and Messengership (their relationship is complete inclusion), and in respect of universality then come Prophethood and Messengership (like three concentric circles). Therefore, every Prophet is a Guardian, but every Guardian is not a Prophet, and this also applies to the relationship of the Messenger with the Prophet(S) and the saints. So in the view of Ibn 'Arabī a Prophet is a saint who has knowledge of the hidden and certain precepts through divine revelation that cannot be known in any ordinary way, but a Messenger is a Prophet and a saint who is aware of the obligation of delivering divine messages to people and has a divine responsibility. Therefore, a Messenger owns three positions whereas a Prophet has two. Shabistarī believes Prophethood is no other than sainthood manifested in creation and this world:

"The Prophet(S) is as a sun, the saint as a moon
It is set over against him in the point 'I am with God'."
"Prophethood is resplendent in its own perfection,
The saintship therein is manifest and not hidden.
But the saintship in a saint is concealed,
Whereas in a prophet it is shown forth openly".[2]

---

1. *Kashf al-Maḥjūb*, 267.
2. *The Mystic Rose Garden*, Verses No. 339- 341.

These three titles mainly differ in that "the Guardian" (*walī*) is one of the divine Names and, therefore, it always demands a manifestation, whereas the Prophet(S) and Messenger are not among the divine Names and don't always need to be manifested or represented and, therefore, they may be terminated (the termination of Messengership and Prophethood). Mawlānā states:

> "Therefore in every epoch [after Muḥammad] a saint arises [to act as his vicegerent]: the probation [of the people] lasts until the Resurrection."[1]

It can be said that sainthood is the soul and foundation of Prophethood and Messengership for Prophethood and Messengership historically follow certain conditions and are sometimes terminated. Indeed these two are divine responsibilities for organizing the virtuous life of man in this world, whereas sainthood has no such essential relation with the world and thus Prophets and Messengers may lose their positions in the other world but they will always keep their state of "sainthood".

Ibn 'Arabī believes that the Prophets and Messengers are the manifestations of the reality of the existential Perfect Man. He calls this existential reality "the Muḥammadan Reality", because its most perfect manifestation throughout human history has been Muḥammad Ibn 'Abdullāh, the Seal of the Prophets (A.S.), though other Prophets and Messengers have also been the manifestations of this reality (which is called the greatest manifestation, the creating Real, the first determination, and the Muḥammadan light). Rūmī on the Muḥammadan reality and its relation with Adam (A.S.) writes:

> "If in appearance I am born of Adam, in reality I am the forefather of [every] forefather,
> Since the worship of the angels was [rendered] to him

1. *Mathnawī*, Book II, Verse No. 815.

for my sake, and he ascended to the Seventh Heaven on my account".[1]

Jīlī states in this regard:

Some of the prophets and the saints are perfect but some are more perfect; nevertheless, none of them has the determination of Muḥammad (S). That reality has been one being from the beginning of existence and will be so eternally, but it appears in different forms and shapes and in respect of those determinations has been called by different names. The original name of this reality is Muḥammad, its nickname is Abu al-Qāsim, its epithet is 'Abdullāh or the servant of Allah and its noble title is Shams al-Dīn or the sun of religion, and according to its different forms and manifestations it is also called by some other names.....[2]

Shabistarī also maintains:

"The first appearance of prophethood was in Adam,
And its perfection was in the Seal of the prophets.
"Saintship lingers behind while it makes a journey,
And like a point makes another circuit in the world".[3]
"The light of the Prophet (S) is a mighty sun,
Now shining in Moses, now in Adam".[4]
"The time of our lord is the meridian line,
For he is purified from all the shadows of darkness".[5]
"But since a prophet is most perfect through prophethood,
He is of necessity more excellent than any saint.

1. Ibid,Verse No. 527 – 8.
2. *Al-Insān al-Kāmil*, vol. 2, 71, 75.
3. *The Mystic Rose Garden*, Verses No. 369- 370.
4. Ibid,Verse No. 377.
5. Ibid,Verse No. 380.

Saintship will be all shown forth in the 'Seal of the Saints';
The last point will be finished in the first".[1]

Evidently by the Muḥammadan reality the mystics following the school of Ibn 'Arabī do not mean the person of the Seal of the Prophet(S), but in the words of Ibn 'Arabī it is a generative being (called by philosophers the first Intelligence), a reality whose existence and universality embraces all the world and in respect of sainthood it is the nearest manifestation to the Exalted Real. Thus, it has appeared in the form of all the Prophets and Messengers throughout history and with the appearance of the person of the Seal of the Prophets Muḥammad (S), this kind of manifestation came to an end. According to some traditions this reality (the station of the Muḥammadan Prophethood) existed even when Adam was between water and mud and its manifestation in the form of the saints is interminable and will continue and endure to the Day of Judgment.

Accordingly, the interpretation of Ibn 'Arabī of "Resurrection" is closely related to the Question of "sainthood", for with the appearance of the absolute Seal of the Guardians, who is the terminating point of sainthood and the last person and manifestation of the perfect Man all the secrets of existence and divine realities become manifest, and with his return to divine essence, Which is the origin and goal of all beings the course of the world will end, for he is the means of the preservation and continuity of the world and its ultimate cause. Thus with the termination of the absolute sainthood and its end the world will come to an end and Resurrection will approach. Shabistarī writes:

"Its entirety will be seen in the 'Seal of the saints',
In him will be completed the circuit of the world".[2]

---

1. Ibid,Verses No. 390-391.
2. Ibid,Verse No. 371.

The Absolute and Limited Sainthood

The mystics divide both Prophethood and sainthood into the absolute and the limited. According to Sayyid Ḥaydar Āmulī, the limited Prophethood is the knowledge of the essence of the Real and His Names, attributes and orders and also the delivery of divine realities. It is divided into two kinds:

a. Descriptive Prophethood: knowing and informing about the essence, Names and attributes.

b. Law-giving Prophethood: besides the above mentioned points it deals with introducing divine commands, teaching people the moral precepts and wisdom, and establishing government. This kind of Prophethood is also called Messengership.

Absolute Prophethood, on the other hand, is the real and essential Prophethood which has always been and will be; the true Prophet is aware of the capacity of all beings according to their essence, realities and quiddity, and he mediates the bestowal of rights to each of the recipients according to its capacity and demand. This awareness is due to the eternal teaching of the Real and the owner of this position is called the real Adam, the perfect Man, the great vicegerent, the pole of the poles and the Muḥammadan reality. Traditions such as "The first thing that Allah created was my light, and I was a Prophet when Adam was still between water and mud" describe the owner of this position, who is the origin and goal of all beings.

The absolute sainthood, moreover, is the essence of the absolute Prophethood; it is marked by the attainment of those perfections according to the inner capacity in eternity and their subsistence everlastingly as narrated by the Commander of the Faithful (A.S.): "I was a saint (*walī*) even when Adam was still between water and mud." This absolute sainthood is essentially related to the Muḥammadan reality and by inheritance to the Commander of the

Faithful (A.S.). Ibn 'Arabī believes although all Prophets and saints are his heirs, 'Alī Ibn Abī Ṭālib is the nearest to him, and holds that he is the leader of the people of the world and the secret of all the Prophets, peace be upon them: "A Muḥammadan reality....He was the Master of all the world and the first to be manifested in existence....Of people, the closest to him is 'Alī Ibn Abī Ṭālib, may Allah be pleased with him, the leader of the world and the secret of all the Prophets."

The Seal of Sainthood

The mystics believe as there is a seal of the Prophets, there is a seal of saint in every age. According to the Shiite mystics and many other mystics, the seal of Absolute sainthood is 'Alī Ibn Abī Ṭālib (A.S.) and the seal of the limited sainthood is his son al-Ḥasan Ibn 'Alī al-Mahdī (A.S.). Sayyid Ḥaydar Āmulī on the basis of rational, narrational and intuitive evidence argues for these points extensively in his works and meanwhile critiques the view of Ibn 'Arabī on the seal of sainthood. In the view of some of the commentators of Ibn 'Arabī the latter believes in two or three kinds of sainthood and as a result he believes in the same number of the seals of sainthood and the seals of saints:

1. The seal of the universal sainthood, which he believes corresponds with the sainthood of 'Īsā (A.S.).
2. The seal of the Absolute Muḥammadan sainthood, which he maintains is the Imām al-Mahdī (A.S.) but in some other places he states it is Imām 'Alī (A.S.).
3. The seal of the limited Muḥammadan sainthood, which in some of the places he states is manifested in some people of his time, but in *Fuṣūṣ* and *al-Futūḥāt* he probably maintains it belongs to him.

The Knowledge of the Sainthood. In the view of Ibn 'Arabī the knowledge of the saint, which is a trans-rational mode of knowledge and derives from counting the divine Names and manifesting them, is the legacy of Muḥammad (S), who (according to traditions) is given all the wisdom and Allah's words, which are endless. In Mawlānā's words:

"O son, the saints are God's children: [both] in [their] absence and presence [He is] well aware [of what befalls them]".[1]

The Supremacy of Guardianship. Ibn 'Arabī in his explanation of some of the Sufis' view that sainthood is superior to Prophethood and Messengership states that when two or three designations and positions are found simultaneously in one person we may say sainthood is higher than Prophethood and Messengership, and thus the Messengers and the Prophets would differ according to their difference in sainthood. He states:

If one person gathers in himself two or three virtues and positions, in respect of being a Guardian and a mystic his position would be more complete and more perfect than being a Messenger or a legislator (Prophet). So if you hear one of the people of Allah saying or reported as saying that Guardianship or sainthood (*wilāyat*) is superior to Prophethood he means what we mentioned already, that is, the Messenger in respect of being a saint is more perfect than he is as a prophet or a Messenger, and the mentioned speaker does not mean to say the position of the following Guardian (meaning following the religious law) is higher that the (followed) Messenger.[2]

Sayyid Ḥaydar Āmulī having explained the views of the mystics including Ibn 'Arabī on this point writes:

As a result the rank of Imām 'Alī (A.S.) and the rank of the immaculate Imams in respect of sainthood is higher than the sainthood of the prophets and messengers (with the exception of the

1. *Mathnawī*, Book III, Verse No. 79.
2. Ibn 'Arabī , *Fuṣūṣ al-Ḥikam*, 135- 136.

seal of the Messengers). This is so, however, only in respect of sainthood; otherwise there is no higher rank than Prophethood and Messengership, for the saints and guardians always depend on the messengers and the prophets in religious laws and divine orders.[1]

He further adds, "The mistake of the Ismā'īlīs and Nuṣayrīs (among the Esoteric) is due to their ignorance of this point. They observed that the interior is superior to the exterior and that sainthood is the essence of Prophethood and, therefore, professed that the saints are superior to the Prophets. However, they did not notice that the superiority of the sainthood of the Prophet (S) to his Prophethood is not an indication of the superiority of the sainthood of the saint to the sainthood of the Prophet (S) or his person.

The authority of the Saint. In the viewpoint of Ibn 'Arabī one of the distinctive features of the saint and the perfect Man is the ability to exercise his power in the world, which is done with the help of the divine Names and their manifestation through the mediation of the saint. Mawlānā writes:

"The saints possess power [derived] from God: they turn back the arrow that has sped from its course."[2]

The important point here is the question of "creation by determination", which in the view of Ibn 'Arabī is due to the saint and the perfect Man as the perfect manifestation of the divine creativity, in the sense that the mystic can influence a thing only by concentrating his spiritual power and even create an object which did not exist before. In short he is given the power to influence and subdue everything. Ibn 'Arabī by comparing "determination" and the common imagination, by which we can create everything we desire in the mind, states that the mystic can induce the same state in the external world. He argues that "the

---

1. *Jāmi' al-Asrār*, 386-387.
2. *Mathnawī*, Book I, Verse No. 1669.

mystic by his determination can create something outside his determination (his spirit), and it is his determination that preserves that which he has thus created."

Questions

1. How does Ibn 'Arabī explain the position of man (the perfect Man) in the world of existence and the necessity of his existence?
2. Explain the features of the perfect Man.
3. Does unity of Acts lead to determinism? Explain.
4. Discuss the four domains of man as the little world in mysticism.
5. Compare and contrast the ranks of the soul and the spirit.
6. What are the seven subtle substances? Explain their relationship with each of the four worlds (the world of human nature, dominion, almightiness, and divinity).
7. Discuss the rank of sainthood and its divisions.
8. Explain the relationship between the three titles of sainthood, Prophethood, and Messengership from the viewpoint of Ibn 'Arabī and compare them with each other.
9. What do the mystics following the school of Ibn 'Arabī mean by the Muḥammadan reality? Explain.
10. Discuss the relationship between "Resurrection" and "sainthood" in the view of Ibn 'Arabī.
11. Discuss the question of the Seal of sainthood in Ibn 'Arabī's view.
12. Explain the "Creation by determination" as discussed by Ibn 'Arabī.

Appendixes

Appendix One: Authority of the Mystical Beliefs

I. William Payne Alston (1921-2009)

Alston argues that belief in mystical experiences, such as God or spiritual essences, is among the foundational beliefs which immediately reflect our experience—as belief in the reality of the material world is one of the foundational beliefs in the sensible experience—and its reliability is equal to that of the sensible experience.

In Alston's view, if we think of reliable knowledge as "the justified true belief", belief in the results of mystical experience and the mystics' sayings–like the contents of empirical experiences–are justified and can be taken as a foundation for other beliefs or arguments. He claims that those foundational beliefs which are based on inner experiences are representational beliefs or dependent on manifestation and states that both kinds of experience are initially justified and confirmable unless there is evidence to the contrary.

To explain, on the basis of Foundationalism he classifies beliefs arguing they are either basic beliefs which do not depend on other beliefs and are the basis of some other beliefs or they are nonbasic beliefs. Each of these two are also either related to the external world or inner intuitions. For example, a sensory basic belief is like the shaking of the trees, a sensory nonbasic belief is like the existence of wind, an inner basic belief is like feeling pain, and an inner nonbasic belief is like disorder in the nerve system. Alston holds that in both domains an inference of a nonbasic belief from basic beliefs is justified and logical. He maintains that the sources of human perceptions are: 1. Sensual perception (external sense); 2. Introspection (inner sense); 3. Memory; 4. Intellect (both demonstrative and intuitive); 5. The testimony of others (narration), and 6. The heart which is the means of mystical intuition. He believes perceptions resulting from the first and the sixth sources are alike and have equal epistemological and cognitive value. His view on the authority of the mystical experience for the subject and also for others is justified by the two principles of Richard Swinburne, namely the principles of Testimony and Credulity, which he accepts.

The principle of Testimony is related to the moral truth of others' testimony and the principle of credulity is related to the logical truth of their speech. To prove the validity and justification of the mystics' speech on the basis of the principle of testimony, it is argued that what is stated by others is true unless it is proved to be to the contrary, for example, when it is in contradiction with a stronger belief. This principle also applies to the speech of the mystics. The other question raised here is that even if their speech is morally true, why should one think their speech is logical and true in content and they are not mistaken. Here we turn to the second principle, namely the principle of Credulity: Everything is actually as it appears unless there is evidence to the contrary, that is, it is proved to be illusory. This principle refers to the following equation: It seems A exists = A exists. Indeed through this principle we always resist the possibility of misperception in our empirical daily experiences and say, for example, there *is* a tree and snow *is* white rather than it seems to me there is a tree or it seems to me the snow is white. There is no structural difference in this regard between sensual and mystical experiences, that is, in mystical experiences there is also no difference between "there is" and "It seems to be." So there is no difference between the Mystic's "there is an angel" and "there is a tree" for in both cases there is something seen clearly and it is reported. Alston is aware of the possible objections regarding the difference between sensual and mystical experiences. Nevertheless he does not think these differences are an important cause of the negation of this rule. To explain, it may be objected that sensual perception is universal and enduring whereas mystical perceptions are personal and limited only to a few and they are temporary findings in certain times; therefore, the generalization of the principle of credulity in the latter case is questionable. Alston's answer to this objection is that there is no logical relationship between "universality" and "reliability" or between "minority" and "unreliability" and falsehood. For example, some of the rational truths like understanding complicated mathematical formulas are also limited to a few and even some sensual perceptions, such as recognizing a particular smell or hearing a particular voice are sometimes limited to only a few people. Thus, he contends restricting the principle of credulity to only sensory perceptions is founded on a kind of epistemological dictatorship.

The other objection is that because sensual perceptions are universal and can be evaluated according to the alterations of the states and perceivers (subjects), the principle of credulity is confined to them. His answer to this objection is similar to that one he gave to the preceding one that is, when there is no way to demonstrate something it does not mean it is false. For example, we do not do that in relation to inner feelings; we hold that the feeling of pain indicates the existence of pain and we do not look for a way to prove the existence of pain.

II. Charlie Dunbar Broad (1887 –1971)

Broad the English Philosopher argues that on the basis of his mystical experience the mystic reports of certain events which people of no mystical experience have no right to question or refute, for in this respects they are like a five year old child who wants to judge the adults' love or speak of their sexual desires. Therefore, the only judge on such issues is the mystic himself; however because the mystics are often people of strong passion but weak analysis and in consequence sometimes differences and contradictions are seen in their reports, the common elements in their reports must be considered. Considering these common elements and shared centre the differences in expressions are mainly due to their different cultures and traditional conditions and beliefs.

Broad holds that the mystics' experiences are founded on reliable reasons which he demonstrates in the following argument:

1. There is a considerable consensus among the mystics on the reality they have experienced or witnessed.
2. When there is a noticeable agreement among the observers on the subject of their experience, the reasonable inference is that their observations and experiences correspond with reality, unless there is decisive and categorical evidence to the contrary.
3. There is no conclusive proof that the mystical states and experiences are illusory.
4. Therefore, the view that the mystical experiences are real is a logical inference.

To explain, Broad in an analogy initially divides people into three groups in regard of their religious and mystical experiences. He states that people in regard of their appreciation of music are divided into three groups: 1. Those who have no appreciation of music, 2. Those who have a simple appreciation of music, 3. Those who have a deep appreciation of music, and rather they are musicians themselves. In regard of religious experience likewise some people have no religious experience, some have a simple understanding of the religious or mystical experience (common religious people), and finally a few people have the highest understanding. Following his explanation of the differences between the two cases Broad argues that despite some differences the comparison has at least one important result, that is, a person who does not understand music but claims he is an expert in music and arrogantly looks down at musicians must be an ignorant and conceited person rather than an eminent thinker. Likewise, people with no religious experience who think they are superior to men of religious experience must be suspected in their views and ideas.

Second, Broad discusses the religious and mystical experiences common to mystics and religious people in all times and ages all over the world and also the reasons of some differences in the mystics' expressions. To explain the common views entertained by the subjects of these experiences he offers two theories: 1. One may suggest that the mystic face an aspect of reality that is unknown to the common people in their daily experience, 2. It is supposed that all the mystics are deluded.

Third, to identify which of the two theories is more reasonable Broad argues that the mystics speak of certain events and unanimously accept some issues which are unknown to us. It is important to see that their agreement and reports approaches which of the following:

a. The consensus of biologists equipped with microscopes and the report of cells and what takes place in them, which cannot be seen by the naked eyes.

b. People who have consumed alcohol or opium and the report of snakes or mice around them that we don't see.

c. Some who are born blind getting their eyesight and informing other blinds of certain colours and things around them that cannot be perceived by the latter.

Having said that he adds that the main question is whether the common experience of the religious mystics is more similar to the biologists' report on the structure of the cells which they see in the microscope, or the report of the opium eaters and alcoholics on the mice and snakes they seen in their rooms, or that of the few blinds after getting their eyesight on colours and describing it to other blind people.

Broad in his evaluation states that the reports of the mystics is not like the biologists' report on the cell and its mechanism, for although we do not know how to work with microscope or analyze the data collected through the observations, but we have general knowledge of the function of lenses and their validity (we are aware of the laws dominating the optical devices). However, we have no knowledge of the laws ruling over the genesis of different kinds of mystical experience. Moreover, the mystic reports a world other than the world of nature, and the report of the mystic is different from the reports of the consumers of alcohol and opium, such as seeing animals around them, for they claim they see things of the kind of sensible things, which are not different from things other people see and expect. However, the views accepted commonly by the religious mystics (which are not of the kind of sensible things expected to be seen by others, and as a result) are not incompatible with what we perceive through our senses. These views are related to the general structure and order of the world and also the relations of man with other parts of the world and in general have but little relationship with daily events and, therefore, are not likely to contradict them. In short, because of their different subjects of perception, there is no homogeneity between the reports or the consensus of the mystics and the reports and consensus of the alcoholic or opium addicts.

Accordingly, the reports of the mystics and their common experience are like the reports on colours given by a born blind after getting his eyesight to other blind people; in other words, he is a person who has gained a special vision or insight that is denied to others. Thus, on the basis of our daily practical experience, it is not unwise to trust such reports unless there is reason enough to show they are false or illusory, as it is also done with sensual and empirical reports. He concludes by arguing that if in the experiences of people who differ in time, place and culture there is a common core that is accepted by all and all of them give the same interpretation of the cognitive content of their experience, it would be logical to think there is consensus because they have met with an objective aspect of reality, unless there is evidence to the contrary.

Finally, he tries to answer the objection that targets the third premise of his argument, that is, the physical weakness or the special symptoms indicating the psychological disorder or abnormality of the undertakers of the religious and mystical experience which questions their claims and indicate their falsehood. Broad's answer comes in four parts.

First, as a revoking answer, many of the founders of religions, mystics and saints had a high degree of endurance and capacity for organization and management.

Second, it is very likely that many of the scientists of empirical sciences and artists mentally and physically are not normal and some of them are indeed odd in their behavior.

Third, if we theoretically assume that there is an aspect of the world that exists outside the domain of common people's knowledge and insight, it is very likely that one needs the degree of mental and physical abnormality to be released from the concerns of perception and to establish an epistemic relationship with this aspect of reality. So, it is naturally true and much expected that those who claim a special kind of knowledge are often physically and mentally abnormal. Indeed it may be necessary to be a little mad in order to find an opening to the trans-sensible world.

Fourth, if mystical experiences are true, it is very likely that they lead to the abnormal behavior of those who strongly undergo such experiences. If the people of mystical and religious experiences have a recurrent relationship with a certain aspect of reality (that is unknown to people), such people will live in two worlds, whereas common people live only in one world. They may be compared to a person who looks into life with one naked eye and another armed with a microscope. Those who have undergone the religious experience base their behavior on that aspect of reality which is only known by them and important to them.

Appendix Two: The Considerations of Existence and the Essence of the Real

One of the questions of the mystics and philosophers is that which considerations or aspects of existence can be attributed to the essence of the Real. In theoretical mysticism the essence of the Real is known to be absolute and in its absoluteness it is unknowable, inaccessible and above all the qualities and attributes that man can understand. Whatever is said and thought about Him is in fact limiting Him and is incompatible with His absolute and undetermined essence. Therefore, the Real in His unconditional sublimity is unknowable, the most hidden and the secret of the secrets. He is above the speech of the speakers, the thought of the thinkers and the vision of the mystics. It is the state of silence and witnessing the dark light or the highest level of mystical vision (the station of the mystics' weakness) that cannot be exceeded. From the ontological perspective of theoretical mysticism even words such as God (the worshipped) or Allah in religions, the Necessary being in philosophy, or the Creator and Maker in theology indicate certain determinations of that Absolute rather than His essence. Nevertheless, since no one can speak of a subject without restricting it verbally, the mystics often use the term "the Real" in reference to the Absolute. Thus, even in the most sublime mystical experiences, namely oneness and annihilation and subsistence, the Real in the rank of absoluteness and oneness will remain unknown to all except for Him, and this is because of the essential limitation of man's knowledge.

Therefore, although silence is the best description of the Unknown, in philosophy and theoretical mysticism one thing can be attributed to the essence of the Real, namely existence. For in one sense in the field of philosophical thought existence is the vaguest term but at the same time it is in the highest level of being unconditioned. It is on this basis that the students of the school of Ibn 'Arabī believe that the essence of the Real is the instance of the concept of "being unconditioned as the source of division" and their view in this regard differs with that of the philosophers.

To explain, among the mentioned aspects there is no difference between the philosophers and the mystics that the Exalted Real is neither being conditioned by a thing restricted and limited nor is a being unconditioned as a division (which corresponds with the Act of the Real). However, the philosophers on the basis of their accepted principles (in Peripatetic philosophy the primacy and difference of existence and in transcendental philosophy the primacy and gradation of existence) believe the Necessary being is "being unconditioned" but the mystics on the basis of the personal unity of existence hold that being unconditioned is the rank of unity rather than essence. They state that the rank of essence is "being unconditioned as the source of division" which remains unknown and it is the domain of bewilderment.

Mullā Ṣadrā in this regard states that for the mystics the unconditioned being is the rank of unity and for philosophers it is the entire reality of the Necessary being. Moreover, for the mystics it is the unconditioned being that shows the reality of the Exalted Real, for this aspect is devoid of any qualification even that of transcendence (which itself leads to a kind of limitation).

The Real in this rank has neither a cognitive relation with the knowledge of man or any other kind of knowledge, nor an existential relation of the kind of appearance (manifestation) or causality, etc.

Accordingly, in theoretical mysticism whenever the Real's appearance, causality or manifestations in the ascending or descending arcs is discussed or His life giving, life taking or presence is mentioned, the issue is related to His absolute Act, that is, being unconditioned as a division (ever-expanding existence) which in fact is the manifestation of the Real's existence. Thus, Mullā Ṣadrā follows the method of the philosophers in some of his works and clearly predicates the Necessary being of the absolute existence, namely reality unconditioned by existence, rather than being unconditioned. He argues if the Exalted Real were otherwise (unconditioned), there would have been many flaws and deficiencies. In the mystical chapters of *Asfār*, at least in one place, he is inclined to the view of the mystics.

It should be noted that the three aspects in philosophy and even in transcendental philosophy are founded on the diversity of being though it is the graded diversity and typical unity of existence. In other words, all the mentioned aspects have a share and portion in existence. Therefore, in transcendental philosophy being unconditioned or the essence of the Necessary being, being conditioned by absoluteness or His Act, and being conditioned by a thing or His creation have a portion of the reality of existence and their diversity is graded like their unity. However, in mysticism all these three are the different determinations of the Necessary being and none of them has a separate or independent existential reality. In other words, their diversity is phenomenal rather than existential and the essence of the Real is being unconditioned as the source of division, which is pure existence.

The other point is that in theoretical mysticism (unlike philosophy) the three mentioned aspects are not based on existence, for in mysticism existence is a personal One and other than the Real has no portion in existence; in other words, existence is confined to being unconditioned as the division and the portion of others is mere manifestation and representation rather than existence and being. Therefore, in mysticism the function of the mentioned aspects is to represent and determinate the Necessary being. Accordingly, it cannot be said that if it was not for the quality of universality, the extended emanation would have also been Necessary.

In sum, for the mystic being unconditioned of determination, diversity and manifestation is the station of unity. Being conditioned by the determination of the attributes is the different Names of the Real, such as being determined by divinity is God. Being conditioned by all the determinations of attributes is called the station of Oneness and the Name Allah. On the other hand, being conditioned by particular and phenomenal determinations in the form of particular emanations is the manifestations and representations of existence. Being unconditioned as a division which is seen along with other divisions and is qualified by absoluteness is the holy emanation and pervasive manifestation. It is this being which is inside all things but not by the way of mixing with them and is outside all things but not by the way of separation. Finally, being unconditioned as the source of division, which is unconditioned of any quality and even that of absoluteness is the station of essence and absolute divine identity, a station that cannot be manifested, understood or distinguished and it is beyond explanation and description.

The discourse of the mystic on the essence of the Real is always related to His manifestation and Acts. In a non-manifested state

He is indescribable and is unknown in His absoluteness, and the highest vision of the mystics, namely the manifestation of the essence, is also witnessing the Real in a particular kind of His manifestation. Therefore, the worldview of the mystic is an existence-oriented worldview and in other words it is centred in the Real. The Real is also being unconditioned as the source of division and His other Names such as the One, the Unique, the Necessary being, the Creator, the Light, the Worshipped and Lord are the determinations of that absolute existence, as others and all the entire universe are also pure determinations rather than degrees of light or accidental lights.

Existence and Light

Having mentioned light and existence it is important to note here the difference between the Illuminationist philosophy of Suhrawardī and existential theosophy of Ibn 'Arabī. The expression "the light of existence" in the discourse of Ibn 'Arabī and his followers like Shabistarī is a precise expression that indicates a deep relationship—to the limit of objectivity—between mystical epistemology and ontology, which keeps them away from the error of the Illuminationist philosophy. To explain, as it was mentioned the epistemology of the mystics is founded on the illuminations and revelations they derive from the light of existence (divine lights and gleams) and in one word light, but their ontology is rooted in existence.

In the view of Ibn 'Arabī and his followers these two are one reality and one being which encompass the person's inside and outside, and his intuition, heart, mind and conscience, and all that we call knowledge or known objects, the external world or the mind or intuition are nothing other than determinations of that Absolute being. Accordingly, the expression "the light of existence" is a compound term indicating unity. In Illuminationist philosophy, however, these two are separate and Suhrawardī, who is more a philosopher with a mystical tendency rather than a mystic with a philosophical inclination and has had some mystical experiences and has elaborated on the gleams of light, believes in the primacy of quiddity. His mysticism, therefore, is limited to Angelology and the knowledge of the world of the Imagination and Intelligence, and finally God remains Pure and Transcendent. As evidenced by his works no mention is made of the oneness of existence and his interpretation of mystical expressions such as "I am the Real" (though he honours the mystical words of Ḥallāj a lot) does not exceed the level of unity of vision.

Bibliography

'Abd al-Wahhāb Sha'rānī, *al-Kibrīt al-Aḥmar*, (Cairo: Maṭba'at Muṣṭafā al-Bābī, 1959).

'Abd al-Wahhāb Sha'rānī, *al-Yawāqīt wa al-Jawāhir*, (Cairo: Maṭba'at Muṣṭafā al-Babī, 1959).

'Abdulkarīm Jīlī, *al-Insān al-Kāmil*, (Cairo: Matba'at Muṣṭafā al-Babī, 1402).

'Abdulkarīm Jīlī, *Sharḥ Mushkilāt al-Futūḥāt al-Makkiyya*, (Kuwait: Dar So'ad al-Sabāḥ, 1992).

'Abdulkarīm Surūsh, *Qumār 'Āshiqānih*, (Tehran: Mu'assasa Farhangī Ṣirāṭ, 1379 S.A.H).

'Abdurraḥmān Jāmī, *al-Durrat al-Fākhira*, ed. Nicholas Hir & Musawī Bihbahānī, (Tehran: Intishārāt Mc Gill, 1358 S.A.H).

'Abdulraḥmān Jāmī, *Ashi'at al-Luma'āt*, ed. Rabbānī, (Tehran: Kitābkhānih Hāmidī,d).

'Abdurrazzāq Kāshānī, *Iṣṭilāḥāt al-Ṣūfiyya*, (Qum: Intishārāt Bīdār, 1370 S.A.H).

'Abdurrazzāq Kāshānī, *Laṭā'if al-A'lām*, (Tehran: Nashr Mīrāth Maktūb, 1379 S.A.H).

'Abdurrazzāq Kāshānī, *Sharḥ Fuṣūṣ al-Ḥikam*, (Qum: Intishārāt Bīdār, 1363 S.A.H).

'Abdurrazzāq Kāshānī, *Ta'wīlāt* (Tafsīr Ibn 'Arabī), ed.Ghā'ib, (Tehran: Intishārāt Nāṣir Khusraw, d).

'Abdurrazzāq Lāhījī, *Gawhar Murād*, (Tehran: Kitābfurūshī Islāmiyya, 1365 S.A.H).

'Abdurrazzāq Lāhījī, *Shawāriq al-Ilhām*, (Tehran: Maktabat al-Fārābī, 1401 A.H).

'Abdurrraḥmān Jāmī, *Lawāmi' wa Lawāyiḥ*, (Tehran: Kitābfurūshī Manūchihrī , 1360 S.A.H).

'Abdurrraḥmān Jāmī, *Naqd al-Nuṣūṣ*, ed. William Chittick, (Tehran: Anjuman Ḥikmat wa Falsafa, 1356 S.A.H).

‘Abdurrraḥmān Jāmī, *Sharḥ Rubā‘iyyāt*, (Tehran: Kitābfurūshī Manūchihrī, 1360 S.A.H).

‘Abu’l Ḥasan Tahānawī, *Kashshāf Iṣṭilāḥāt al-Funūn*, ed. ‘Alī Dahraj, (Beirut: Maktabat Lobnan, 1996).

Abū Naṣr Sarrrāj Ṭusī, *al-Luma‘ fī al-Taṣawwuf*, (Tehran: Asātīr, 1382 S.A.H).

Abul‘alā ‘Afīfī, *Ta‘līqāt ala Fuṣūṣ al-Ḥikam*, (Tehran: Intishārāt al-Zahrā, 1366 S.A.H).

‘Alā’ al-Dawla Simnānī, *Muṣannafāt Farsī*, (Tehran: Sherkat Intishārāt ‘Ilmī Farhangī, 1369 S.A.H).

Asin Palasiyun, *Ibn ‘Arabī Ḥayātuhū wa Madhhabuhū*, trans. ‘Abdurraḥmān Badawī, (Beirut: Dār al-Qalam, 1979).

‘Azīz al-Dīn Nasafī, *Insān Kāmil*, ed. Marizhen Moleh, (Tehran: Kitābkhānih Ṭahūrī, 1362 S.A.H).

Faḍlullāh Ziānūr, *Wahdat Wujūd*, (Tehran: Intishārāt Zawwār,d).

Fakhr al-Dīn‘Arāqī, *Luma‘āt*, ed. Najīb Mayil Hirawī, (Tehran: Intishārāt Mawlā, 1363 S.A.H).

Farīd al-Dīn‘Aṭṭār, *Manṭiq al-Ṭayr*, (Tehran: Bungāh Tarjumih wa Nashr Kitāb, 1356 S.A.H).

Farīd al-Dīn‘Aṭṭār, *Tadhkirat al-Awliyā‘*, ed.Isti‘lāmī, (Tehran: Zawwar, 1380 S.A.H).

Ghulām Riḍā A‘wānī, *Ḥikmat wa Hunar Ma‘nawī Dar Islam*, (Tehran: Intishārāt Garus, 1375 S.A.H).

Ḥasan Ḥasanzādih Āmulī, *Wahdat az Dīdgāh ‘Arif wa Ḥakīm*, (Tehran: Intishārāt Fajr, 1362 S.A.H).

Henri Bergson, *Du Sarcheshmeh Akhlāq wa Dīn*, (Tehran: Sherkat Sahāmī Inteshār, 1358 S.A.H).

Ḥusayn Ibn ‘Abdullāh Ibn Sīnā, *al-Ishārāt wa al-Tanbīhāt*, vol. 3, (Tehran: Daftar Nashr Kitāb, 1403 A.H.).

Jalāl Sattārī, *Madkhalī bar Ramz-shināsī ‘Irfānī*, (Tehran: Nashr Markaz, 1372 S.A.H).

Jalāluddīn Dawānī, *Risālat Zora‘*, ed. Aḥmad Tuysirkānī, (Iṣfahān: Madrisih Amīr al-Mu’minīn, 1364 S.A.H).

Javādī Āmulī, ‘Abdullāh, *Tahrīr Tamhīd al-Qawā‘id*, (Tehran: Intishārāt al-Zahrā, 1372 S.A.H).

Karl Raimund Popper, *Usṭūrih Chārchūb*, trans. Pāyā, (Tehran: Ṭarḥ-e No, 1379 S.A.H).

Khāwaja Hawrā' Maghribī, *Nūr Waḥdat*, (Tehran: Intishārāt Nūr Fāṭima, 1361 S.A.H).

Maḥmūd Ghurāb, *al-Fiqh 'inda al- Shaykh al-Akbar*, (Damascus: Dār al-Fikr, 1401 A.H).

Maḥmūd Ghurāb, *al-Khiyāl, 'Ālam al-Barzakh wa al-Mithāl min Kalām al-Shaykh al-Akbar*, (Damascus: Dār al-Fikr, 1405 A.H).

Maḥmūd Ghurāb, *al-Ṭarīq ilā Allah min kalām al- Shaykh al-Akbar*, (Demascus: Intishārāt Dār al-Fikr,d).

Maḥmūd Ghurāb, *Sharḥ Fuṣūṣ Al-Ḥikam*, (Damascus: Intishārāt Dār al-Fikr, 1405 A.H.).

Maḥmūd Lāhījī, *Mafātīḥ al-I'jāz fī Sharḥ Gulshan Rāz*, ed. Keyvān Samī'ī, (Tehran: Kitābkhānih Sanā'ī).

Majd al-Dīn Baghdādī, *Tuḥfat al-Barara*, trans. Sa'idī Khurāsānī, (Tehran: Intishārāt Marvī, 1368 S.A.H).

Mawlānā Jalāl al-Dīn Balkhī Rūmī, *Ghazaliyyāt Shams*, ed. 'Abbāsī, (Tehran: Nashr Tulū',d).

Mawlānā Jalāl al-Dīn Balkhī Rūmī, *Mathnawī Ma'nawī*, ed. Ramazanī, (Tehran: Kilālih Khāvar Edition,d).

Mawlānā Jalāl al-Dīn Balkhī Rūmī, *Mathnawī Ma'nawī*, ed. A. Surūsh, (Tehran: Intishārāt 'Ilmī wa Farhangī, 1378 S.A.H).

Michael Peterson, *'Aql wa I'tiqād Dīnī*, trans. Sulṭānī & Narāqī, (Tehran: Ṭarḥ-e Nou, 1376 S.A.H).

Mīr Sayyid Sharīf Jurjānī, *al-Ta'rīfāt*, (Tehran: Intishārāt Nāṣir Khusraw,d).

Muḥammad 'Alī Shāh Ābadī, *Rashaḥāt al-Biḥār*, (Tehran: Intishārāt Nihḍat Zanān Musalmān, 1360 S.A.H).

Muḥammad Ḥusayn Ṭabāṭabā'ī, *Rasāel Tawḥīdiyyeh*, (Qum: Namāyishgāh wa Nashr Kitāb, 1365 S.A.H).

Muḥammad Ibn 'Alī Ṣadūq, *al- Tawḥīd*, ed. Ghaffārī, (Qum: Intishārāt Islamī,d).

Muḥammad Iqbal Lahori, *Iḥyā Fikr Dīnī, dar Islam*, trans. Aḥmad Ārām, (Tehran: Intishārāt Risālat Qalam,d).

Muḥammad Iqbal Lahori, *Seyr Falsafa dar Iran*, trans. A. Āryānpūr, (Tehran: Amīr Kabīr, 1383 S.A.H).

Muḥammad Ja'far Lāhījī, *Sharḥ Risāla Mashā'ir*, ed. Āshtiyānī, (Qum: Intishārāt Daftar Tablīghāt Islāmī, d).

Muḥammad Kulaynī, *Uṣūl Kāfī*, ed. 'Alī Akbar Ghaffārī, (Tehran: Intishārāt Islāmiyya, 1363 S.A.H).

Muḥammad Shams Tabrīzī, *Maqālāt Shams*, ed. Ṣamad Muwaḥḥid, (Tehran: Intishārāt Khārazmī, 1369 S.A.H).

Muḥammad Taqī Fa'ālī, *Tajrubi Dīnī wa Mukashifāt 'Irfānī*, (Tehran: Markaz Nashr Pajūhishgāh Farhang wa Andīsheh Islāmī, 1379 S.A.H).

Muḥammad Taqī Fāḍil Tunī, *Ta'līqāt bar Fuṣūṣ al-Ḥikam*, (Tehran: Intishārāt Mawlā, 1360 S.A.H).

Muḥsin Fayḍ Kāshānī, *Mishwāq*, in *Shinākht Shākhiṣ, hā-ey 'Irfānī*, (Tehran: Intishārāt Nūr Fātima, 1363 S.A.H).

Muḥsin Jahāngīrī, *Ibn 'Arabī Chihri-ye Barjasti-ye 'Irfān Islāmī*, (Tehran: Intishārāt Daneshgāh Tehran, 1361 S.A.H).

Muḥyī al-Dīn Muḥammad Ibn 'Arabī, *al-Aḥadiyya*, (Beirut: Dār Iḥyā al-Turāth al-'Arabī,d).

Muḥyī al-Dīn Muḥammad Ibn 'Arabī, *al-Futūḥāt al-Makkiyya*, (4 volumes), (Cairo: n,d).

Muḥyī al-Dīn Muḥammad Ibn 'Arabī, *al-Futūḥāt al-Makkiyya*, ed. 'Uthmān Yaḥyā, (14 volumes), (Cairo: n, 1985- 1994).

Muḥyī al-Dīn Muḥammad Ibn 'Arabī, *al- Jalāla*, (Beirut: Dār Iḥyā al-Turāth al-'Arabī,d).

Muḥyī al-Dīn Muḥammad Ibn 'Arabī, *al-Masā'il*, (Beirut: Dār Iḥyā al-Turāth al-'Arabī,d).

Muḥyī al-Dīn Muḥammad Ibn 'Arabī, *al-Ṣifāt al-Ilāhiyya*, (Beirut: Dār Iḥyā al-Turāth al-'Arabī,d).

Muḥyī al-Dīn Muḥammad Ibn 'Arabī, *'Aqlat al-Mustawfir*, Baghdad Edition, (n,d).

Muḥyī al-Dīn Muḥammad Ibn 'Arabī, *Chāhārdah Risāla 'Irfānī*, ed. Sa'īd Raḥīmīān, (Shīrāz: Intishārāt Kūshāmihr, 1380 S.A.H).

Muḥyī al-Dīn Muḥammad Ibn 'Arabī, *Fuṣūṣ al-Ḥikam*, ed. A. 'Afīfī, (Tehran: Intishārāt al-Zahrā, 1366 S.A.H).

Muḥyī al-Dīn Muḥammad Ibn 'Arabī, *Inshā Al-Dawā'ir*, Leyden Edition, (n,d).

Muḥyī al-Dīn Muḥammad Ibn 'Arabī, *Kashf Al-Ghiṭā*, in *Chāhārdah Risāla 'Irfānī*, ed.Sa'īd Raḥīmīān, (Shīrāz: Intishārāt Kūshāmihr, 1380 S.A.H).

Muḥyī al-Dīn Muḥammad Ibn 'Arabī, *Kashf al-Ma'nā, 'an Sirr Asmā' al-Ḥusnā*, ed.Nilno, (Qum: Nashr Bakhshāyish, 1419 A.H).

Muḥyī al-Dīn Muḥammad Ibn 'Arabī, *Mā Lā Ya'lū 'Aliyh*, ed. Maḥmūd Ghurāb, (Damascus: n,d).

Muḥyī al-Dīn Muḥammad Ibn 'Arabī, *Naghsh al-Fuṣūṣ*, (Beirut: Dār Iḥyā al-Turāth al-'Arabī,d).

Muḥyī al-Dīn Muḥammad Ibn 'Arabī, *Rasā'l Ibn 'Arabī*, (Beirut: Dār Iḥyā al-Turāth al-'Arabī,d).

Muḥyī al-Dīn Muḥammad Ibn 'Arabī, *Tanbīhāt 'alā Uluww al-Ḥaqīqat al-Muḥammadiyya*, (Cairo: Maṭba'at 'Ālam al-Fikr, 1988).

Muḥyiddīn Ilāhī Qumshi'ī, *Ḥikmat Ilāhiī*, (Tehran: Intishārāt Islami,d).

Mullā Hādī Sabzivārī, *Sharḥ al-Asmā' al-Ḥusnā*, (Qum: Intishārāt Baṣīratī,d).

Mullā Ḥusayn Kashifī, *Lubb Lubāb Mathnawī*, ed. Naṣrullāh Taqavī, (Tehran: Maṭbū'āt Afshārī, 1362 S.A.H).

Murtaḍā Muṭahharī, *Kulliyyāt 'Ulūm Islāmī*, (Qum: Intishārāt Islāmī, Jāmi'a Mudarrisīn,d).

Murtaḍā Muṭahharī, *Maqālāt Falsafī*, (Qum: Intishārāt Ṣadrā, 1369 S.A.H).

Murtaḍā Muṭahharī, *Sharḥ Mabsūṭ Manẓūma*, (Tehran: Intishārāt Ḥikmat, 1363 – 1369 S.A.H).

Muṣliḥ al-Dīn Sa'dī, *Kuliyyāt Sa'dī*, (Tehran: Mu'assasa Intishārāt Amīr Kabīr, 1367 S.A.H).

Nahād Khayyateh, *Dirāsa fī Tajruba al-Ṣūfiyya*, (Beirut: Dar al-Ma'rifat, 1414).

Najm al-Dīn Rāzī, *Mirṣād al-'Ibād*, ed. Amīn Riyāḥī, (Tehran: Intishārāt 'Ilmī wa Farhangī, 1366 S.A.H).

Naṣīr al-Dīn Muḥammad Ṭūsī, *Awsāf al-Ashrāf*, (Tehran: Intishārāt Hudā, 1361 S.A.H).

Rudolph, Otto, *Mafhūm 'Amr Qudsī*, trans. Humāyūn Himmatī, (Tehran: Intishārāt Naqsh Jahān, 1380 S.A.H).

Rūḥullah Khumeinī, *Miṣbāḥ al-Hidāyat*, (Tehran: Payām Āzadī, 1360 S.A.H).

Rūḥullah Khumeinī, *Ta'līqāt, 'alā Fuṣūh al-Ḥikam*, (Qum: Intishārāt Pāsdār Islām, 1406 A.H).

Rūzbihān Baqlī Shīrāzī, *Sharḥ Shatḥiyyāt*, (Tehran: Kitābkhānih Ṭahūrī, 1382 S.A.H).

Sa'īd al-Dīn Farghanī, *Mashāriq al-Dararī*, ed. Āshtiyānī, (Mashad: Dāneshgāh Mashad, 1357 S.A.H).

Sa'id Raḥīmiyān, "Muqaddama bar Waḥdat Wujūd wa Mawjūd", in *Keyhān Andīshih*, No.55.

Sa'id Raḥīmiyān, *Tajjalī wa Ẓuhūr dar 'Irfān Naẓarī*, (Qum: Intishārāt Daftar Tablīghāt Islāmī, 1376 S.A.H).

Ṣā'in al-Dīn Ibn Turkeh, *Tamhīd al-Qawā'id*, ed. S. J. Āshtiyānī, (Tehran: Anjuman Ḥikmat wa Falsafa, 1360 S.A.H).

Ṣadr al-Dīn Kāshif Dizfūlī, *Manāhij al-Muwaḥḥidīn*, (manuscript) in Kitābkhānih Āyatullāh Mar'ashī Najafī.

Ṣadr al-Dīn Qūnavī, *al-Fukūk*, in *Ḥāshiya Manāzil al-Sā'irīn*, (Tehran: Intishārāt Hāmidī,d)

Ṣadr al-Dīn Qūnavī, *al-Nusūs*, ed. Āshtiyānī, (Tehran: Nashr Dānishgāhī, 1362 S.A.H).

Ṣadr al-Dīn Shīrāzī, *al-Mashā'ir*, ed. Henri Corbin, (Tehran: Intishārāt Ṭahūrī, 1363 S.A.H).

Ṣadr al-Dīn Shīrāzī, *Asfār*, ed. Amīnī & Umīd, (Qum: Intishārāt Muṣṭafawī,d).

Ṣadr al-Dīn Shīrāzī, *Khalq al-A'māl*, (Qum: Intishārāt Muṣṭafawī,d).

Ṣadr al-Dīn Shīrāzī, *Rasā'il*, (Qum: Intishārāt Muṣṭafawī,d).

Ṣadr al-Dīn Shīrāzī, *Shawāhid Al-Rubūbiyya*, ed. S. J. Āshtiyānī, (Tehran: Nashr Daneshgahī, 1360 S.A.H).

Sayyid Ḥeydar Āmulī, *Asrār al- Sharī'a wa Aṭwār al-Ṭarīqa wa Anwār Al- Ḥaqīqa*, (Tehran: Mu'asasa Muṭāli'āt wa Taḥqīqāt Farhangī, 1362 S.A.H).

Sayyid Ḥeydar Āmulī, *Jāmī' al-Asrār*, (Tehran: Intishārāt 'Ilmī wa Farhangī, 1368 S.A.H).

Sayyid Ḥeydar Āmulī, *Naqd al-Nuqūd fī Ma'rifat al-Wujūd*, (Tehran: Intishārāt 'Ilmī wa Farhangī, 1368 S.A.H).

Sayyid Jalāl al-Dīn Āshtiyānī, *Hastī az Naẓar Falsafa wa 'Irfān*, (Tehran: Intishārāt Nihḍat Zanān Musalmān,d).

Sayyid Jalāl al-Dīn Āshtiyānī, *Sharḥ-e Muqaddamah Qayṣarī*, (Qum: Intishārāt Daftar Tablīghāt Islāmī, 1365 S.A.H).

Sayyid Mahdī Baḥrul'ulūm, *Risāla Seyr wa Sulūk*, ed. Ḥusaynī Tehranī, (Tehran: Intishārāt Ḥikmat, 1360 S.A.H).

Sayyid Muḥammad Ḥusayn Ṭabāṭabā'ī, *Nahāyat al-Ḥikma*, (Qum: Intishārāt Islāmī, 1362 S.A.H).

Shāh Maḥmūd Dā'ī Shīrāzī, *Nasāyim Gulshan*, ed. Parvīz 'Abbāsī Dākānī, (Tehran: Intishārāt Ilhām, 1377 S.A.H).

Shams al-Dīn Muḥammad Ḥāfiẓ, *Dīvān*, ed. Ghanī & Qazvīnī, (Tehran: Intishārāt Asāṭīr, 1367 S.A.H).

Sharaf al-Dīn 'Umar Ibn Fāriḍ, *Dīwān*, (Qum: Intishārāt Sharīf al-Raḍī, 1411A.H.).

Sharaf al-Dīn Maḥmūd Qayṣarī, *Rasā'il Qayṣarī*, ed. Āshtiyānī, (Tehran: Anjuman Ḥikmat va Falsafa, 1357 S.A.H).

Sharaf al-Dīn Maḥmūd Qayṣarī, *Sharḥ Fuṣūṣ al-Ḥikam*, (Qum: Intishārāt Bīdār, 1363 S.A.H).

Sharaf al-Dīn Maḥmūd Qayṣarī, *Sharḥ Fuṣūṣ al-Ḥikam,* ed. Āshtiyānī, (Tehran: Intishārāt 'Ilmī wa Farhangī, 1375 S.A.H).

Sharafuddīn Khurāsānī, "Ibn 'Arabī", in *Dā'irat al-Ma'ārif Buzurg Islāmī*, vol. 3.

Sharafuddīn Khurāsānī, *Nukhustīn Fīlsūfān Yūnanī*, (Tehran: Shirkat Sahāmī Kitāb-hā-ye Jībī, 1357 S.A.H).

Shaykh Maḥmūd Shabistarī, "Gulshan Rāz", in *Majmū'a Āthār*.

Shaykh Maḥmūd Shabistarī, *Majmū'a Āthār*, ed. Ṣamad Muwaḥḥid, (Tehran: Kitābkhānih Ṭahūrī, 1371 S.A.H).

Shihāb al-Dīn Suhrawardī, *Ḥikmat al-Ishrāq*, ed. Henri Corbin, (Tehran: Anjuman Ḥikmat wa Falsafa, 1977).

Taqī Pūrnāmdārīān, *Ramz wa Dāstānhā-yi Ramzī dar Adab Fārsī*, (Tehran: Intishārāt 'Ilmī wa Farhangī, 1376 S.A.H).

Terence Walter Stace, *'Irfān wa Falsafa*, trans. B. Khurramshāhī, (Tehran: Intishārāt Surūsh, 1367 S.A.H).

Toshihico Izutsu, *Bunyād Ḥikmat Sabziwārī*, trans. S. J. Mujtabavī, (Tehran: Intishārāt Danishgāh Tehran, 1368 S.A.H).

Toshihico Izutsu, *Khalq Mudām*, trans. Kāviyānī, (Tehran: Intishārāt 'Ilmī wa Farhangī,d).

Toshihico Izutsu, *Sākhtimān Ma'nā'ī, Mafāhīm wa Iṣṭilāḥāt Akhlāqī Qur'an Karīm*, trans. Badri'ī, (Tehran: Intishārāt Qalam, 1360 S.A.H).

Toshihico Izutsu, "*Sākhtimān Tafakkur Falsafī dar Islam*", in *Ḥikmat wa Hunar Ma'nawī Dar Islam*, (Tehran: Intishārāt Garus, 1375 S.A.H).

Toshihico Izutsu, *Sufism wa Taoism*, trans. Gawharī, (Tehran: Intishārāt Rawzanih, 1378 S.A.H).

Toshihico Izutsu, "Taḥlīlī az Waḥdat Wujūd", in *Pajūhish-hā-e Falsafī wa Kalāmī*, No. 17 & 18, (Qum: 1382 S.A.H).

Wien Poradfoot, *Tajrubih Dīnī*, trans. Yazdānī, (Qum: Mu'assasa Farhangī Ṭāhā, 1377 S.A.H).

William James, *Dīn wa Rawān*, trans. Mahdī Qā'inī, vol. 2, (Qum: Intishārāt Dār al-Fikr).

Yaḥyā Yathribī, *Falsafa 'Irfān*, (Qum: Mu'allif, 1366 S.A.H).

Yaḥyā Yathribī, *Nisbat Dīn wa 'Irfān*, (Tehran:Pajūhishgāh Farhang wa Andīshih Islāmī, 1379 S.A.H).

Index

E

F

G

H

Q

R

S

T

www.ingramcontent.com/pod-product-compliance
Ingram Content Group UK Ltd.
Pitfield, Milton Keynes, MK11 3LW, UK
UKHW020145250726
13967UKWH00002B/871